Lo
diano

Jesus said ...
The I AM

Cindy ~
How wonderful to meet
spiritual you! Hope you
enjoy this amazing
book, are inspired, &
will share . . .

Kindly,
Diana C.

3/9/2017

Jesus said . . .
The I AM

C.S. McClintock

Book-Broker Publishers
Port Charlotte, Florida

Book-broker Publishers of Florida
Port Charlotte, FL 33980
Printed in the United States of America

ISBN: 978-151-758-5860
Cover painting by Diana Craun

TABLE OF CONTENTS

FOREWORD

One passage from "*Jesus Said... The I Am;*" defines the book's form and function:

The dazzling presence of this Christ-Light was witnessed in the luminance of Moses, *"When Moses came down from Mount Sinai with the two tablets of testimony in hand... Moses wist not that the skin of his face shone."* (Exodus 34:29)

McClintock writes with the wide-eyed wonder and shining faith of the illuminated. He speaks with authority and documentation to the one-ness, the commonality of the soul. He uses long passages from theosophists and lines from popular music to present his revelation in language both stately and familiar.

He uses the story of an apple to illustrate ascension and rejuvenation. He rips hidebound religious mores that interceded between the soul and the divine. Using historical, scholarly and homespun arguments, McClintock offers a loving yet skeptical look at our place in this Great Soul of a Universe.

In a world that is too much with us, C.S. McClintock offers a gentle and well-informed alternative. Turn away from the fables of original sin, break the shackles of organized religion and institutional cant to find your universe, your connectivity with the God-consciousness, that lies within.

McClintock's series of provocative essays are buttressed by readings in the great theosophical tradition. He illuminates the great I AM that awaits all who are willing to make a journey of faith.

James Abraham

"We are foremost and more importantly, the authors of perfection. The new spiritual shift in thinking reveals that as heavenly life-streams placed on this earth we have the capacity to think only right thoughts!"

Chapter 1

AWAKENING

Our goal is to go from bright to brighter to brightest, from high to higher to highest.

And even in the highest, there is no end to our progress, for God himself is inside each of us and

God at every moment is transcending his own reality.

—***Sri Chinmoy***

The Bible is a wondrous compilation written over hundreds of years from thousands of different pens. It is truth, love, adventure, history, accounts of wars, defeat and victory, stories, similes, practical advice, poetry and parables. It is a treasure trove of spiritual secrets, messages and miracles. It includes a chronicling of the Master Jesus' life and works. Without the benefit of radio, television or the internet, his teachings and healings were personally witnessed by only a very fortunate few thousand.

Most written accounts concerning the Master and his great works did not surface until years after his ascension, yet here we are still trying to fit a pre-modern understanding of his teachings into an advanced age of worldwide intelligence. But thank goodness the old theologies are beginning to yield.

Many lost Gospels have been unearthed in the last few hundred years, some even very recently. The much awaited worldwide spiritual "shift" in thinking is being brought about, readying us to go through yet another door of spiritual awakening. The wise men of today should be ready to assimilate fresh truth, sacred light, whatever its time period or form. Truth is truth whether old or new.

The beauty of life is that we can swing open these formerly closed doors of comprehension and walk through them. We can reverse-engineer the age-old religious interpretations, the human concepts concerning spiritual matters; and rediscover the Universal Laws of Life, tracing them back to Revelations, through Genesis, and even thousands of years before.

We live in a virtual sea of approaches to everything surrounding Jesus. There seems to be a boatload of varying perspectives for every sentence in the Bible concerning the Master. It is so easy for us to nap and let the other guy row our boat or set our course to his. However, we may look up from our slumber one day and wonder where we've been led and why we let another's hand steer our rudder or fashion our belief system.

Has this tack or course been our own chosen destination of thought and conclusion, or another's? That's all the more reason to keep our head above water through our own reasoning and revelation. Perhaps our theological beliefs were anchored in our early childhood then gradually set adrift in a basket.

A man's mind filled only with the accepted
teachings of another man,
is like a chessboard
filled only with the checkered squares.

—***C.S. McClintock***

Prepare yourself for "Good News," most assuredly mind-bending, possibly life-altering, liberating news. If you feel a sense of apprehension or trepidation as you peruse these pages, it's okay, it is to be expected. Even if these words make you feel a bit incredulous, it's okay; this too shall pass. As a seeker of wisdom and Truth your desire should be to reach a more exalted state of awareness, to be stirred, liberated, as you advance on your spiritual journey.

I once wrote a note to Dr. Maya Angelou that it was my soul's sole intention to release, not her "caged bird," but to release the "caged Christ" in every man.

A friend of mine was overcome with tears after reviewing this manuscript. "I knew it, I knew it, I love it!" he exclaimed. "We are all divine, Godly beings as you've said. We're not dregs after all, and we were not born to be sinners, a mindset I have endured for more than thirty years. I feel so uplifted, freed. You write that even a man who seems to be wallowing in the gutter can be transformed back into his original goodness. I was especially moved by your statement about the Christ being inherent to every individual. It should be our 'good pleasure' as you say, to reach for and attain that elevated plateau of understanding. And wow, you said we have the potential 'to be like Jesus!'"

It is my heart's intent through the following pages to bring the Master closer to the human perception; and also to bring our Source, our Creator, closer to conscious awareness. Not only is this celestial essence closer to us than our own heartbeat, our breathing; it is also closer to us than our own hands and feet. These and other secrets of the ages will be found in the following presentation. This energy of Life, this ultimate vibration of spirit just is. As humans we have named this Is-ness: the omnipotent, omnipresent, omniscient energy of the All-that-Is, God, Jehovah, Allah, Brahma, Shiva.

As we shed old mindsets, it will no longer be necessary for us to idolize the Master Jesus or his Mother-idealize them, yes, but hold them in idolatry—no! Hopefully, we are learning that it is not requisite for us to access the "Mother" so that she might contact the "Son" on our behalf, so that in turn he might communicate with his Father in our stead. Neither will we need to go to a mountain top or pray through other individualities once we realize that we and the Father are one. This book declares our Oneness—with the Divine.

For years we have been taught that the Master is like a treasured painting on the wall in a fine museum, roped off from the public. We learned that we had to view him only at a distance because his sovereignty was absolutely untouchable.

But you may be surprised to hear that he is not so unapproachable to us "lowly serfs" as we have been programmed to believe for all these centuries. He is after all, not mounted on a wall. And it is rapidly coming to light that the concept of our unworthiness is being uprooted and ever so slowly replaced with the truth of our original perfection. Our Master Jesus is not up in some far-off ethereal heaven in the sky and sitting at the feet of a judgmental and bearded old man. Further, you will hear that he is not way off in some otherworldly rarefied existence.

Whether you are an Atheist, Humanist, Jew, Gentile, Christian, Muslim or Hindu, know this: Jesus, along with all the ascended enlightened masters and teachers, are standing with you, beside you, right here and now. They may be in what seems to us an invisible dimension, nevertheless they are as present and real as the unseen air we breathe, or the wind that blows our sails.

We can't physically live in two places at once. By the same token, we can't stay in the past spiritually, and seek a spiritual future at the same time. We can open new gateways of enlightenment and walk through them into greater works, or we can choose to stay in one place with the status quo.

Those who are seekers of truth should continually be living in the moment, with each of these moments moving into the next, full of enlightenment, wonder, and promise. The Scriptures, as well as sacred texts from many enlightened writers throughout the ages, provide a unique looking glass for those "with eyes to see."

We humans are not merely dancing particles of matter, nor are we aimless, yet dangling participants in a somewhat confused world. We are brilliant portions of His Light, His I AM-ness, which has been projected into this world as our own personal Christ-Self. We are part and parcel of the Divine Presence, awaiting recognition by our own humanized consciousness. We are to eventually proceed out of the intersection within the "Cross"; where we have helped invent a time and space of spiritually conceived material organisms, our co-creation, a grand design as it were.

We continue to orbit lifetime after lifetime within the constraints of this Cross-roads of time and space. However, the power within is like a magnet, a spiritual magnet drawing us to a higher state in our celestial awareness. After all, are we not limitless divine beings temporarily wearing the Cross? Know ye not that we are all eternal travelers?—"for God himself is inside each of us (as us) and God at every moment is transcending His own reality."

Perhaps our spiritual leaders inadvertently left us afloat, having to discover our own self-transcendence—the ultimate game of hide and seek— which will be addressed presently. Maybe we have been unknowingly programmed and conditioned by particular doctrines or creeds. Many have become weary of all the rhetoric and worn down from all the confusion of religious interpretations. Are we ready to chart our own course, prepared to add to, or even change the convictions we have formulated? More importantly, are we willing to begin anew in the search for the ultimate Truths of our world?

Is this human existence a game our Higher-Self is playing with our human consciousness at the quintessential level? Can you consciously find yourself, your spirit which has been hidden deep within this material paradigm, this "earthly theater for the arts," this majestic world we live in? I'm talking about your *real Self*.

Once again our "dancing the jig"—the cycles of birth and death, death and birth— is coming to a close. The music is about to stop for us. With that ending must come a cessation of anger, hate, envy, jealousy, greed, covetousness, intolerance, judgment— and religious confinement! Can you find a seat at the end of the music, where there is no more stress or strife, where harmony reigns and forgiveness flows abundantly? Whereby the human freely blends with the divine as Jesus and many others have exemplified.

How ridiculous the concept of a limited life cycle, that has been perpetrated upon us. Our life, our consciousness, along with our learning experiences can never be extinguished. The music and our rhythm never ends because our life is eternal. Amen!

The authors of fabled fairy tales of horrors with their hellish connotations have unwittingly mistaken us for foolish sheep and we have followed their directives for more than two thousand years! Unfortunately, in the name of religion, theology, and through personal interpretation we have unintentionally shut so many doors.

Are you still happy to participate in these endless rounds of physical birth and death? Next time around you may not find a book like this one or others like it that will help recalibrate your spiritual GPS—"recalculating" your spiritual journey. After all, as they say, "history repeats itself." My next sojourn, I could possibly be burned at the stake by people like those officials of the early church, for publishing a writing of differing opinion, of new revelation. "The more things change, the more they stay the same." As Yogi Berra said, "It's deja vu all over again!"

The truth is, as we are *individualizations* of the *Supreme Being*, here on earth, with free will, we are the privileged authors of our own fortunes and misfortunes, whether good or bad. How dare we blame a loving "Father" for personal adversities, or for climatic calamities, disasters of mass destruction, or the myriad so called "acts of God," which have in fact been generated by the collective negativity of man's erroneous thoughts and actions.

Sooner or later it is imperative that we learn "nature" is not a power separate from ourselves or our Source. Our conscious thoughts and deeds mirror outward and manifest into our natural world, directly affecting the harmony of our eco-system, our planet. As men, we are independent co-creators, having possible dominion over all the elements. Therefore, Mother Nature will reflect back what man's creative energy gives out, whether harmony or disharmony.

We are foremost and more importantly the authors of perfection. The new spiritual shift in thinking reveals that as heavenly life-streams placed on this earth, we have the capacity to think only right thoughts! As we choose to be righteous beings, we will again witness the Garden of Eden along with its world-wide peace and perfect weather conditions.

Perhaps you were already aware of the fact that, yes, you are a Divine Spiritual Being. You are not just an intellectual mind wearing a physical body, standing alone, destined for the grave, and perhaps waiting for a rapturous deliverance. For how can a coffin hold a conscious spirit, a non-material vibrant entity that has eternal life and eternal freedom? It can't, anymore than a fiery furnace of burning flames can consume HIS own Godly-Spirit, a portion of which we are.

Of course, even a genius like a Stephen Hawking would never admit we bring about the circumstances of our own destiny. And he would most likely say, "How could there be a Supreme Being, a compassionate God?" I would kindly reply, "How could there not be?"

Scientists do not yet understand how all is derived first from Spirit—Before Abraham was, before Adam was, and before atoms were— I AM.

Jesus said *the* I AM.

The Father most tender, Father of all,
my immense God—I his atom.

—***Elizabeth Ann Seton***

"As we choose to be righteous beings, we will again witness the Garden of Eden along with its world-wide peace . . .

"I am a rock, the wind, a plant, a tree ... I am also you ...
Everything that exists is a unique facet of Me,
individualized again and again."

Chapter 2

REALIZING THE I AM

In the faces of men and women
I see God.

—**Walt Whitman**

Hello there—It is Me, Your Creator, the All-in-All, All Consciousness, every atom, cell and particle, the visible and the invisible. Nothing can be outside of Me, because, the "I" is the I AM, the "All there Is," the One and only Power there ever has been or ever will be. It is Me, living all Life, all individualities and personalities: I am a rock, the wind, rain, a plant, a tree, an insect, a bird, an animal, etc.; at the same moment, I am also you, the fireman, policeman, soldier, dentist, veterinarian, schoolteacher, minister, rabbi, a salesman, painter, musician, poet, pilot, construction worker, or yachtsman. I am the medical doctor, the housewife, mother, dancer, writer, athlete, or the child. Everything that exists is a unique facet of Me, the pure essence and energy that is Love, individualized again and again.

Yes, "I" am continuously dividing Myself proportionately into zillions of droplets or focal points of consciousness in a myriad of varying shapes and forms with endless functions, complexities, activities, creativities and interactions in my infinite Ocean of Being. I am very capable of maintaining and sustaining all these experiences at the same time, in fact, a zillion times ad infinitum. Truth is, to Me there are no numbers or measurements, there is no time or space. It is only Me, the I AM-God, the One Source, over and over and over, replicated in a kaleidoscope of activity, color, design, beauty and wonder.

You will never understand Me completely, the All of Me, through the intellect or through science; although these will be greatly enhanced proportionate to your acknowledgement of My Spirit as the basis of all human exploration, discovery and invention.

All that is created is in actuality my One I AM, playing all the roles, being all form, making every prodigal journey, each with individualized free will at the helm; creating vast experiences of learning all within Myself— for Me. The "I" is Me, Myself, you, them, thine, yours, mine, ours. As the Master said, "The Father within me doeth the works," not myself as Jesus doing the works, but the I AM within me.

It is the "I" that prevaileth, that moves the planets, brings order to our days, that manifests miracles and heals the sick. It was Jesus who came to reveal this secret of the universe, the secret of *the* I AM within all men, and to show forth My works. I AM all that Is, all phenomenon, and you are individualities of Me, my phenomena.

Furthermore, this greatest secret ever told, reveals that some of your human translations left out that tiny article in Jesus' sayings, the word "*the*." Though he came to furnish the supreme example for all to follow, Jesus never meant to portray himself as the only way, nor the only light of the world; and he never implied that anyone had to go through him, personally, as "the doorway" in order to find Me, God.

The theory of Jesus being the only way and only door was strictly a manmade concept helping the early church form a new and strict disciplined orthodoxy. He was speaking for Me when he declared that *the* I AM, the Father within, was "the way," "the rock," the foundation to follow, and that this Kingdom of Heaven, this Kingdom of the perfect I AM was within everyone! The omission of the word "the" may have happened inadvertently through many mistranslations over time, or perhaps through personal interpretation.

A possible mistake, the omission of this one word preceding I AM statements, though seemingly insignificant, has had a huge and very critical influence in altering the meaning of My dear Jesus' teachings. That mistake has hindered you on your journey, your pathway toward remembrance of Me, The Divine.

This mistake has taught you to distance yourself from Me, rendering you somewhat handicapped and uncertain.

This mistake has left you less adept in the full understanding of the Christ-Spirit, the Father within.

This mistake has left you unaware of the demonstration, the activity of My Christ-Spirit within YOU.

The I AM is the Christ-presence, that Jesus showed and tried to convey as present in all men, not just in himself. "Let thine eye be single." Let your full focus of thought be centered. Know ye not that this "I" is singular, yet occurring and consciously operating throughout every facet of creation?

He taught that the ever-present and all-wise God, "the I AM" abides in all states and stages of our experience. It makes no difference if an individual expresses the most heinous and horrific acts, or if he lives the most honorable and exemplary peace-filled life; all individualities from the most selfish mortal and material personality, to the most spiritually inspired and metaphysically enlightened, have the potential to expand their understanding and know that the I AM, is the Life and Light within themselves, no matter how dimly some may be discerning this extraordinary spiritual fact.

(John 14:6) *"I am"*(the I AM is) *the way, the truth, and the life; no man cometh unto the Father, but by me."*

The brilliance of Mary Baker Eddy succinctly stated, "The 'I' referred to in the text is not a person, it is a principle. It is not a man, it is God. Jesus said, *'The words that I speak unto you I speak not of myself'*...Jesus was not Christ; Christ was but another name for God, and it was an honorary title bestowed on Jesus for his great goodness. In the original texts the term God took its origin from the word good, —hence the term Christ Jesus, a good man.

"In the passage *'I am the way, the truth, and the life,'* the 'I' alluded to is God—the divine Principle of the man Jesus and was that which guided his way... one fact in Jesus' history is clearly apparent; namely that his Principle, rule and method of healing involved no drugs, dogma, or doctrine to aid his work. A person does not heal another." (An individual who understands the Divine Principle helps to facilitate the healing process.)

"...therefore a person is not the power that heals the sick... we can ask a person to doctor our sickness and to forgive our sins, and that is all we can do, but we can do more than that with a Principle, we can work it for ourselves to this result. In the text, *'I am the way, the truth, and the life, no man cometh unto the Father, but by me,'* we naturally ask, what is this way referred to? The way and the demonstration thereof is through the understanding of its Principle by which we can produce the harmony."

By the hand of their own free will, some may choose to ignore their better Self, their higher consciousness, ME, and follow mortal-mindedness, their own ego, with a clouded perception to the negative side, and whether through thought, deed, or both, wind up placing themselves in the gutter instead of shining forth in good works.

In such cases, the I AM within them may be hidden behind layer upon layer of misconception and misbehavior, but I, God, am ever there within, nonetheless. Whether you call it a fallen angel or a fallen man, "fallen" merely refers to the temporary descending of consciousness right within the angel or man's own Godly-Being. You are never fallen or lost to Me, the I AM! You can never fall out of My Omnipresence. Remember no matter where you make your bed there I AM…there AM I in the midst of you. Why? Because you are living one of My infinite number of lives. There is no life that is not My own.

Therefore, please allow every man, as My individualization, to follow the beat of a different drummer if he so chooses. No group or sect should be forcing or proselytizing their beliefs or agenda upon the rest of the world.

My great prophets such as Jesus, Buddha and Mohammad cannot intervene in your life to save you from yourself, your selfishness. Only you are responsible and accountable for "thine own" free-willing.

"Got Jesus?"… If you do, are you then totally loving, forgiving, selfless, and non-judgmental, especially in the matter of a person's color or creed? The Master instructed you to judge not, yet some of you go all around the world claiming to be "holier than thou!" Think about it! Possibly you have allowed yourself to be somewhat misled in thinking that you have the only truth and have the right to interfere in another's sacred spiritual learning journey.

You must realize that the spiritual core of your Being, My Christ-Presence is ever enforcing a kind of balancing, a sort of righting effect much like what you call a GPS guidance system. My spiritual guidance system is ever correcting, guiding, governing—protecting and leading to each next step toward your refining, regenerating and reforming.

Though you may never see or feel the wholesomeness or the divinity of certain individuals in this lifetime, you can be assured that the balancing and workings of My Universal Law of Life, which is the law of right, the law of love, goes on adjusting, correcting, and instructing, every one of My precious souls, even after what you call "here." Yes, it is sometimes hard to fathom what some people have done while using My life, while others wisely glorify Me with all their might! No matter how out of control some may seem to be, whatever course they have chosen, wherever they have made their bed, it remains My spirit and My body they have temporarily misdirected during their earthly learning experiences, erroneously thinking that their lives actually belonged to themselves!

When the chaff is removed, the wheat will stand alone in its purest form just as I have planned. The now discarded chaff will be put to the purifying fire and burned as part of its very own regeneration process; its now invisible energies will soon be re-manifested in a new configuration.

As the life leaves a human body, this physical form, whether through cremation or deterioration through burial, man's spirit, like the wheat, continues its eternal journey. Similar to the magnetic forces of gravity, the energies and elements that made up a physical form, even if invisible are still alive; they now collect and orbit around the non-visible spirit/soul to re-manifest over and over again. You mistakenly think life has ended for the spirit and the body, but nothing is ever lost or left to chance; in every instance all things are being renewed. Not a speck of My energy or identity is ever lost.

> *When we pass, it's the beginning of something else.*
> *We are all unfinished songs, pictures to be drawn.*
>
> —***Celine Dion***

Many do not realize that the energy a human misuses to think and create evil or negativity is eventually purified with this same refining process, the Law of Adjustment. Through the violet flame of transmutation all erred energy is crystallized back into pure love. Originally, imagination and free will were bestowed upon the people for the creative magnification and expression of good alone!

Just as surely as the wheat has been separated from the chaff, so will the spirit be separated from the physical body. Furthermore any negative creations man carries in his soul as baggage from one sojourn to the next must be transformed. Since graduation from material form and the earth is required of every lifestream, you will inherently want to progress forward. As long as you are not taking any senseless backward steps, you will find yourselves gradually ascending this plane of existence.

Your level of thinking, through your spiritual vibration or frequency will always project into your next experience. Then, the outcome will again determine your new level, whether it be pro or con, working with the I AM of your inner goodness, or rather against it. You are involved in somewhat of a circular learning curve, a centripetal force, forever drawing and gravitating you closer to your inner axis, your Christ-Self. And My magnetism never lets go, never wanes, because It is the very activity and nature of the Christ, at every turn; until you become conscious of that Life vibrantly living every one of you, loving every one of you— Living MY I AM in us, as us! All creation works in consonance, rhythmically, synergistically, and harmoniously. Please, dear ones, contemplate these spiritual facts to live by.

Those who have turned away from perceiving Me as a mighty potentate in the sky, judgmental and distant, are beginning to understand Me as I truly AM, the Presence of Love, the Source of all Being, an omnipotent Energy forever bubbling forth new creativity, invention, design and purpose for Us as Us. You call Me Divine and so I AM. But I am not a mystery or an enigma. I am an understandable ever-presence, urging forth ideas for you to manifest in your human journey. You are on the threshold of knowing that My thoughts need not necessarily be higher than your thoughts, My ways than your ways. What a happy day for Us!

When I said "Hello there, this is your Creator," I didn't mean for you to think of Me as a mysterious presence from somewhere outside yourself or imagine Me speaking to you from a celestial throne in the clouds, light-years away. Nor did I mean for you to think of Me merely as a "parent" or "friend" either, as many tell you to do. I am not "outside" and separate from you like a distant voice or even a closest relation. I am the Real, the True feeling and essence, God, that resides within your very heart, mind and soul. My Spirit is your spirit, the life of your being.

I am the one and the same God that your brother Jesus revered, your Source, Father of all that is. He told you that "of himself," personally, "he could do nothing," he said that the "Father," Me, the I AM within, "doeth the works." Never did he imply that he personally was the only I AM. As all of you are My beloved sons, he, however earned the right to be the appointed, the anointed one, showing forth "The Way."

What he did say is that the I Am is the way,
the I Am is the truth and the life,
the I Am is the resurrection and the life everlasting,
the I Am is the ascension into the light,
the I Am is the Light—Father—God.

How that little word "the" was omitted from the I AM statements is beyond Me! Perhaps it happened one day when an eager listener heard these words according to his own perception. Maybe its meaning was left out later as My sayings got passed from person to person before they were ever written down. How it happened now seems insignificant compared to the importance of this Truth coming to light once again!

There is a new shift in spiritual awareness, consciousness, a turning away from the literal and limited, toward the enlightened and illumined. Oh how I've waited for this day! So very much more than simply a grammatical error; the recognition of this correction is of paramount importance. It is pivotal to the understanding of all My dear Jesus' teachings, parables and healings. And "the" greater works will follow.

So you see, when you reach out to Me, I am already right here. I have always been honest and forthright with you. Understand this, there is never a need "to reach out," you only need reach "in," be still and listen, and consciously recognize Me within. For your erroneous human thoughts "are not My thoughts." So "take no thought for yourself," that is, your mortal self, for "I Am with you always." Know this also, that there is no such thing as "you and I" as separate entities. There is only the "I," for we are One.

Two thousand years and four thousand religions later, the new light thrown on the significance of "the I AM" within each of you is as revolutionary to our world as Jesus' teachings were to the Mosaic law-driven Jewish scholars. The luminosity of this new light will be felt not only in the pulpit but in every modern-day disciple.

The recognition of this Truth will not diminish the good works you have accomplished thus far, but will add new impetus to the realization and power of your individual Christ-Presence, causing greater works to ensue, a grander inner peace to be achieved. This truth, this principle, could be the great "savior" men are seeking. As your Creator I say unto you, "let thine eye be single" in the discernment of this monumental Truth. This singular focus will bring you peace, "the peace which passeth all understanding." My I AM means peace to all men, which in turn brings harmony to all conditions of our world... including climatic. The I AM is My Consciousness, which threads throughout all life forms whether visible or invisible ... *the* I AM ... that I am is the Healing "Father."

You can be assured that,
all that I have is thine,
but, only when you have
gained the wisdom to access it.

—*C.S. McClintock*

We will each find the light in our own way and eventually take on spiritual wings and mentally fly higher ... seeing the light of the spirit within every divine creature ... this Spirit is WHO WE ARE!

This Presence is the life-consciousness within every individual life-stream, and animates this and all the infinite number of universes.

Chapter 3

NOW YOU SEE ME

To believe you are separate from your Source
is to remain consciously separate
from your own Higher Self.

—***C.S. McClintock***

The I AM is God, the Source of love, wisdom and power in all creation. We limit and diminish the significance of the "I Am" statements in the Scriptures when we reduce the meaning of these two immeasurable words to mere persons or events unrelated to ourselves or to our own lives. The I Am is the very spirit, the core of our being. It is the identity to which Jesus, Moses and others referred in speaking of the SUPREME INFINITE ONE. This Presence is the life-consciousness within every individual life-stream and animates this and all the infinite number of universes.

Some teachings have a more abstract idea as to God and law, while this new, old instruction explains God to be an individualized presence at once within and above us, in which our spiritually rich physical form abides. It gives one a sense of something more concrete, rather than just conceptual. Most people seem to have a concept of God as abstract and incomprehensible, rather than a focused presence, a loving and living Being to whom you can talk; who hears and answers your prayers. As the enlightened Guy Ballard along with Alice Schutz stated, "Contemplate your I AM Presence; try to get a feeling of its reality—as a living, all-wise Being."

"Pour your love into It and it is possible to feel a response from It. Some people think they cannot love a Being unseen to them, or not present to their physical touch. Yet we can generate a feeling of love by thinking about a child or person we care for very much. In that same way you can pour love into your I AM God Presence. Although It has often been ignored and forgotten, through the ages It has kept on giving us life."

Try very hard to perceive with me that ... It is the purest form of you.

1. BEFORE ABRAHAM: (John 8:57)

"Jesus said unto them, verily, verily, I say unto you, Before Abraham was, (the) I Am"(was).

Before Abraham was, the I Am was. Since before Abraham, the I Am has eternally existed.

2. BREAD: (John 6:47-53)

"for the bread of God is he which cometh down from heaven, and giveth life unto the world... (the) I Am (is) that bread of life, (the) I Am (is) the living bread which came down from heaven: if any man eat of this bread, he shall live forever."

The I Am is our bread of life—our spirit.

3. LIGHT: (John 8:12)

(The) "I am (is) the light of the world: he that followeth me (the presence within me) shall not walk in darkness, but shall have the light of life."

The I Am is the light of the world.

4. Gate (or DOOR): (John 10:7-10)

"Verily, verily, I say unto you, (the) I Am (is) the door of the sheep. All that came before me are thieves and robbers: but the sheep did not hear them. (The) I Am (is) the door: by me if any man enter in, he shall be saved, (from ignorance) and shall go in and out, and find pasture. The thief (misunderstanding of Truth and Divinity) cometh not, but for to steal, and to kill, and to destroy: (the) I Am (has) come that they might have life, and that they might have it more abundantly".

The I Am is the door, opening Truth and understanding to man's eternal life.

5. SHEPHERD: (John 10:11)

(The) I Am (is) the good shepherd: the good shepherd giveth his life for the sheep. (The) I Am (is) the good shepherd and know my sheep, and am known of mine. Jesus said to the Jews who were questioning him, is it not written in your law, I said, ye are gods."

The I Am is the good shepherd...ye are portions of God's own awareness.

6. RAISE THE DEAD: (John 11:25-25)

"Jesus said unto Martha, (The) I Am (is) the resurrection and the life: he that believeth in me, though he were dead (unaware or dead to the truth), shall he live: and whosoever liveth and believeth in me shall never die.(consciously) Believest thou this ?"

The I Am is the "Me," the Father within, the resurrection and the life.

7. THE WAY THE TRUTH AND THE LIFE: (John 14:6-28)

"Jesus saith unto Thomas, (the) I Am (is) the way, the truth, and the life: no man cometh unto the Father, but by me (by the I Am—the Christ in every man).

"If ye had known me, ye should have known my Father also: and from henceforth ye know him, and have seen him. Jesus saith to Philip, he that hath seen me hath seen the Father: believest thou not that (the) I Am in (is) the Father, and the Father in me" (and you)?

"The words that I speak unto you I speak not of myself: but the Father (The I Am) that dwelleth in me, he doeth the works."

"Believe me that I am (the I Am is) in the Father and the Father (is) in me: or else believe me for the very work's sake. Verily, verily, I say unto you, he that believeth in me (the I Am), the works that I do shall he do also: and greater works than these shall he do: because I go unto my Father" (in prayer and meditation, just as you should do).

"And whatsoever ye shall ask in my name, that will I (the I Am) do, that the Father may be glorified in the Son"... (and in all his sons, my brothers and sisters).

"If ye shall ask anything in my name, (my nature), I (the I Am) will do it."

"Peace I leave with you, my peace I give unto you: not as the world giveth, give I unto you. Let not your heart be troubled, neither let it be afraid."

"I go unto (draw from) the Father : for my Father (the I Am) is greater than I." (for we are all sons, individualizations of the one Father, Source).

The I Am is the way, the truth and the life.

8. THE VINE AND THE BRANCHES (John 15:1-5)

(The) "I Am" (is) the true vine, and my Father is the husbandman and you are the branches. Every branch that beareth not fruit, he taketh away: and every branch that beareth fruit, he purgeth it, that it may bring forth more fruit."

"Abide in me, and I in you. As the branch cannot bear fruit of itself, except it abide in the vine: no more can ye abide in me. (The) I Am (is) "the vine, ye are the branches: he that abideth in me, and I in him, the same bringeth forth much friut: for without me (the I Am) ye can do nothing."

The I Am is the vine, and you are its branches.

"Whom say ye that I am?" (Matthew: 16:15)

Peter gave the optimal answer when he replied, *"Thou art the Christ,"* meaning that he perceived the Christ activity of the I AM Presence in Jesus. He had the mental vision to discern the infinite principle, the ever-operative I AM, God manifest in Jesus and innate to every individual; unseen to the physical eye, yet fully discernible to spiritual awareness.

Peter must have glimpsed the omnipotent nature of the Christ, the activity of the God-Consciousness that had stirred those around him through the Master himself, and had been illustrated by virtue of his teachings and healings.

Surely this eager disciple must have felt privileged and thrilled to see this beautiful Presence at work. Jesus called it the *"Father within."* He also said that he (as a man) *"can of mine own self do nothing,"* meaning that it is the Father within us, *"who doeth the works."* He was declaring that this Divine Power that is Love (Father, Spirit) was the Source, the I AM, acting through It's Christ activity within all men. Peter had to be profoundly moved when he reached the enlightened epiphany, the understanding that all of us are capable of going and "doing likewise," doing the "greater works"—greater than even The Master performed!

Jesus' well-known response affirmed that Peter's advanced state of spiritual insight was a "rock," a solid foundation to build upon. Upon this rock of enlightenment will you build your full understanding. Peter realized that his own body-temple-church held this foundation within. The Master knew that this recognition heralded the Christ-awareness within Peter, who no longer saw himself as separate from God, which too, was his personal Presence. He and the other disciples were becoming cognizant of "the fullness of the Christ," that highest consciousness that was also within themselves.

These Apostles now knew that they were becoming qualified to go out, preach to the multitudes, heal the infirm, and teach the message to receptive hearts. The twelve were being made aware that they carried this new revelation, this "rock" of understanding, this I Am Presence within their own body-temple. It was time now to go and share this "Good News!"

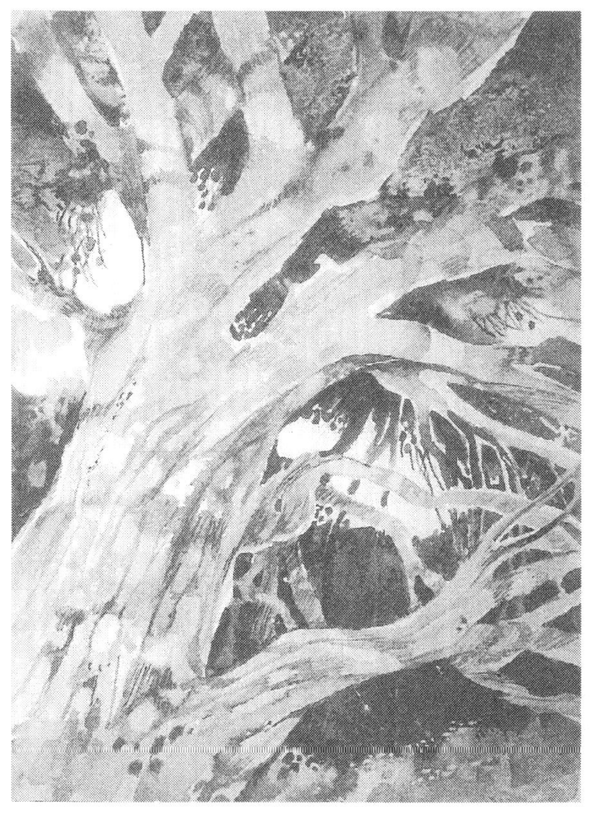

The I AM is the vine, and you are its branches.

Are we still waiting and waiting the dawning of our own illumination?

Chapter 4

THE LIGHT WITHIN

It is a sad fate for a man to die
too well known to everybody else,
and still unknown to himself.

—***Francis Bacon***

Imagine individuals from centuries past being transported into a twenty-first century home. They would find themselves stumbling in the dark with candles in hand, seeking light. All the while, unbeknownst to themselves, the lamps and chandeliers are full of light bulbs. Electrical switches are everywhere.

So there they are, unaware of all the switches, oblivious to the abundance of lighting power, the electricity running through a myriad of wires within the walls. After all, they are literally from the "Dark Ages." A dogmatic neighbor, knocking at the door exclaims "You'll have to stay in the dark. There is no oil available and there are no oil lamps to be found. When we find them, we may need to slay some whales." They stop seeking, and nod in agreement that the morning light will eventually come. So they sleep and wait, sleep and wait—staying in the dark.

Metaphorically speaking, we humans have a wealth of light within, awaiting our discovery. Know ye not that *"Ye are the light of the world?"* (Matthew 5:14) However, in order to activate this energy, this inner illumination, we must first know that there is a switch. This energy source within us can be accessed and turned on at any given moment.

Jesus had the God-sense, the good sense, to know that the Kingdom of Heaven, the Kingdom of Light, the Christ-Light, is within each of us. He came to shake us up and wake us up from our spiritual slumber, and deliver us and all people from the darkness we had grown accustomed to. The truth of life, the truth of being, within the Spiritual-Self is our individual light radiating, alive and pulsating just below the surface, awaiting discovery.

The Pharisees and Sadducees with their religious rituals and strict doctrine, felt completely threatened by this one man from Galilee. He roamed the countryside, shining his brilliant Light, sharing the simplicity of his message, speaking freely, outwardly loving and healing the masses. Both government and religious factions felt the need to squelch this independent thinker along with his teachings.

Decades of being identified as condemned guilt-ridden and lowly sinners by the hierarchy of government and religion had taken its toll on men and women. Jesus' message of spiritual individuality and dominion was that we didn't have to wait for the daylight of a future salvation, but that the divine "electrical circuitry," the Kingdom of Heaven, of harmony and wholeness, was already at hand, right here and right now.

That was two thousand years ago. Thought has substantially progressed over the last twenty centuries—or has it? Some religious denominations still retain their armies, as a show of power, or in some cases to protect the wealth they've accumulated over the centuries. Other overly-zealous organizations like cults denounce and ostracize their parishioners if they refuse to comply with written creeds or if they chose to leave the fold.

Religion was intended to comfort, heal, and teach, not frighten people into submission. There is no need of coercion, for the Light of truth will naturally *"draw all men unto me."* (the I Am) (John 12:32)

Like those transplanted folks from the Dark Ages, are we still waiting for the dawn of our own illumination? It makes one wonder how a new light-bearer, a spiritual teacher would be received today, especially if his message was a bit contrary to the present teachings of the status quo. Possibly he would be healing the infirm. He could be encouraging people to love and forgive one another, care for all life and show forth their individual light.

The purity and simplicity of his message would be without all the rhetoric and dogma, without the tedious tenets, creeds, and complicated rituals. He would be teaching that our salvation would be found within ourselves, not bestowed upon us from an outside source. If this new teacher came with short-cropped hair, wearing casual attire in lieu of a robe and sandals, would we recognize him? Would the Sadducees and Pharisees of today shun him, cast him out and possibly worse—again?

Unfortunately the ego of man has gotten in our way, casting a shadow, causing a chasm between ourselves and the Master, shielding us from his Light. It started with a few men of power bent on controlling the masses, keeping the people in subjugation with the darkness of ignorance. If the statement is correct that "the truth will set us free," then these same self-serving individuals were keeping people sequestered from the truth.

Partaking of uplifting services in a church, synagogue, temple or mosque are wonderful experiences. It should be an inspirational privilege for all to congregate and sing hymns of praise without having to be driven by man-made edicts and doctrine. Attending services should voluntarily bring adults, as well as their offspring, closer to the spiritual understanding of their own Christly-Self, their inner light. However, when adults in congregations have been made to feel a sense of guilt for not attending services, they consequently pass this guilt along to their children, dimming the child's enthusiasm for inspired learning.

Controlling a group of sheep flocked together, sometimes requires sheep-herding dogs nipping at their heels. Where religions of the past are concerned, the clergy, priests, nuns, or their armies, were in some cases required to "nip at the heels" of the masses. Only by keeping the people subdued and mentally in the dark, through guilt, condemnation, and illiteracy, could the church make their parishioners heed their authority regarding all matters church and state. Worse, they expected a certain percentage of the peoples' earnings, so elaborate shrines and temples could be built, fine robes could be donned, and golden chalices would grace the alters. The flocks were kept under an iron fist and sometimes went hungry. This type of oppression was not just endemic to, or belonging only to the third world countries.

Ruling powers couldn't let their subjects speak out freely to question their methods or doctrine. There was no telling what might happen if the masses actually knew the freedoms of thought they should be experiencing. First of all, the powers that be would keep the people docile and uneducated as long as they could get away with it. Then, if some began speaking their own mind, speaking openly, they would be pronounced heretics.

Those who did question this subjugation and oppression had to be dealt with; the hierarchy could not let them get out of control, out of hand. Furthermore, by doing away with these so-called heretics and these protest-ant or Protestant non-conformists, rulers would be teaching a lesson and at the same time scaring all the people back into submission. In the past, rulers would make examples of these free thinkers by lopping off their heads, or burning them at the stake. Today there are those who would still tend to discredit free thinkers, claiming their ideas violate the generally accepted teachings of a given religion, deeming this rejection as heretical, apostasy, blasphemy and deserving of punishment, in some cases death—all because of their differing viewpoint.

One of the greatest independent thinking minds in our world's history, the brilliant and spiritually enlightened Albert Einstein tells us in his book, *The World As I See It*: "I maintain that *cosmic religious feeling* is the strongest and noblest incitement to scientific research and spiritual enlightenment. It is very difficult to explain this feeling to any one who is entirely without it, especially as there is no anthropomorphic conception of God corresponding to it." (anthropomorphic—the explanation of what is not human as though it were—in other words making God more humanlike than divine).

"Primitive religions are based entirely on fear," said Einstein. "In the higher levels of civilized peoples, religion conforms to a standard of right behavior, with a preponderance toward morality.

"In primitive man it is fear that evokes religious notions—fear of hunger, wild beasts, sickness, or the after-death experience.

"The human mind creates for itself more or less analogous beings on whose wills and actions these fearful happenings depend. One's objective is to secure the favor of these beings by carrying out actions and offering sacrifices which, according to the tradition handed down from generation to generation, propitiate them or make them well disposed toward we mortals. I am speaking of the religions of *fear*.

"This type of religion is stabilized by the formation of a special priestly caste which sets up as a 'mediator' between the people and the beings they fear, and erects a predominating influence on this basis. Man would indeed be in a poor way if he had to be restrained by fear and punishment, in hope of reward after death.

"In many cases the leader or ruler whose position depends on other factors, or a privileged class, combines priestly functions with its secular authority in order to make the latter more secure; or the political rulers and the priestly caste make common cause in their own interests.

"The *social feelings* are another source of the crystallization of religion. Fathers and mothers and the leaders of larger human communities are mortal and fallible. The desire for guidance, love, and support prompts men to form the social or moral conception of God. This is the God of Providence who protects, disposes, rewards, and punishes; the God who according to the width of the believer's outlook, loves and cherishes the life of the tribe or of the human race; or even life as such, the comforter in sorrow and unsatisfied longing, who preserves the souls of the dead. This is the social or moral conception of God. However, development from a religion of fear to a moral religion is a great step in a religion's life."

Einstein concludes by saying: "Feeling and desire are the motivating forces behind all human endeavor and human creation... It is therefore easy to see why early religions had always fought against science and independent spiritual progression, and hence, persecuted said devotees."

When people left Europe to come to the new world, many were hoping to escape both oppressive secular and religious rulers. Our forefathers knew exactly what freedoms they were looking for. Freedom of individual thought and expression was a foregone conclusion. Those great leaders wanted to establish a country whereby all men were known to be created equal, with equal rights and opportunities. They sought a life, country governed by the people and for the people instead of by the rule of kings or priests, lords or earls. They desired freedom from taxation without representation; freedom to speak out no matter what the topic, including speaking out against religious persecution. They insisted on freedom of religion and, in some cases, freedom from religion.

Thankfully, our forefathers were being guided by the light within. They insisted on the good sense of the freedom and liberty of human rights. Most important, they valued every individual's spiritual rights. These brave people labored to denounce and reverse the dominance and dogma that had been imposed upon them from centuries past.

Today the proverbial switch has been turned on. Neon lights on churches, high definition television evangelists, and colorful worldwide web broadcasts proclaim the Scriptural message in every way, shape and form imaginable. Unlike Franklin or the two mice in Ratatouille, we no longer have to fly our kite during a thunderstorm in order to get a jolt of reality. It's the 21st century; electricity has already been discovered and finally, so has the truth, the truth that sets men free, free to navigate their own individual course. Yet even today we must sift through all the rhetoric to find Truth, the true nuggets.

Two thousand years ago, a great man called Jesus walked the earth, teaching us the good news, proclaiming that we each have an abundance of light, a power source within, in fact all that we will ever need. He reversed the negative currents of darkness imposed by the oppressors of his day. I hope we will stay alert and awake, never to sleep and wait again, nor will we be reticent or oblivious to our own loving light. Never should we allow our divine incandescence to be dimmed, denied, or regulated by anyone, by any group anywhere at any time.

Our spirituality, our God-given inner luminescence and radiance, is not to be hidden, dictated or formed by others, distanced, or made to appear inaccessible!

Whether you have reached this enlightened understanding or not, all of us are indeed, each, illumined individualizations, focal points of His Brilliance—*"the light of the world, a city that is set on an hill that cannot be hid."* (Matthew 5:14)

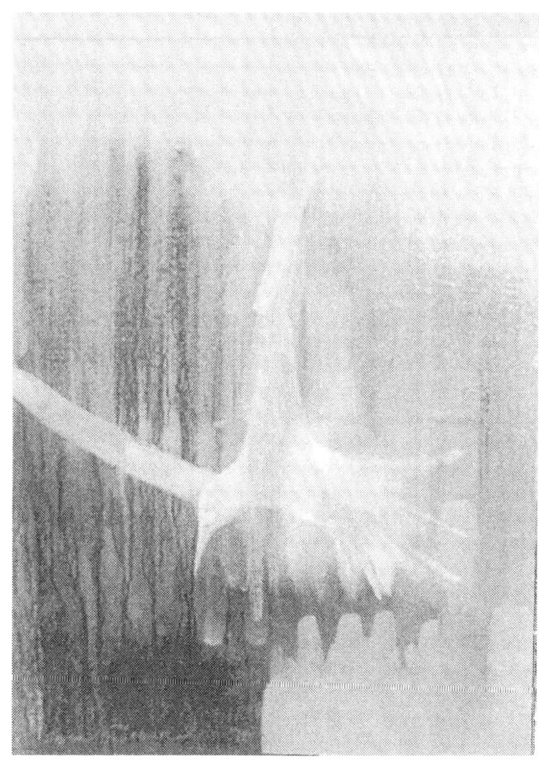

... the truth of being, within the Spiritual-Self is our individual light raiating, alive and pulsating just below the surface, awaiting discovery.

Perhaps you would journey to a cathedral of a very different nature… a beautiful forest where you would commune with the wildlife and listen to a wondrous choir of birds singing…

Chapter 5

GO TO CHURCH

Man must be arched and buttressed from within,
else the temple waivers to dust.

—***Marcus Aurelius***

To seek spiritual nourishment you might travel to a church, a synagogue, a mosque, or perhaps you would journey to a cathedral of a very different nature. You could be in a beautiful forest where you would commune with the wildlife and listen to a wondrous choir of birds singing, much like the Franciscan Friar, St. Francis of Assisi did.

When you seek spiritual nourishment wherever it might be, the edifice, the temple, the material form does not consecrate the man. The man who recognizes the Christ within himself and holds to this very personal I Am Presence understanding, is aglow, and shall consecrate the sanctuary. He carries about him an aura of enlightenment. You are a "light unto the world."

Acknowledgement of this higher vibration or Godly-Energy, this luminescence travels with you, it becomes you.

When Jesus said to Peter, *"I will give unto thee the keys of the Kingdom of Heaven... and I will build my church upon this rock,"* the Master never implied a physical edifice: We were to build our spiritual foundation upon a *solid understanding*, that is, the Rock of the Christ, the Father within, the I Am. The God-Consciousness is within all of us, within all life. As I Corinthians 6:19 states, *"Know ye not that your body is the temple, church, the sanctuary, of the Living God?"*

We may pray to find our keys, our phone, find a job, restore health to our body, but how often do we pray to be more enlightened spiritually? We should learn that we do not go to God for business or for dollars, nor do we go to Him for health or for personal accumulation. We go to God for God, and connecting with Him we have all. We can't have "all," while we keep seeking a separate "my." There is no room for Me and thee, says God, for I fill all space. I am a jealous God, and there is no room for aught but Me, Me alone. I am *the I Am*. And I Am All, which includes all facets of my individualizations.

'The Father that dwelleth in me, He doeth the works.

Christ liveth in me... greater is He that is in you, than he that is in the world

He performeth the thing that is appointed for me...

The Lord will perfect that which concerneth me."

In most all these quotations, the text is referring to a *He*, but do we understand that this "He" is the I Am within ourselves? If so, in this way, we are better able to understand the Master when he says, *"He that seeth me seeth Him that sent me—I and my Father are one."* You and our Father are one.

There is no need to seek outside ourselves, our personal church for power or for answers to meet our human needs. This infinite invisible One, is our true identity; He dwells within our very own body-temple. When we meditate within our own church-consciousness, we are touching the Him of our garment. Knowing this, *"The Lord will perfect that which concerneth me."* (Psalms 38:8) He performs that which is given us to do. Perceiving that He is within us, that All is within, is the conviction, that immediately takes our gaze from out there, outside ourselves, and prevents us from believing that there is somebody in this world who can help our demonstration or someone or some thing that can hinder it. It also keeps us from believing that we need temporal influence and pull to get ahead, or that we need to add something to ourselves that we do not already have.

We instead must know this; the One Power is already within, which includes both the inner and the outer world. When we have connected with this Higher-Self, it is up to us to let the Christ "liveth" our lives. Be stilled; quiet your free will, your human thoughts, and then let His consciousness supersede ours.

This power is an invisible something. Call It the Christ,— the I Am, call It God or Allah, call It the Father within, call It what you will— the spirit of God within man, the transcendental Consciousness, or the Presence—but realize that although It is invisible to the human eye, It stays present whether you understand it or not, whether you acknowledge it or not. It is your Source, the All-There-Is. To deny that your life is literally *His spirit* within your body, would be like denying the all-inclusive invisible forces of gravity in our Earth. Spirit is infinite, It is Love, Wisdom and Power, and yet is closer to you than your own breathing.

If you mount up to heaven,

It goes there with you...

If you make your bed in hell, you will find It there;

If you "Walk through the valley of the shadow of death," fear not, It is with you.

The Kingdom of God is within you. (His Spirit is your spirit)

You "live, and move, and have your being" in God, and conversely God lives in you, as you.

We hear the greatest of worldly thinkers explaining to us how we "live and move" in God, and that He lives in us. How are we perceiving these profound statements of Truth? Do we think, oh how beautiful and how sweet these words sound; but I'm just a lowly Joe, too insignificant to matter to God? And how could He ever have time for me or my individual needs?

We should realize that this temple-church we think of as our body is God's house, His home and sanctuary. We must understand that His Spirit is our spirit, the life that resides inside, and He lets our consciousness, through free will, creatively direct this Presence or Energy for His experiences. Yes, we are having His experiences, so keep them honorable!

"Behold the tabernacle of God is with men,
and He will dwell with them."

—***Revelation 21:3***

Therefore, true prayer within this Holy Church of our worldly body would consist of quieting our human ego, thoughts and desires, to create a tranquil stillness. This is why the Master exhorted us to "go within" our own temple-church, our "closet" as it were. We are asked to take no thought for ourselves. Please see with me—though not easy for human comprehension—that your Spirit is actually not your own, but His.

The body-temple holds our consciousness, and is the intersection, the meeting place between our God life and our human life, where the boundaries of a presumed separation between divine knowing and human thought disappear. It is the high ground where all *dualism fades away*—the human versus the divine, good verses evil; and our mental view takes in the entire panorama of the *supremacy of One God, One Mind, One Spirit.* This intersection is the blending juncture of our consciousness, our sub-conscience and our super-conscience, as our human mind elevates into our Christ-mind.

Whether we recognize this as fact or not, this is the highest state of human perception as it relates to our physical tabernacle. This is the conscious awareness that consecrates the edifice, the sanctuary, upon our entry.

Churches should be points of light on the ever undulating sea of truth leading us into the Golden Age filled with the riches of wisdom and compassion. They should provide inspired teaching and quiet respite for this blending of the human with the divine.

There is a difference between religion and spirituality—hopefully one day this will not be so. Until that day comes, prayer, whether in a building or a wildlife preserve, will remain the catalyst for spiritual advancement, human needs met, and a "more abundant" peace filled life.

Do you ever wonder why religions are losing their flocks on a mass scale? Could the false teachings, man-made concepts and the fairytale visions of well meaning prophets be part of their own undoing? This is a hell of a question some are bedeviled with.

I myself am disappointed to hear the predictions that by the year 2050 religions as we now know them may be totally dissolved. We see it happening as every type of inventive ploy is being utilized to draw and "mob the masses" into religious sanctuaries. Men of the cloth must become willing to question and even revise their platforms built upon early man-made doctrines.

To paraphrase a portion of Bishop John Spong's message: Far more than most people realize, the worship services in all Christian churches originated in 13th century understanding and practices. In that medieval era human life was mostly denigrated and devalued, particularly the accepted view toward women. Even in their hymns people had been taught to regard themselves as "wretches" and "worms." Their perception of life at that time was something to be escaped, not something beautiful and to be revered.

There was not even a Bible as we now know it until the end of the 1st century. Paul's letters were the first of what we currently recognize as the scriptures. Stories of Jesus were largely oral traditions shared by persons group to group. Such sharing was uniquely effective in opening thought to the presence of the Holy Spirit within. Home fellowships were the yeast that effected listening ears, impelling and expanding a greater inner growth and change.

The word "church" in Greek means "the called-out ones." Jesus' teaching was to "call out" from within individuals the "living waters," the Holy Spirit, indeed something recognized to be "beautiful and to be revered."

You must learn to be still in the midst of activity,
and to be vibrantly alive in repose.

—***Indira Gandhi***

For many, taking the Bible literally has become equated with being a "good Christian." Many religions often inadvertently preach self-righteous intolerance. Instead, we should have unconditional love and respect for all variations of inspired thought whether they be found in small groups or within organized edifices such as mega churches.

People are dying for truth. They are literally leaving this physical existence without answers. Possibly they will receive more clarification next time around. As Chardin so eloquently suggests, sooner or later we must learn that we are not human beings trying to have a spiritual experience, we are in fact spiritual beings having a human experience.

I once was under the illusion
that there was only man and no God,
until I came to the enlightened conclusion
that there is only God… being man.

—***C.S. McClintock***

During the twentieth century, the remarkable Joel Goldsmith healed thousands of people around the world. This is what he had to say regarding prayer. Hear ye him:

"There is no way to pray other than to make of one's self a stillness, in quietness, a peacefulness, and a listening ear. Prayer that contains words and thoughts meant to reach God is not really prayer at all. True prayer has neither words nor thoughts because it has no desires except one: to know God's will, to know Him aright, to be a fitting instrument for His grace. With that one exception, prayer is desire-less, without want of material possessions It is a desireless state of being which opens the way for God's will to be known and made evident.

"Prayer is an inner stillness that waits for God's thoughts--'For my thoughts are not your thoughts, neither are your ways my ways.'

"Therefore, let us be still with our thoughts and our ways, and let us hear God's thoughts, and by listening, let us come to know God's ways:

" '*Thou will keep him in perfect peace whose mind is stayed on thee.*' Thou wilt keep me in perfect peace in proportion as my mind is stayed on Thee. '*Thou leadest me beside the still waters. Thou makest me to lie down in green pastures.*'

"What must I do? Only acknowledge that because the Lord is my shepherd I need not fear. I shall not want. He feedeth me in the wilderness and setteth a table before me. My function is not to ask or to tell this All-knowing Intelligence, but rather to listen and be still.

"Prayer is acknowledging God as Omnipotence, Omniscience, and Omnipresence—All power, All knowledge, and All presence. Prayer is being still, being in repose, so that omnipotence may establish itself in our consciousness, omniscience impart itself to us, and omnipresence reveal its presence to us. Prayer does not bring God to us. Prayer does not bring God's grace to us: prayer reveals God and God's grace to be active where we are, right within ourselves."

Joel continues,"The most important part of prayer is that listening or receptive attitude which is a state of pure humility:

"Speak, Lord; Your servant is listening. I am not turning to You to have You do my will, as though You were my servant and I could direct You to provide me with supply, health, home, or companionship. I am not coming to You as though I had greater wisdom than You, and therefore, knew what to pray for. I come to You in true humility, for I realize that I can of my own self do nothing. I do not even know how to pray, or what to pray for.

"Therefore, Father, let Your Spirit make intercession with my spirit. Speak, Lord, that Your will may be made manifest in my experience. You are my shepherd; I shall never want. Your grace is my sufficiency in all things.

"So it is in this state of receptivity, in this state of opening ourselves in humility to the will and the grace of God—whether it happens the first day, in our continuous prayerful mode, or the hundred and first day is not important—eventually it happens, and we recognize that we are already filled with the Spirit of God, we have activated the Christ within. We have finally touched it. There is an inner warmth, an inner stillness, an inner peace.

"Sometimes, if we continue listening closely, there is even the still small voice assuring us, 'I have never left you. I will never leave you,' or sometimes, 'I am your bread and your wine and your water.' It does not make any difference whether it comes symbolically or in words, whether it comes in thoughts, or whether it comes just as a feeling, a sensing, or a release. But it is an assurance; 'God is closer to me than breathing and nearer than hands and feet. He knows my needs before I do, and it is His good pleasure to give me the kingdom.'

"Prayer is attunement, at-one-ment, with God. Through prayer, our eternal relationship with the Father is revealed. But for that oneness to become realized consciousness, we must come to the throne of God pure of heart, free of desires, and in a state of forgiveness; with every barrier removed, seeking only communion, and praying the prayer of acknowledgement and affirmation. In that purity, selflessness and desirelessness, we are holding ourselves in the highest esteem, and we enter the inner sanctuary, and from that high point of vision behold His Kingdom on earth as it is in heaven."

God's grace is the beginning
the middle and the end.
When you pray for God's grace,
you are like someone standing neck deep in water,
and yet crying for water.

—***Ramana Maharishi***

Practical application

Joel Goldsmith goes on to say how we can show forth God's will:

"Thy will be done" through us ... Even though in reality *God* constitutes our spirit, our consciousness, and we therefore already possess the full and complete perfect spiritual consciousness, this is only a demonstrable availability in proportion to our awareness of that truth. It will not be demonstrably available if our lives are lived by performing our daily tasks with little or no conscious realization of a spiritual Presence and Power within ourselves.

"Without a continuous, conscious recognition of this Presence, we are subject to the mass human consciousness, and if it happens to be a year of universal prosperity or of collective good health, we probably will share in it. On the other hand, if it happens to be a year of economic depression or a year of epidemics, we will share in that, as well.

"The only way to avoid being a part of that mass mind, which results in the kind of robot-like life that is lived by the majority of human beings, is to begin and end our day, and to continue throughout the day, praying without ceasing, by recognizing that we ourselves are not living our own life, nor is anyone else living it for us, but that God is living it; God in the midst of me is mighty. There is a divine Presence that goes before me to 'make the crooked places straight.' There is a spiritual Presence and Power within me that is the law of resurrection unto my entire experience, unto my business and my body, my profession and my health. There is a spiritual Influence within me, a spiritual Presence that restores even the lost years of the locusts.

"The continued recognition of the Presence and Power of God within our very own being is what separates us from the masses, and enables us to live a God-governed life, a life lived under the law, the substance, and the activity of God, the Presence and the Power of God. But only by acknowledging Him in all our ways, keeping our mind stayed on Him—only this separates us from the mass influence, saves us from the collective experience, and enables us to be a law unto ourselves.

"The Master made it clear that God has no pleasure in our sacrifices. He also made it clear that man was not made for the Sabbath, but that the Sabbath was made for man, that worshipping in holy mountains or even in holy temples, has no value. Above all things he made it clear that we should take no thought for our life, what we should eat, or what we should drink, or wherewithal we should be clothed, and he may even have gone on and added, "housed," too.

"It is true that over and over again, he said, 'Ask, and it shall be given unto you; seek and ye shall find; knock, and it shall be opened unto you.' But he also explained what we were to ask for: bread, and he told us what 'bread' is. The bread that he was talking about had no relationship to baker's bread. The bread to which he was referring is the bread of life; ... the I Am is the bread of life."

Goldsmith adds:

"Just what is 'bread?' Nearly every Christian church repeats incorrectly in its communion service, when it is said that 'I am the bread,' referring to Jesus. First of all, he never said, 'I am.' This is a mistranslation. He continually conveyed, 'I can of mine own self do nothing.' Throughout his ministry, he expounded that 'THE I AM' is the bread, the truth, the way, and the life. It is the All-in-All. Further, he related the I Am to be the God, Spirit, within every man, and all life forms.

"Thus, when we pray for daily bread, we should remember what bread we are praying for. This bread is Christly substance. This bread feeds us with the understanding that the spirit of God is within us. We are praying that this enlightenment be given to us, that God's grace be made evident to us. We should pray as though we really understood the master's teaching of two thousand years ago, that the Kingdom of God is within us.

"The reason we never understood the real meaning of the bread is because we read the Bible with the conditioning we had received in our childhood and from our early religious teaching, and not with an unconditioned and open mind. This is the way with many of us; we have accepted our childhood teachings, never questioning them, and never realizing that sometimes we need to think and reason for ourselves.

"Father, even though I know that the Kingdom of God is within me, reveal it to me now. If I have forgotten this great truth, if the mesmerism of human teachings and living have consciously separated me from it, open my eyes that I may see, open my ears that I may hear.

"All we have to do is turn within and pray, but not as though we were praying to a human being, to a human mother or father who has a piece of candy to give us, a toy, or a new dress. To pray in that way is to humanize God. It is trying to make God over into the image and likeness of a man, a Santa Claus. We may as well know once and for all, that our God is not in the business of putting presents under Christmas trees, not even for good children.

"The gift of supply is not to be found in this world—not for you and not for me. There is no supply 'out there' at all. All supply is embodied within our consciousness; it is omnipresent in our consciousness. Supply is infinite. We can never increase it; it is already all that the Father has.

"The only bread that we can have, and the only bread that will come back to us, is the bread that we cast on the waters. What we do not give out cannot come back. What we do give out cannot fail to return to us; it is earmarked for us, and no one can touch it without burning his fingers. So spend your 'energy,' your daily bread, wisely.

"We are not merely finite human beings; we are the life of God in individual expression, embodying everything necessary for our experience. It is much like an individual seed. It contains within itself everything necessary for its unfoldment and development into a full-grown tree with fruit on it. The tiny seed, by virtue of an activity within itself, draws unto itself from its surroundings its particular needs without taking anything from the tree or the plant next to it.

"So it is with us, our good appears to come to us through outside activities—a business, a profession, or through some other person. Even though we seem to be drawing our supply from these sources, nevertheless it cannot come to us unless we set in motion the activity of consciousness within ourselves that draws back into us that which is already our own.

"In this stage of spiritual unfoldment, we learn that our participation in a spiritual activity and our desire to contribute to the betterment of mankind and to be active in some service, that is to benefit others, is the 'putting out' of the bread that is to return to us. This is the truth which every 'mystic' has known. The secret is giving, not getting; outpouring, not withholding; selflessness, not selfishness. It is only in proportion to the outpouring of ourselves, to our dedication and service to others, and to what we give out, that our fruits may return to us."

Now, nothing in this physical world is adequate to describe and explain the ways of the Spirit, the Oneness, the God-ness, the All-in-All, the Life that lives all Life. Jesus used parables, many Masters and Teachers have employed analogies and metaphors. Religions and other forms of worship have adored God, celebrated Him, and paid homage to Him.

And, yes, we are the better for every whited steeple dotting our countryside and gracing our metropolises. Every house of worship, filled with folded hands and the sound of grateful hymns, blesses our world.

From the book GOD WE ARE

My friend, Dr. Jack Bruns had this to say concerning intuiting the Holy Spirit, after a lady of his congregation had questioned an inspired word of knowledge she had received:

"Your skepticism is natural... spiritual powers work toward specific ends... the intuitive nature of early Christianity and the psychic nature of spiritual communication and communion are open to believers today. This event demonstrates the deep spiritual communion of the living God, the Holy Spirit, which goes far beyond the literalism offered by today's Christianity. I believe those who rely on the written scripture *exclusively* are afraid of the Holy Spirit.

"They prefer to use the scriptures to dominate and indoctrinate those in the pews. They want to create fearful robots marching in step to established doctrine. Such persons are prevented from experiencing the love and joy of God which Jesus demonstrated though his life and teachings. Literalists run from the new life made possible by the encounter of God through the coming of the Holy Spirit at Pentecost." Bruns later left his ministry to pursue a more concentrated calling.

The newer generations as well as some of the older are no longer fearful or respectful of tired elementary disciplines. Younger people no longer see judgment and persecution as a right of particular sects. They and all people do however understand the idea of loving and forgiving. Collective thought is slowly turning away from all things ritualistic, yet at the same time is still hungry and yearning for deeper spiritual understanding and enlightenment.

How many times have we heard that so and so was a "God-fearing" person? How far removed from truth is this oxymoron of old ideology. The All There Is is Love, without fear, without end. Again, there is not a man-like being judging us from the sky before whom we should quake and are compelled constantly to beg for mercy. As a minister recently said, perhaps this is why worship seems so misunderstood, and at times, unpleasant and boring to people in the 21st century.

As we advance out of the literal and fearful practices of medieval based worship, no longer are we seeing God at a distance, a far-off "grand" Father-figure in the clouds. We draw closer and closer until we feel at one with Him, a true communication and communion, at one with His Supreme Sovereignty. As we humble ourselves, we draw nigh unto that Great Holy Omnipotence in which we abide. We realize we are not God's "subjects," but are *each God's individuality expressing Him-Self through our self,* as Godly Divine Beings. And in prayer we are learning to enter "our closet," where our innermost stillness resides.

Though we may hold a computer in our hands, we still have to take action to connect to the internet, so the two may become one in operation. In like manner we must actively turn our consciousness away from material cares in order to connect with the divine internet, the universal circuitry of our Source, the ultimate "processor," and operate as one with that Source. When you realize that All is "Thee," including me and thee, and connect internally with this knowing, you are blending with the divine supply which meets all human needs. *"Seek ye first the kingdom of God, and his righteousness, and all these things shall be added unto you."* (Matthew 6:33)

There we can pray, no longer with a prayer of petition and pleading to that which is unapproachable. We have become one with "that mind," that same conscious awareness, "which was in Christ Jesus." We are then "thinking out from God," and not "up to God." We will pray with affirmation and declaration. Whether in a church of our own choosing, or in the quiet of our own body, temple-church, we can worship, adore and know Him.

The Master clearly indicates throughout his teachings that the time has come when man must make each and every day a spiritual Sabbath by knowing and doing all things in a spiritual light, moment to moment. He gave us one comprehensive prayer that meets all our needs:

"Our Father which art in heaven,
Hallowed be thy name.
Thy kingdom come.
Thy will be done on earth, as it is in heaven.
Give us this day our daily bread; (our daily spiritual energy)
And forgive us our debts, as we forgive our
debtors. (trespasses, trespassers)

And lead us not into temptation, but deliver us from evil; (the suggestion of evil, negativity)

For Thine is the kingdom, and the power, and the glory, forever."

Amen

Whether we recognize it or not, all life is yearning to be lifted higher and higher to a more vibrant frequency, emanating radiance. Our theologies have the opportunity to take us there, if they will expand out of the dark ages and remove the limitations created by veils of doctrine and creed that consciously hold us in a less than divine state.

The new spiritual shift, whether with or without organized religions, is rising, and taking us from the literal to the Celestial. We are light-beings, light-bodies, and light-bearers foreordained to illuminate our own "temple," our own son-ship.

The one eternal lesson for us all
is how better we can love
and bring peace to our surroundings.

Chapter 6

DEDICATION

Motivated not by human ego but by Divine Will
makes man a devoted and active instrument of the Supreme

—***Krishna***

Perhaps you remember Goethe's words, "Talent develops itself in solitude; character in the stream of life." In the 1880s Henry Drummond later put it this way, "Talent develops itself in solitude, the talent of prayer, faith, meditation, of seeing the unseen; character grows in the stream of the world's life. That chiefly is where men are to learn love… and learn that love is the greatest commodity in the world… The business of our lives is to be fitted with the characteristics thereof.

"That is the supreme work to which we need to address ourselves on this earth, to learn love. Is life not full of opportunities for learning compassion? Every man and woman every day has a thousand of them. The world is not a playground; it is a schoolroom. Life is not a holiday, but an education. The one eternal lesson for us all is how better we can love.

"What makes a man a good cricketer, is practice. What makes a man a good artist, a good sculptor, a good musician, is practice. What makes a man a good man, practice, nothing else. If a man does not exercise his arm, he does not develop bicep muscles; and if a man does not exercise his soul, he acquires no muscle in his soul, no strength of character, no vigor of moral fiber, no beauty of spiritual growth. Love is not a thing of enthusiastic emotion. It is a rich, strong, manly, vigorous expression of the whole round Christian type character—the Christ-like nature in its fullest development. The constituents of this great character are only to be built up by ceaseless practice.

"What was Christ doing in the carpenter's shop? He was practicing. Though perfect, we read that he learned obedience, and grew in wisdom and in favor with God. Do not quarrel, therefore with your lot in life. Do not complain of its never ceasing cares, its petty environment, the vexations you have to stand, the small and sordid souls you have to live and work with. This is your practice which God appoints you... working to make yourself more patient, humble, generous, unselfish, kind and courteous."

Baird T. Spalding, in writing about a great leader of our time, stated:

"Gandhi studied the situation of non-violence for twenty years before he began his work, becoming a very deep student of it. Great work is being done by the illumined. 'What the Father sees in secret, He will reward you openly,' is not an idle statement but it reveals the manner in which all things come into being in the outer world. We follow the noisy people into bypaths and lose the path of life that moves in stillness through our own individual being."

Gautama the Buddha gave up family and wealth seeking truth, finding moderation to be the way, the "middle way," with sacrifice, service, honesty, but mostly teaching ethics, compassion, and sharing life in a loving fashion. When someone sent him anger or hate, he sent them back love in return. Five hundred years before Jesus, Gautama spoke of men "touching the hem of my garment." And said, "Returning anger for anger changes nothing." Of course, he knew that we reap what we sow, and that change can only come from "loving the least of my brethren."

Hate is not conquered by hate,
Hate is conquered by love.

—***Gautama the Buddha***

Much can be gained from looking into the insights and writings of many of history's highly enlightened individuals. I have infinite respect for Jesus in what he practiced and all he accomplished. He is my ideal, given that he studied tirelessly and demonstrated every bit of what he preached. Most importantly, he saw all of us as his brothers and sisters, indeed, as his equal. Jesus gave his whole life, beginning in early childhood, to his spiritual mission. We too, have that same inner potential and talent to accomplish our spiritual mission as well, whether we currently realize it or not. He focused on the job at hand, practicing love wherever he went, on the hillside, in the marketplace, by the sea shore. He gave of himself 100 percent. What percentage of ourselves, our time, have we given toward following his example? Five percent? 10 percent? He surely never intended to be idolized by the people of earth... instead perhaps idealized. He is my ideal!

In the 1990s, there was a popular saying, "I want to be like Mike." This statement, of course, was directed toward the greatest basketball player to ever play the game. That person would be my good friend, Michael Jordan. The fact of the matter is this, as many have found out, you could work your whole lifetime, with all earnestness and dedication, with the one single goal in mind, that of being like Mike, and it probably won't happen. Unless you were fortunate enough to grow to six foot six inches or better, and could jump 40 inches straight up off the ground, and have a competitive nature like a bulldog, there's no way you are going to "be like Mike."

I can diagnose a person's temperature by using a thermometer or placing my hand upon a child's forehead. I can even prescribe an aspirin or flu tablets. But an individual with a medical degree knows one hundred times more than I—hmm—actually he knows thousands of times more than I. A doctor would have studied for years, including having had hands-on experience.

My point is this: you would have a better chance of working your whole lifetime with an ethical and spiritual goal in mind, the goal of practicing the ways of the Christ, than to try and miraculously grow six to twelve inches taller to be like Mike, or aspire to become a renowned doctor. Actually each of us is inherently more qualified to "be like Jesus!" There are no physical or scholastic aptitude requirements for following the Master. He would say to us, it is so very, very simple. How simple you may ask? Practice, practice, practicing "The Way."

Of course there is nothing wrong with having role models, whether they be sports stars, movie stars, teachers, parents or a close friend. But we must constantly ask ourselves—are we emulating them for their highest qualities or for their personality and popularity? Are we wanting to add to the best we already possess within ourselves, or are we trying to lose ourselves in their aura because of our own inner feelings of dissatisfaction and

insecurity? We must look for the motives in our admiration of others and ask ourselves often what it is we are admiring? Do we follow an ideal for fame, self-satisfaction, ego, pride, or perhaps because someone else expects it of us?

It is the Christ qualities that must become the role model for each and every one of us. And adding these to our character only results in bringing greater strength and winning achievement to every talent we may pursue. The practice of goodness is its own prize every time! Have you ever considered that someone may be seeing you as their role model?

Jesus told us that the Spirit, Father, within himself, is none other than the very same Spirit, Father, within ourselves. All that is required of us is to simply "go and do likewise." We have all the qualities, all the ingredients and components of brotherly-kindness, patience and love that the Master had. Our physical and spiritual person, identical to his, is comprised in totality, of divine love, wisdom and power. The wisdom of love is your power. If we practice what the Master taught, if all our thoughts are loving and forgiving, and we stay focused on our spiritual nature, we would see that we can be like him and express God on earth. To paraphrase Shakespeare, though we may be but small, we can be fierce! Yes, fierce and compassionate concerning our spiritual growth.

Nothing great in this world has ever been accomplished without passion.

—***Hegel***

Picture your whole day filled with only loving thoughts, ideas, and actions. Wow! See how simple heaven on earth can be. We would be returning to our original, harmonious, Garden of

Eden. Think about it, no negative thoughts, words or deeds. We would be living our lives with "that mind which was also in Christ Jesus." Hopefully learning to love what we are doing and in turn doing what we love.

Even Beethoven was continually practicing, refining and refinishing his musical compositions. Are we continually refining, re-polishing our character, and becoming our own best critic?

Gandhi once told us, "One can hardly do anything in the way of accomplishing universal peace until he has found peace within his own nature and he cannot find peace in his own nature until he has been long enough truly in touch with the unseen forces which move toward the common good. There is no question but that the individual first must be at peace."

A peace-filled consciousness is a disciplined consciousness. Being still, demonstrating dominion from within, is the first step toward achieving any worthwhile goal. Remember, Talent develops itself in solitude, the talent of prayer, faith, of meditation. It takes great practice to quiet the mind which is continually racing to get ahead in this world, to make its mark, make a name for ourselves, get that award. Only when the mind is stilled can we practice being our true spiritual selves, which readies us for the next step, developing our character, which grows in the mainstream of the world's life.

This is the Christ-like nature in its fullest development. The constituents of this great character are only to be built up by ceaseless practice. So... *"Seek ye first the kingdom of God, and his righteousness; and all these things shall be added unto you."* (Matthew 6:32)

Jesus said something like this to the wise man: How can I tell you of heavenly matters, when you are not understanding of this world? What moves within man also moves within the

universe. To know himself in some of these most simple things is his key to great understanding and power, no matter the height of his endeavors. Dedication to the practice of being more like an enlightened Master, should be the unwritten goal of every man. Where are we on this quest?

Nothing happens unless first a dream.

—***Carl Sandburg***

I think humanly we should aspire to be more like a Mother Teresa, Buddha, Lao-Tze, Rumi, a Master Jesus, in their example of teaching and serving our fellow man. With the highest regard and respect we should give thanks to all our brothers and sisters who answered their calling to come to the cloth, and have become ministers of the world. Ninety-nine percent of these dedicated individuals put their egos aside in order to do God's, Allah's work on earth. They are brave and selfless, no matter their creed, they deserve no less than our highest admiration and gracious thanks. *"... he that is greatest among you will be your servant."* (Matthew 23:11)

And these dedicated religious individuals are literally the "greatest" among us. Whether they have professed it aloud or not, I congratulate them; for they are truly practicing to be like Jesus.

We must first become master of our own vessel, our own consciousness. Taking the road that is very straightforward, narrow and specific, is "The Way" toward total control of one's human self. This then prepares us to reach out to others in service with love, compassion and forgiveness.

Are we developing our spiritual talents on the way to our own Master's degree? Are we even practicing touching the "hem" of our innate potential?

The one eternal lesson for us all is how better we can love and bring peace to our surroundings. The one eternal question is, how long will it take each of us to come to this understanding?

ALL THERE IS... IS LOVE
GOD IS LOVE
WE ARE LOVE
GOD WE ARE

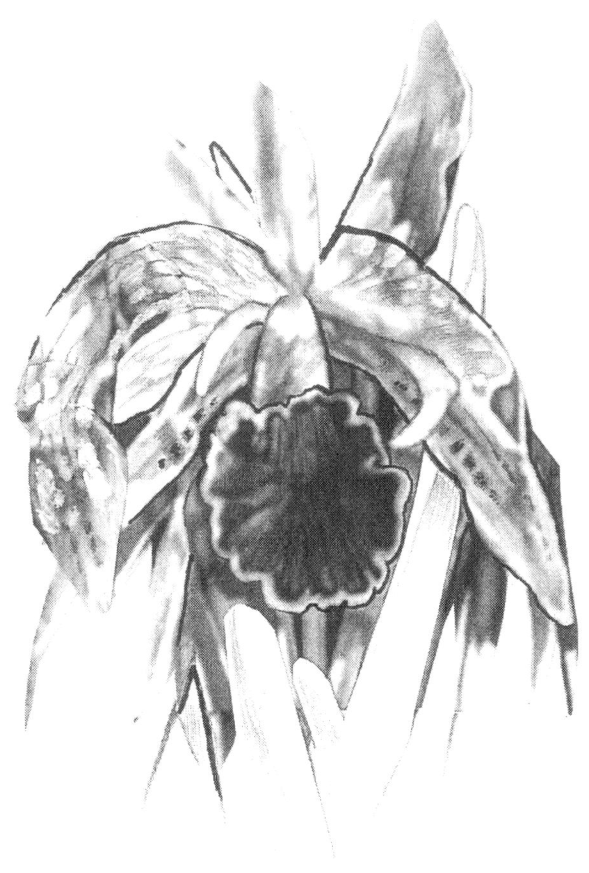

Like an orchid that gets its nourishment from the sunshine, rain and air… people have flowered to the highest understanding… praying to offset the world's accumulated negative energies of greed, hate, anger, and stress.

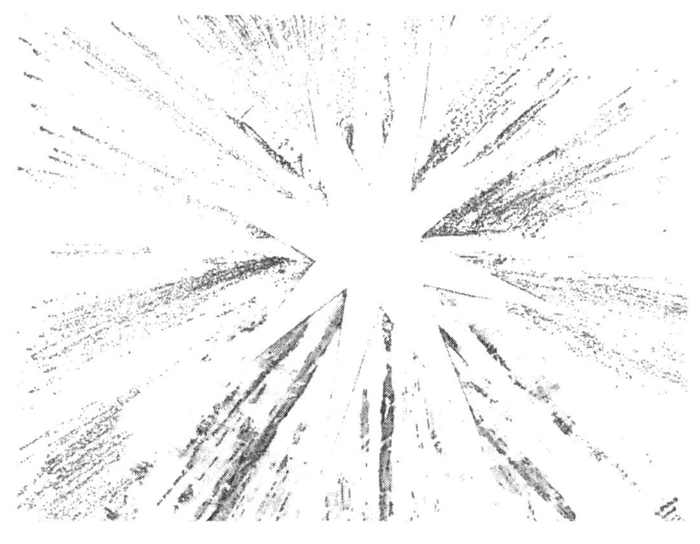

We, as well as Jesus, are spiritual rays of light from a Central Sun, so to speak. Each shining forth uniquely, none greater than another. But, in our limited understanding and expression, some may shine brighter because of the intensity of their heightened spiritual efforts.

Chapter 7

GO AND DO LIKEWISE

Earth's crammed with heaven
and every common bush afire with God.

—***Elizabeth Barrett Browning***

Our divinity

Divinity is not the antithesis of humanity—it is the full magnification thereof. We human beings divide ourselves into groups, fraternities, sects, organizations and nations of different races, colors, religions, genders, nationalities. Yet along with this diversity, we seldom view ourselves and others equally, much less as divine. And when we look toward the Master we divorce ourselves from any conceivable way of being equal to him, let alone emulating him and doing likewise; or the possibility of our being "afire with God."

The time has come for the truth to be told, the truth that sets all men free, that truth which "passeth" all human understanding.

Since the beginning of man's existence on earth the clock has been ticking. By this time, the 21st century, we should be spiritually advanced enough, intelligent enough, to listen, reason and understand for whom the bell tolls, the time is nigh. Don't you hear the resonating tones in your ear? It is your Higher-Self calling for you to come home to your own Christ-Self. The ringing is loud and clear, for each of us to seek and find, "go and do." The ministers of today have answered this "clarion call" and are doing "likewise," taking up the cross.

Christmas morning has arrived. Just take a look at the children's faces. Yes, we are those children, and we smile because we understand that our Master and Teacher, Jesus arrived on this day. His gift to us is to know our own Christliness. Are we ready to receive this gift, to acknowledge and embrace it?

We need to realize that he came to let us know we are his brother, we have the potential to be like him. Remember, Jesus was considered to be a great Jewish prophet, perhaps even the greatest man ever; until approximately 325 A D when two individuals, the pagan Roman Emperor Constantine along with the Roman Catholic Pope, in the midst of bitter argument over Biblical translations, decided to bestow the title of "God" upon him.

Ruling powers

This was a subtle transfer of ruling power meant to enhance, strengthen these two governing bodies, the Roman Empire and the Catholic Church, as they developed their new religion eventually called Christianity. They were seeking a combination of political and religious, governmental control. They wanted to leave behind the worshiping of many gods, i.e. Zeus, Apollo, Poseidon, etc. in order to unify the people of their empire under one new deity. Christianity would soon be gaining strength throughout the land, following the teachings of the master prophet Jesus. These two sovereigns wanted to jump on board and take advantage of the wave of rising enthusiasm that a great many had for this master teacher, albeit with ulterior motives.

However, proclaiming Jesus as a "god," making him their one and only deity, would come to inhibit the emulation of him as is still witnessed today throughout religions. The crowning of this recently proclaimed god, deified and distanced Jesus from the people, making him less approachable, except through the clergy in rote prayers and elaborate rituals. We might do well to remember that originally Jesus was not a Christian, Muhammad was not a Muslim, Buddha was not a Buddhist. Devout followers later very conscientiously tried to pattern and name these religions after the teachings of these avatars.

The pagan-like worship that evolved, the idolizing of a man, was in direct contradiction to what the Master taught and practiced. Mao Zedong stated that "Religion is the opium of the masses." In addition, as early as 1843 Karl Marx similarly had this to say, "Religion is the sigh of the oppressed creature, the heart of a heartless world, and the soul of soulless conditions. It is the opium of the people." More succinctly Marx continued, "The first requisite for the happiness of the people is the abolition of religion."

Why would these powerful men utter such displeasure at the concept of religion? Perhaps because Marx and others knew that people can easily be duped and stupefied by so-called righteous, yet tyrannical leaders, in the name of God or Allah. Yet today, in the free world, we love our Christianity, and are grateful to have unlimited religious choices. We just choose not to be squeezed doctrinally into a straitjacket!

We should cherish the freedom to further our spirituality by thinking for ourselves, seeking truth from within, and independently reading differing points of view; like studying the earliest teachings of Jesus as was part of the Gnostic practice of old, before the Catholic inquisition.

In order to help continue their dominance over the people, these sovereigns were setting up and building a system of rules, regulations and decrees. The old pharisaic doctrines were being fashioned anew, yet the rigidity and oppressive control was once again being duplicated, only in different form, and now under the auspices of a different name, "Christianity." This was the very dominance and dogma our Master ironically had fought so openly against, and for which he was crucified by the clergy.

In reality Jesus was no more "God" than we are—that is, no more of God than we are, for in truth we are all equal portions or individualizations of consciousness within our One Source. No one is to be idolized over another. We all have the right, the privilege of being just as much of the One Source as Jesus exemplified. Over a long period of time, we have simply been programmed to believe the contrary. The early Gentiles along with the ruling bodies had unwittingly thrown layers of misinterpretation and misunderstanding over the original Jewish, Hebrew written stories concerning the Master.

It was also at this point in time when dualism gained a substantial momentum—human versus divine, spiritual versus material, heaven versus hell—as the collective consciousness struggled to find its mental footing and purpose for existence. Oppression and confusion was rampant and causing men to seek a way out of their misery and doom. Whether self-imposed or not, they were desperate.

Symbols and sacrifices

This new theology fashioned around setting the man Jesus up as a singular god, at the same time declared him to be the "sacrificial lamb." In actuality he had been lovingly forgiving us for our sinning ways and admonishing us to think more with our divine capabilities than with a selfish lower human free will. Yet per pagan philosophy, the church pronounced him to be the one, the lamb, to take on the "responsibility" of the world's sins, past, present and future, as if to eradicate the individual accountability of 7 billion souls. In our modern-day sense of things this should seem illogical and absurd! In addition, the already lowly subjects were being trained submissively to beg for mercy and forgiveness. The responsibility of the people's errant sowing was to be waived off through confession and rote supplication.

The concept of a sacrificial lamb with blood and body sacrifice was thus initiated within the church, the transubstantiation, if you will; as well as further manipulation through requisite ceremonies in order to help control the people under this new regime of an institutional system of beliefs, creeds and convictions.

The appeasing pagan concept of sacrificial offering to the gods, continues in the trappings of today's more sophisticated rituals, in symbolically bathing in or drinking the wine as "blood," and eating the "bread," as the "body" of the man Jesus.

We need to realize that this communal sacrifice was appropriated from the pagan-like and cannibalistic ceremonial events of ancient times. It was the Greek, Roman, and Aztec ritual to sacrifice sheep, goats, and people to appease their gods. Egyptians and others also practiced human sacrifice—and the Mayans offered up the lives of young boys to their deity.

Regardless of the reasoning for such primitive practices, it is quite obvious that many symbolic words in Jesus' allegories and parables, which were intended to have deep spiritual import, were instead turned into literal and materialistic mantras and rituals which continue to this day.

As the collective consciousness moves further away from hollow ceremony and ritual, the more enlightened meaning of many of Jesus' messages, especially those uttered at the Last Supper, will glow with new transparency. We will then *drink* more deeply the import of his timeless words, and *ingest* more fully the embodiment of his works.

The literal and symbolic must finally give way to the spiritual at all points. It is a wise adage that says: The more literal and material worship becomes, the less spiritual it is.

A new spiritual shift on our planet has recently taken place and a lifting of our consciousness is evident as we begin leaving behind aged precepts for the new old wisdom of the ages. As Episcopal Bishop Spong reminds us, the message from the pulpit and many of our hymns still perpetuate the guilt being driven into us as "lowly wretched sinners," creating within the church a marketplace for needed forgiveness, and a pleading for mercy, from an all- loving God who is said to have taken his own Son's life! Bishop Spong, with tongue in cheek, calls this eternal punishment for our sins, "the gift that keeps on giving," as the church requires our continual penance, when it should be confirming and teaching our potential for righteousness and our innate divinity.

The law of love

Hear ye him! When he declares the Father in me, the spirit within, "he doeth the works, not me," this means the same Father, Spirit, which is within ourselves, and we ought to be affirming our capabilities of doing the "greater works" which he commanded us to do. Jesus was the "elect" Son, the supreme example, to be sure, but not the only son as these sovereigns would have had us believe. For indeed, we are all his brothers and sisters in a universal family as the "sons of God."

Through misinterpretation, some theologians have taught that Jesus came to earth like a benevolent rich uncle to pay our debts, to pay for our sins. Again, how shallow the thought process. There is no logic or reasoning in this conjured up and baseless age-old premise. We must understand that each man is responsible for his own evils, whether Jim Jones, David Koresh, or a Hitler. Under the system of "vicarious atonement" that has Jesus paying our debts, even a Fuhrer could be let off the hook for his own transgressions, atrocities, such as a Holocaust.

This leaves us with a quagmire of a question: Imagine if Adolf Hitler, before his death had asked a priest to forgive him of all his sins? Are we to suppose that a priest has the wherewithal to relieve another human being of their heinous criminal acts, transferring and laying all his indiscretions at the feet of the Master, with no conscious reformation earned, no lessons learned? Should we somehow assume that Jesus will give him immediate pardon with 6 million absolutions?

If in your own garden you have seeded, inflicted 250 million injuries...do you actually think someone else will reap this harvest for you? Can you hear the Master saying, how utterly ludicrous and nonsensical—the Law states that each man is responsible for his own salvation!

Thankfully, the planetary shift in a new spiritual awareness is taking root. The literal interpretations of the early teachings and pre-modern ideas of vicarious atonement and a vengeful God are being transformed and replaced with the understanding and acceptance of the overarching Universal Law of Adjustment, the divine principle of worldly and spiritual individual accountability.

How will a child or an adult, for instance, learn his or her lessons of hard knocks if not individually disciplined for his errant behavior? How will a country learn from its erred behavior, if its leaders are not brought to justice? Only through personal transformation can the perpetrator be absolved of his sins. The depth of a person's or a nation's error, sinning, will of itself constitute the magnitude of its self-imposed punishment.

The Master has even so much as said he is not going to learn your ABCs or your multiplication tables for you; to survive and succeed in this world you must learn them for yourself, "work out your own salvation." Neither will he wipe your debts away. Where would be the lesson?

Universal Law requires that sins, evils, transgressions, be adjusted and transmuted personally. This omnipotent and impartial Law of Love is not meant to be so much a punisher, as it is a patient teacher. Could this be why Jesus told us repeatedly not to stand in judgment or be critical of others? That is not our place, their judgment will automatically be forthcoming.

The true mission

Jesus' sole purpose was to teach us "The Way" to be conscious of and governed by the fact that we are all divine life-streams, divine individualities, equal in every way, not just humanly, but with the same spiritual capabilities as well. We seem to have lost sight of the fact that the Master's sublime mission was to reveal God-Consciousness to mankind.

Every life, every consciousness, all spiritual forms and all physical forms are vibrant and alive, actively bearing witness to their Creator. All is maintained, sustained, and supported by the spirit of the One Energy, One Source, One Consciousness. It is omnipresent, omnipotent, omniscient, eternity, infinity. We call it God, Allah, Shiva, or the All-that-Is. It is Love, energy, with no beginning, no end, all pervasive. It is All-in-All. "All there is is love, love, love is all there is," sang John, Paul, George and Ringo.

The Master clearly practiced dominion over the elements—knowing that all facets of this magnificent and beneficent creation have consciousness, intelligent purpose and function, even that which we call inanimate and inert matter.

Atoms, particles, molecules, electrons, neutrons, cells, gases, all elements contain and express their own individually governed intelligence, because each is derived from the One Source that is Love, Wisdom and Power. We too, being the vibrant light, the greatest and most magnificent of all creations, the "suns" of the most High, need to recognize and appreciate that we are each individualized and en-lightened Life-streams of consciousness within the One God/Love/Energy. Knowing this we come to the all-important fact that we are every one, perfectly equivalent suns of God.

We, as well as Jesus, are spiritual rays of light from a Central Sun, so to speak. Each shining forth uniquely, none greater than another. But, in our limited understanding and expression, some may shine brighter because of the intensity of their heightened spiritual efforts.

Each of us can be likened to an equal drop of ocean water, in the Sea of Eternity Some sons have come to understand their true spiritual nature much quicker than others, their true, divine son-ship. Some are yet sleeping. Still others have never forgotten their celestial status and thus, behold, the entry of Jesus! He recognized the power within the Christ, or divine nature, the Godliness within himself. However he never made a claim of being any different than any other person, never taught that we were beneath him or were unworthy. Quite the contrary.

The fact is, he saw us as his brothers and sisters and exhorted us to see ourselves as his counterpart and "follow" him. How could he possibly ask us to go and do likewise, if we too weren't presently endowed with the same divine qualities and with the full potential and capabilities of raising the Christ within ourselves? He knew that just as within himself, the Light of God was the Source of life in each one of us, within all men and including all facets of creation.

Presence of the Christ

Please remember, the "Christ" is not exclusive only to Jesus. "The Christ" was a title bestowed upon him for his recognition of Our Father, Our Source, the I Am within; a title or term, which implies the greatest degree of spirituality understood, and expressed in human form.

The Christ is the I Am projecting its Presence into this realm, thus becoming the Christ-Presence on earth. It can be thought of as the dynamic activity, the "verb" if you will, of the I Am, the God-Presence. It is the activity that stirs, heals, regenerates and elevates consciousness, body and spirit. It stays pure in "My Kingdom", but extends itself into "this world" through one's consecration, purity and unselfed love.

The acknowledgement of this Presence was demonstrated by Jesus through his miraculous works. Does he ask much of us? Absolutely! But are we willing to step onto the straight and narrow pathway? He encourages us to take our mortal-minded thinking upwards, up, up and away, elevating above the material senses; raising our conscious awareness into our higher-self-consciousness, where our own individual Christ patiently awaits its ascending discovery.

He asks us to raise our spiritual awareness to heights previously unknown to all but a few, whereby we too might go out and heal the sick, make the lame walk, and raise the dead. He thought divinely while he walked among us humanly. He tried to advance us by showing we have dominion over the elements, by levitating himself over the seas, manifesting loaves and fishes, turning water into wine, and calming the storms.

His Sermon on the Mount was the "how to" for the ages. He asks us to talk about his example and share the "The Old, Old Story" of love and forgiveness, compassion, ethics and integrity.

Everything to do with the Master is showing us how to be his equal. In the East, 500 years before Jesus, Gautama the Buddha wrote, " the Christ can be attained." Not added to ourselves, but the prana of life-force energy and power realized from within. We are each individual expressions and experiences of the One and the same Divine Source. Jesus and other especially enlightened beings throughout time, have, through their teachings, tried to further advance the concept of our own equivalent and unique individual light.

Jesus and Buddha have this in common,
that their form of ethics... is not an ethic of action,
but an ethic of inner perfection.

—Albert Schweitzer

The very first followers of the Master saw themselves as his brothers and his aspiring equals. They set out to "do likewise" aspiring "to be like Jesus" in his compassionate teachings of our righteousness. This pure and simple spiritual mission was gaining much momentum with its message of love and healing, until brashly interrupted with the humanly imposed theology accompanied by Emperor's edicts, religious armies and inquisitions, declaring their subjects not worthy of having spiritual aspirations of their own.

The living Jesus was bound and hindered by the new church creed as per scriptural interpretation according to the scholars who were more concerned about their reputations and keeping their lives, than revealing truth.

In writing "The Third Jesus," Deepak Chopra considered hundreds of Gospel verses before completing his manuscript to convey the whole range of what Jesus really had to say, even when he appeared negative or discouraging. Contrary to conventional wisdom, the picture we have of a smiling, benign Jesus is only half the story; he was just as capable of anger, harshness and even dismissal of those who could not or would not understand him.

Chopra had to choose from dozens of New Testament translations, in compiling his writings, discovering the contrast in the different versions to be startling. He found the many differing Biblical translations to be a very thorny issue indeed. The early writers of the Bible had Jesus seemingly to float in a kind of intentional otherworldliness, always keeping us at a vast distance from him.

Chopra reminds us that the Master's teachings are truly learned only when you become and live the teaching. Love is deeply instinctive in all of us. Yet innate as love is, we do not always exhibit this divine quality. At times we choose to be completely unloving. The lesson of Love that Jesus taught is that divine love is so full of grace it causes a transformation within the human, a disciplining effect which changes a person's whole being.

Doing likewise

To go and do likewise is being a modern-day disciple of the Master, meaning to live daily by the truths he taught, beginning first by holding oneself in the highest regard, and being fully representative of the Master and his compassion. We must love and forgive, forgiving 70 times seven if need be, and accept our perceived shortcomings of others—"for what is that to thee?"

We should share love and light, "preaching the Gospel," with our actions spreading the good news. Your actions will be respected much more than mere hollow words.

Example is not the main thing
in influencing others.
It is the only thing.

—***Albert Schweitzer***

Jesus said *"judge not lest ye be judged."* Should his so-called "devout" followers of today be so critical and judgmental of their brothers and sisters, emphatically declaring how wrong they think they are? How off-course they think others are, if they don't all follow the same doctrine or creed as the criticizer!

True judgment ultimately comes from the Law of the Universe adjusting each in its own time. Yes, individual atonement is determined by these laws through our own Christ-Presence, continually correcting our creative energies misspent through errant thoughts and actions, in being judgmental or unkind, or in matters which we call sin.

"Vengeance is mine saith the Lord." This "Lord," of course, is none other than our own individual higher consciousness, our Christ-Self, which is always watching and has no concept of evil, just as the sun which only knows light, has no concept of darkness. However, its illumining presence works on correcting our childish errors and shadowed thoughts and deeds. Its parenting affection sees through our mistakes and insists on our perfection.

The parent loves the child regardless of his mistakes. By the laws of the universe, the discomfort of our own transgressions will be our punisher and teacher, correcting our misdeeds as surely as a boomerang returns in flight.

It is time that we brought peace to our world and calm to our atmosphere. Stilling the storms begins within each person that inhabits this earth. Anger and hate, wars and turbulence in our world are a disturbed manifestation, a temporal creation born from man's errant thinking. Jesus would say, "Go and sin no more," temper your thinking, carefully keeping all your thoughts caring. A thousand years of peace starts within each person. So go now and lose the concepts of anger, envy, greed, etc. Think about it for a moment, harmony, no hate or condemnation allowed, no anger-management needed!

We tend to keep the Master at arm's length, or possibly a universe away. All the while, he is our big brother, our guide and protector ever beside us. Some think he is unreachable unless a stipulated doctrine is adhered to, or certain words are mouthed in a specific mantra. Others have been taught that a particular measure of confession, or the admission that one is a sinner will help pave the way. All this procedure, pomp and circumstance, rhetoric and dogma creates layer upon layer of separation between us and The Master. It leaves us *A Thousand Miles From Nowhere*, as echoed in the popular country song by Dwight Yokam.

If we could at least begin to cut through some of these medieval mindsets, we would feel closer and closer to the man who lived to love and show us that we too have a Christed-Self—undiscovered.

There is a vast difference between "closeness" and "oneness." Jesus emphasized *oneness* throughout his works, to remove every vestige of imagined separation between the Father and all his sons.

Exemplification

Again, everything to do with Jesus was to furnish an example, a lesson, to exemplify how we also, can realize our own God-Self.

As he was the Son of God, so we too are the sons and daughters of God. He went about healing and doing good works, just as we should desire to do. The Master forgave, showing us how to forgive. He illustrated his mastery and dominion over outer conditions. We too can learn to still the storms of weather as well the turbulence within society. His love, compassion and forgiveness for others was unparalleled. We too can aspire to love with the same vigor of Divine Love that he expressed.

All that he did and said has import to our immediate experience and understanding. Even in something so mystical and celestial as his immaculate conception, perhaps we are to discern that we also, are somehow immaculately conceived *spiritually*, regardless of our temporal physicality. We have possibly become so focused on the wonder of a virgin birth, miraculous as it may seem, we neglect to discern or glean from it the spiritual message concerning ourselves. Could this event have possibly been telling us that our real self, our Spiritual-Self, is also conceived spiritually; even before we appear physically and are brought forth by two caring human parents?

Spiritually we are each an "immaculate conception" in the Omnipotent Spirit, God,—originally pure, innocent and perfect in spirit. We will eventually come to accept that our temple-form, our present body is only a temporary vehicle to be used for our creative earthly endeavors.

The Master was also showing us things about our own immortality… that there is no death, not only for himself, but no death for us either. As the infinite, the Spirit of all configurations, continues on, so do its individual expressions, such as you and I, along with all of His creations.

There is no such thing as death, only a continuation, because God is Life—God is all there is or ever will be. He is we, only changing and advancing forms. The ending of one form, does not take away life, but rather, is a metamorphosis evolving us into the next shape or characteristics required for the sojourn to follow, like the caterpillar transforming into the butterfly.

Life is perpetual. The Life, our life, goes on, for all lives are eternal. Death of a material vehicle, a body, is nothing to be feared, but intended to be a wonderful pause and rejuvenating, a transforming process. "Death is like changing our clothes," says the Dalai Lama. Immortality is not some vague and hazy existence, a sort of afterlife where we drift aimlessly in the clouds.

We will have experience after experience, as our Great Teacher illustrated in showing himself after his resurrection. We will continue to add to our life's purpose and achieve higher and higher attainments. Though we may not be able to see and understand it all, still, we can have faith that this particular physical life, is but another parentheses in our own eternality. Our continuation goes on, filling our soul with yet another round of wonderment.

Our Lord has written the promise of\resurrection,
not in books alone but in every leaf in springtime.

—***Martin Luther***

Individualizations of One Source

This Life, the God-Consciousness, of which we are a part, is an active, productive entity working together in harmony for the good of the whole. The One Intelligence splits and divides proportionately into an infinite number of conscious shapes, forms, colors, and endless individualities, such as the marvel of you and I; including the planet we exist upon, and all universes yet to be discovered. Cells, atoms, micro-organisms, drops, pools, vapors, all take part in having zillions of varying experiences in an infinite number of creations, shapes and configurations.

The cycle of originating, dividing, expressing, originating and returning never comes to a stop. Leaves unfurl and clouds may form, seasons come and go. Change is forever active within the whole and individually expressive. Each creation is circulating, and evolving on different levels, vibrations, or frequencies, each with unique purpose, function and intelligence; but all the while revolving, swirling within the one ocean of the All-that-Is, the Source of all.

We as magnificent human beings, need to realize that we are part of this remarkable process of action, forever creating and expressing, forever participating, revolving and evolving through a myriad of experiences within the whole of omnipresent Life.

Jesus tried to show us that this magnificent power source is Love, that all Life is God in varying forms of energy and experiences, and that we should have this life "more abundantly." In the Divine there is no mortal measurement of time, no wall that cannot be walked through, and therein no disease, hate, or torment. Harmony reigns. Couldn't we for one moment step outside of our presupposed religious views of God, man and the universe as the Master did? How our eyes would be opened. What wonders we might behold!

Imagine a pool of H_2O and how it is comprised of tiny droplets, each undergoing its own journey. This illustration might help us to understand our own sojourns: We might think of each drop in this pool elevating, quickening itself—then after a time comes the ultimate elevation—ascending itself to the clouds—and once again dropping from the heavens to the ground creating streams, beautiful lakes, oceans ... and then again cycling, finding itself returning to the heavens ...

Everything flows, nothing stays still.

—***Heraclitus***

In like manner, there are an infinite number of experiences in the continuing spiritual journey of our individual lifetimes. All uniquely important and distinct. It takes an endless amount of harmonizing and perfecting activity to comprise the whole of our being. Love, God, divides, replicates into zillions of forms, with purpose and consciousness. From this divine perspective we can begin to see the face of God in all life.

As Emmet Fox put it so eloquently, "If God did not individualize himself, there would be only the one experience; as it is, there are as many universes as there are individualities to form them through thinking." Scientists are only now beginning to understand the ephemeral nature of the human body, to contemplate parallel universes, and the infinitude of possibilities that are beyond mere human comprehension and calculation.

As we advance and progress in our spiritual understanding, no longer will we indulge any anger, hate, disease and pestilence, or hunger and war. Harmony reigns. We can regain the Christ perspective of seeing all things made with spiritual energy and integrity, and have the capacity to value and protect them.

It took a more highly evolved and enlightened individual consciousness, like the Master, to come and help direct our earthly schoolroom toward the advancement of elevated thought, especially for the dominion of mind over matter, and to the infinite possibilities goodness provides.

No longer will we view God as an ancient, bearded man in the sky throwing lightening bolts at us, or judging us from afar. God is infinite, forever active, creative, Love, Energy. Period!

The dynamics

The dynamics of Jesus' teachings seemed very advanced, even to his disciples, but when they applied his principles of love,

meditation and consecration, they healed much like he did, and perpetuated his mission valiantly. We should be ready for thinking and doing likewise. We might also be eagerly awaiting the new shift in consciousness that welcomes the opportunity to bring into our lives the heretofore hidden, yet deeply important aspects of the Christ ideals that Jesus presented to the world.

Throughout the history of mankind, there have been those from all corners of the world who have come close to "doing likewise." Several that we are aware of, in our not so distant past, who dedicated a large portion of their lives to manifesting healing works, were Smith Wigglesworth, Mary Baker Eddy, Joel Goldsmith, Guy Ballard and Bruno Groening, just to name a few. These people worked, studied and trained with tireless prayer and devotion, and as a result, healed thousands of people, including raising the dead, giving sight to the blind, and enabling the crippled to walk.

They heard the bells tolling, calling them to emulate the Master. However, they first had to embrace the truth of their own inner capacity to do the greater works that were set before them.

Their individual stories are wide and varied, yet one common denominator rings true. Each of these modern healers was able to say "I can of my own self do nothing." It is the Christ-Spirit, the Father within me "who doeth the works." Each of us has an important role to play in this world. We have the full potential to heal as well, if we would passionately embrace the desire to do so in consecrated practice.

Smith Wigglesworth believed that healing came through faith, and he was flexible about the methods he employed. They say he was never seen without a Bible in his hands. He ministered at many churches throughout Yorkshire, England on the outskirts of Sheffield, as well as having an international ministry.

Wigglesworth made a commitment to God that he would not sleep at night before he had won a soul for Christ every day. He turned to God consistently for physical health, and raised several people from the dead, including his wife. At a meeting in Washington, D. C., a young woman on crutches, who had never walked before, upon hearing his emphatic words of the Christ and his Truth, suddenly dropped her crutches and began walking. (http;/wikipedia.org/wiki/Smith Wigglesworth)

In Boston during the late 1800s Mary Baker Eddy healed thousands during her years as a Church Leader and devoted follower of Jesus' teachings. One of her many, many healing works involved a child and its mother. Sometime during the summer of 1865 or 1866, Mrs. Norton took her son, George, to Lynn Beach for a day's outing. George being about seven years of age, had been carried on a pillow since birth, having been born with a deformity commonly known as club-feet, both feet being turned backward. Consequently he had never walked.

Mrs. Norton laid the child on the sand and left him alone while she unhitched the horse and went for water. On her return, the child had disappeared. The mother quickly found him down the beach by the water, and walking, with a woman holding his hand. Soon he was taking steps on his own and from that time was able to walk. The healer and the mother looked into each other's eyes and wept ...then they thanked God for this miraculous healing.

(*Mary Baker Eddy: Christian Healer*—Amplified Edition)

Joel Goldsmith is considered to be one of the most inspired spiritual healers and Christian mystics of the 20th century. For many years Mr. Goldsmith devoted himself to silent healing prayer. When calls came in for healing assistance, he would immediately drop everything and reach the Christ-Presence within himself in prayer. He felt the Christ-Spirit in himself touching the Christ within the needy patient and would later write about the insights he received.

Though possibly continents apart, often instantaneous healings were verified. By the end of his life, he had prayed for—and assisted the healing of—thousands of people around the world. (http:/www.spirit site.com/writing/joegol/)

The healings of Guy Ballard, numbered in the twenty thousands. He was a very enlightened spiritual master who is said to have ascended in the mid 1900s. (reference also Godfrey Ray King.)

Bruno Groening, a German mystic and healer, spoke of God as the Father of all people, who sends help and healing through the "Healing Stream," the I Am Presence within each individual, regardless of their religion or nationality. Groening himself had been conscripted into the Germany Army during World War II. After being drafted he stated that he would not kill another human being. Not only did he refuse to carry a weapon, but he refused to even fight. Because of this refusal he came very close to being executed.

During the 1940s and '50s he was so well known for his healing works that newspapers reported as many as 30,000 people from all over Europe daily visiting his town seeking his healing help.

They are able because they think they are able.

—***Virgil***

When we are humble and expectant, we too can become able. As the Apostle Paul said, *"the natural man receiveth not the things of the spirit."* Nelson Mandela is what one would call a perfect example of a "natural man," a regular man. However, he was so imbued with love and forgiveness and so spiritually in tune, that he also heard the bells toll, and answered the call. Within himself he recognized his capacity for doing the greater works.

Mandela healed a whole nation with "the things of the spirit." Formerly a country without, he gave to it a heart. Every man that has gone and done "likewise" should have his angelic story told!

I love to tell the story
Of unseen things above,
Of Jesus and his glory,
Of Jesus and his love,
I love to tell the story
Because I know 'tis true,
It satisfies my longing
As nothing else can do.

I love to tell the story,
It is my theme in glory
To tell the old, old story
Of Jesus and his love.

I love to tell the story,
'Tis pleasant to repeat
What seems, each time I tell it,
More wonderfully sweet.
I love to tell the story,
For some have never heard
The message of salvation
From God's own holy word.
I love to tell the story,

It is my theme in glory
To tell the old, old story
Of Jesus and his love.

I love to tell the story,
For those who know it best
Seem hungering and thirsting
To hear it like the rest'
I love to tell the story,
To sing the new, new song
That is the old, old story
That I have loved so long.
I love to tell the story,
It is my theme in glory
To tell the old, old story—Of Jesus and his love.
Of Jesus and his love.

The Old, Old Story—
Miss Katherine Hankey, 1866

Our choices set our path … whether it be positive or negative
not a pathway waiting for us in an afterlife,
but the course we've chosen right here, right now.

Chapter 8

THE PATH OF NO RETURN

"As a man thinketh, so he is."

—***Proverbs* 23:7**

The origin of our human experiences, the course that continues to unfold before us, begins with a single thought. This single thought-seed grows and grows, expanding into a pathway. Because of one vision held in our consciousness, our new course is being plotted. This picture, this mental vision, might consist of anything or anyone in our world.

We might see a very attractive person, at school, in the workplace, in a store, a club, or just walking across a street or campus, in daylight or at night. We may become infatuated or overly obsessed. We might be angry at a neighbor, co-worker, close friend or relative. We may become resentful and embroiled in hatefulness. We've allowed our mind to be fixated on desire, anger, jealousy and possibly covetousness. We hold this vision in our head, it won't let go.

Or our attention could be focused on an article of clothing in a store, a handbag or a piece of jewelry, a music CD of the songs we love. We may have become mesmerized, in the most subtle of ways, with an unscrupulous desire to possess. We hold this vision in our consciousness, it won't let go.

Perhaps you have a taste of success, and it is very pleasing to the palate. You have begun playing a musical instrument, and with that little bit of success you're hooked; an unusual feeling of delight accompanies your new accomplishments.

This emotion is coming from deep within you. It won't let go. It could be your first trophy or blue ribbon in art, for painting, a music solo, or a sports experience with a ball, golf club, a bat, a racquet; or it could be an award for tumbling, swimming or equestrian.

This sensation could be of an instant success nature, the feeling a child prodigy might encounter. Emotions of aggrandizement might be taking over, unknowingly filling your ego with personal pride, and gloating. Or you could be out on a first date in an automobile, with a multitude of other kinds of heightened passions you've never experienced before. In either case your emotions are spiraling. They won't let go of your senses. They won't turn loose. A possible uncharted pathway, a new course in your life's experience is being set.

We always attract into our lives
whatever we think about most,
believe in most strongly,
expect on the deepest level,
and imagine most vividly.

—***Shakti Gawain***

In some cases, the visions you are holding in your mind could be growing like unwanted seeds. The wave of emotions that is stirring you could overpower your control center for reasoning and ethics. Possibly your ego has become inflated. Perhaps you have become full of yourself.

A freight train of sensations, lusts and wants, could be steaming down your pathway. Overwhelmed by desire, attraction or rage, in five seconds you have made a decision that could dramatically change people's lives, especially your own. All of a sudden, you have put your hands on your neighbor or relative's person, or you have pocketed the item in a store. You have in a moment's madness, during a fierce argument, pulled out a weapon and struck, or pulled a trigger. You've looked down at your cell phone for two seconds too long, and suddenly your new course in life is an inescapable head-on collision.

Let's hope the emotional avalanche of the senses doesn't steer us away from our natural divine pathway, or destroy us. The uplifting congratulations we might receive at our first recital of music or dance, any new endeavor in theatre, artwork, or a game, can be a good thing and turn into an inspiring encouragement toward higher achievements in our life's work, spiraling us upward.

The opposite or down-side may lead us more in the direction of an overwhelming sense of self-importance. These feelings, these visions coming from our original thought-seeds, can carry us on a wave of positive or negative emotions. If not scrutinized, they can sometimes wind up leading us into errant acts, depression or possibly thoughts of suicide.

Even what may seem a harmless and fleeting loss of focus to our thoughts at an important moment in time, could spin us out

of control and leave us in a place we never intended to go—possibly upon the rocks and shoals.

My heart is being turmoiled in these earthly bouts,
still I believe in Oneness and peace with the spirit.
I speak of evil doings, yet I believe not in doubt.
Please see me through the contradictions
within my soul.

—***Ada Richey***

We must police our thoughts, our mind, very dutifully and carefully, because where our vision is, that's exactly where we are placing ourselves, one thought at a time, or one obsessive vision at a time. That's quite a chore to undertake, when you consider an individual may have 50,000 thoughts a day to be examined and edited. Our choices, however, set our course on the path of no return, whether it be positive or negative. This is not a pathway waiting for us in an afterlife, but the course we've chosen right here, right now.

Where is our vision? Are we motivated by ego and pride, consumed with lust, hate, anger, or the love of possessions? Do we feed our thought-moments with visions of self aggrandizement, and judgment, or with selflessness, humility and good will toward our fellowman?

What Jesus insisted upon was a certain spirit in one's conduct. He was careful to teach ethical principles, knowing that when the spirit is right, details will harmoniously take care of themselves. We are constantly nurturing our own thought-seeds. These repetitiously link together forming hopefully a spirit-filled manifesto.

We have the capability to co-creatively cultivate right thought and ideas. The process of observing our own character flaws

allows us to weed out the unwanted weaker links, permitting only the productive, beneficial, unselfed thoughts to take root and flourish.

The Golden Rule in Christianity is: Think about others as you would wish them to think about you. When the spirit of thought is righteous, the outcome or manifestation will be also.

To become addicted to a substance of any kind; or to become overly attached to a particular person, place or thing, begins with a single idea which multiplied becomes an obsession. A sort of mind control or mesmerism has taken over our free will and we may find it manipulating our actions. Uncontrolled influences can turn into a very subtle form of self-sabotage. But they are never at all "outside" our domain of self control. We constantly have the ability to determine our path.

A little kingdom I possess,
where thoughts and feelings dwell;
and very hard the task I find
of governing it well.

—***Louisa May Alcott***

It has been said that all day long the thoughts occupying your mind, your "secret place," as Jesus calls it, are molding your destiny for good or evil. In point of fact, the truth is that the whole of life's experience is but the outer expression of our inner thinking.

Minute by minute we can determine the quality of our visions and how we shall think; the reality is we always do choose and therefore our lives are just the very result of the kind of thoughts we have chosen to entertain. Thus our lives are of our own ordering, our own creation, hence there is perfect justice in the universe.

There is no suffering for another man's original sin, but the reaping of a harvest that we ourselves have sown. We have free will, yet our free will characterizes our choice of expression. *As a man thinketh so is he.*

Understand and accept the teachings of the Master and make an honest effort to practice them in every department of your daily life. Seek systematically to destroy in yourself everything which you know should not be there. Things such as selfishness, pride, vanity, sensuality, self-righteousness, jealousy, self-pity, resentment, condemnation, and such, need to be weeded out. And furthermore starve them to death by refusing them expression, giving them no recognition with sustenance from your consciousness.

If you extend the right thought loyally to every person and all of creation, and especially to the people or things you dislike, then you are worthy to be called the salt of the earth.

Shepherd diligently your flock of ideas. Stay very aware of the energy, weight and importance given your motives. Humanity's almost ceaseless broadcasting of every kind of irritable and destructive feeling is the greatest crime in the universe against the law of love.

The Law of Love is the law of balance, harmony and perfection. It is "the Golden Mean" of truth. It is broken by what we call "sin," which is nothing more than the discord caused by our feelings and actions, in other words, creations of our erred thoughts.

A man sooner or later discovers
that he is the master gardener of his soul...
A man is literally what he thinks.

—***James Allen***

We will come to realize and recognize that the sinister and destructive forces made manifest on this earth and in its atmosphere are humanly generated, and will mark you by your thoughts and feelings. They have entered the affairs of individuals or nations through lack of control in the emotions of our daily personal experiences.

Destructive thoughts cannot express themselves as actions, events, or become physical things, except by passing through the emotional world of human thought and feeling. It is in this phase of manifestation, that the activity of coalescing the physical atom upon thought forms takes place.

The conditions in life we call old age, lack of memory, disease, and every other failure in the world of human experience, are the effects upon the body structure of stressful and discordant feelings, sometimes accruing over many, many years. We individuals, through our control of the human consciousness must make the effort to rise out of this condition by our own free will.

In order to transcend these limitations permanently, we must express dominion over them, we must leash our own thoughts and feelings. No one can hope to rid his life of misery, discord, disease and destruction until he takes conscious control of his every waking thought. Such discipline does require determined, continuous conscientious effort because the thoughts and feelings of 90 percent of humanity run as uncontrolled and free as stray cats.

To give expression to the discordant thoughts and feelings in one's self is the course of least resistance, the habitual activity of the undeveloped, immature or undisciplined individual who willfully refuses to understand the law of his own being and neglects to bring the personal self, which is his instrument of expression, into obedience to that law. Unfortunately, he suffers the consequences. Youth and the undisciplined adult may not only be impetuous but think themselves to be bullet-proof and invincible with their "you only-live-once" attitude.

A young person's tattoo read
'you only live once.'
I very much wanted to reply,
yes, in your present form,
but how many more lives
will you have to struggle through
paying back, just this sojourn's debts.

—***C.S. McClintock***

Controlling your mind can sometimes seem as difficult as stopping a freight train that is quickly moving downhill. But ideas advance one thought at a time, and can be handled one thought at a time. Letting the unwanted ones go, we can turn them loose and can deprive them of their stimulus, their negative energy.

We will decide if we are going to let the emotions of our mind take control of our future experiences, or if we are going to take control of our mind. Our every "next thought" is the creator of our destiny. It is true that "When a defining moment comes along, you either define the moment or the moment defines you," as Kevin Costner says in the movie, *Tin Cup*.

It does not in the least matter what your life's present circumstances may be, or what difficulties you may have to struggle against. You will eventually be able to triumph over them all and you will determine your own unique pathway. Feeling your own dominion, you will not only make your demonstration in the quickest possible fashion, but you will be in a very positive and literal sense, a healing and illumining influence on all around you. You will be a blessing to the whole human race. As startling and wonderful as this may sound, you will be a light unto the world!

It takes a conscious willingness to learn from lessons along the way. We won't always get it right. We all have made mistakes on the blackboard of life's experiences by skipping a beat to our rhythm or missing a step in our jog along the path. No matter how badly we've missed the mark, all can be forgiven. Even the most capitol of sins, errors and wrongdoings can and will be pardoned and eventually erased, commensurate with the lesson learned, through genuine repentance and transformation.

As baseball great, Darrell Strawberry once stated concerning the fallibility of the human character, "We are not mistakes, we just make mistakes."

The Lord's Prayer admonishes us, *"Forgive us our debts, our trespasses, as we forgive our debtors and our trespassers..."*

But wait, have we really been willing to forgive? Do we sue our trespassers at the drop of a hat? Do we say we will never forgive so and so for what they did or didn't do? What they did or did not say? Are we earnest in our supplication as we repetitiously mouth our beautiful Lord's Prayer with no particular thought or feeling within the meaning of the word forgiveness, actual forgiveness?

The Universal Law of Adjustment dictates that we must first bury our pride and make a concentrated effort to forgive others before we can be forgiven— and yes we can forgive one thought at a time, a step at a time, one person at a time. Only then will our own soul's blackboard of life's mistakes be erased and cleared by the grace of God, within our own Christ-Self.

We have the inherent capacity to keep our thoughts higher-minded. We can be busy in this world, yet in the same moment be practicing our dominion over it. We can be at our best in any career or profession; our best in any extenuating situation or dire circumstance, and simultaneously practice maintaining our true being, our innate marvelous Spiritual-Self. We can keep the divine in the human one thought at a time, every time.

When refusing to indulge uncontrolled "stray cat " thoughts and emotions, one finds a remarkable sense of achievement in the true feeling of spiritual discipline and dominion in one's consciousness. A worthy goal would be total thought control; bringing to a halt the clatter and chatter of the outside world, stilling our mind to the peace of quietness, where we can connect "on-line" to our inner voice, our higher intuitions, divine reasoning— we will gather the harvest of our good thoughts and good deeds.

We may never return to the exact same time and place on old pathways regretted. We usually don't get a chance to do it over again in the very same manner. However, if we've stumbled, we can and we will find ourselves karmically returning to old pathways in order to rectify and heal past mistakes. We may need to forgive ourselves, along with others, or just let go of the past, learn from it, and move forward. Hopefully, we will then take the steps needed in the present to adjust matters in whatever manner we are prayerfully led.

Now, for every good new path taken, excellently directed, with thoughts and actions well-chosen, we will keep moving forward with only grateful memories of lessons learned, and nothing to regret, never to look back. Every day, a new challenge awaits our creative decisions. These fresh starts are one of life's great gifts, the gifts of the Spirit.

The Christly-Way will be our new way. Feel its Fatherly guidance. This Way will fill our hearts and minds with gladness and direct our deeds. It will be our only vision, and we will gladly say of this Christly-Way—"It won't let go!"

Men's courses foreshadow certain ends... But if the courses be departed from, the ends will change.

—***Charles Dickens***

*Perhaps our human existence, our wheel of life,
only appears to be moving forward... perhaps we only imagine
we are living in a forward time frame.*

Chapter 9

TIMELESSNESS

I realize that time and space exist only on the periphery of the creative world which is like a disk rotating with dazzling speed. But I within myself, am timeless, spaceless eternity. And while I am resting within myself my eternal being fills space and everything living in it: I am the only reality, I am Life, I am that I AM.

—***Elisabeth Haich***

Contemplating time

We mortals are unworthy opponents in the enormity of the struggle against time and aging. It is said by many brilliant men that in actuality there is no such thing as time. In fact, they say it is only a man-made phenomenon, a concept invented for human convenience.

In the reality of the spiritual realm, the non-physical, within the eternality of the One Supreme Source there is no time measurement. The more we consciously perceive the spiritual import of this fact the less impact time and aging will have on our physical existence, and eventually *"there should be time no longer."* (Revelation 10:6)

The definition given by Webster says time is: Every moment there ever has been or ever will be. Time is also defined as: A system of measuring duration. Well, is it even possible for a human being to grasp the concept of no time? In *The Beverly Hillbillys,* Jethro Bodine might have come to this conclusion and remarked, "Even with this big brain of mine and a sixth grade education, I still can't figure out the notion that there is no reality to time!"

If everything in our world could move at the speed of light, there would be only the continuous now. In other words, if all our movements were naturally at that speed then there would be almost no aging, no duration of existence, no lapse of time, no past or future, no going backward or forward. There would only be events happening in the now. Hard to imagine, but extremely interesting to contemplate.

In this paradigm of timelessness, perhaps one very talented musician could play all the instruments in a symphony and sing all the vocals at the same instant, performing his concert simultaneously. But wait a minute—didn't Stevie Wonder already do that with his album, *Songs In The Key of Life*? Or perhaps one actor could play all the roles in a Broadway show or a movie. Hmm—Eddy Murphy played several roles when he was *Coming to America*. He would need only to change his appearance, while busily changing his costumes, so as to interact with himself, all in that same moment!

These are scenarios we cannot yet wrap our mind around. Even Einstein's speed of light still involves a relative system of measuring duration. However, we can use the knowledge we are gaining about the concept of time to help us quicken our dominion over the body and the aging process; not to mention over the limitations a time-sense throws in the way of our true identity, as an immortal entity. Hopefully we are approaching the more enlightened understanding that the All-there-Is is GOD and God manifestation, which abides in TIMELESSNESS... and oh by the way, that includes you and I!

The Divine order

In the absolute there cannot be time and eternity. The one is limited, while the other is unlimited. However, in our human existence, clocks and calendars bring structure, order and punctuality to our lives.

So here we are, as in all points of our spiritual advancement, still finding ourselves somewhat limited while living smack in the vastness of the unlimited. Yet in this three-dimensional world we have our time, and we have our positives and negatives. Hence we name this 3-D human learning experience a "schoolroom."

Webster states very simplistically, the meaning of reality: Something real. A quality, state, or fact of being real. While we contemplate the reality or rather the lack of reality of time, we can see that it has virtually no import in the spiritual realm, only in the material. Again, time has been created as a man-made convenience depicting different portions of our day as we orbit and rotate from nighttime to daytime. It helps to keep our human activities orderly. Hopefully this holds us closer to the Divine order. And that's a good thing.

Even a stopped clock is right
twice a day.

—***Marie von Ebner-Eschenbach***

Let us consider another mind-bender: A child is not a man, yet a child is in an early stage of being a mature human. In like manner, it could be said that physical man is in an early stage of returning consciously to his own God-Self, spiritual likeness, his original immortal blueprint. As he matures thus, he gradually elevates above the common constraints of time and limitation.

Remember, All is God; therefore all that exists, all creations, all nuclei, all forms, including atoms, cells, molecules, gases, etc—all are Him, as spiritual entities, eternal creations. All is the action of One Energy forever moving, circulating, ever evolving without end.

Though we are only in the infancy of beginning to grasp this monumental truth, everything we see and experience is in actuality some phase of the All-that-Is, evidenced forth. All spirits are a part of the One Source.. and everything materially manifested is God. So the question naturally presents itself—who are we and what are we doing here? Why—maybe my spirit doesn't really belong to me! And what if my body of material substance doesn't even belong to me?

In that case, I must therefore be an individualization of Him and His Spirit, using God's Infinite Body. As an embodiment of Himself, I must be a distinct continuation, a portion of, or an expression of His timeless Spirit, albeit in human form.

If we could only imagine the endless formations of manifestation He might effectively wear throughout all universes, unique forms determined by their own particular planetary environment. How egotistical we must be in thinking that we are possibly the only intelligent form of life throughout infinity!

Continuing this line of thought, in my present experience, the only reason I would need a name and a certain shape or form would be for others and myself to recognize this particular activity of me that God is going through.

I am privileged to have been given the FREE WILL THINKING to use HIS SPIRIT and HIS BODY as I so desire at this point in time. However, I was under the mistaken impression that they both, body and spirit, belonged to me! I was also operating under the erroneous assumption that there was God and me. I couldn't have been more wrong. There is only God being me, being you, and all formations as individualities, expressions of Himself, simultaneously!

I also thought that my allotted time here on earth was my only existence, my only life. Wrong again! Over and over we continue to recycle, regenerate, reinvent ourselves. Living eternally means just that; eternity can only be defined as the totality of existence without beginning or end; so, in human terminology, infinite time.

It has been said by many that even Jesus lived 30 lifetimes in this particular schoolroom, of earth. Some of us spiritual individualities may require hundreds of sojourns or even thousands of lifetimes through this masterpiece of a theater, this Edenic garden, in order to gain our Master's degree over the limitations of time and the senses. Turns out that time, while useful, is an embryonic stage of our maturation out of a physical conscience into the timeless identity of our spiritual consciousness, the Christ-I Am.

The child does not yet look like a man. Time by all appearances does not yet look to us like eternity. Our childlike thought will eventually grow into this understanding. Do we dare to contemplate that "all things" may actually be happening in the now of this moment—and that these all things are His experiences?

Time frames

To paraphrase the author Curtis White: Are we merely matter made up of obedient neutrons, attributing our behavior to our genes, our DNA and allotted an average life-span? Or as portrayed in the movie *Men in Black*, are we more like manly robots with little ETs manipulating the body from a computer in our head? Far from it.

One day we will learn that we are so much more than just a body, albeit a divine physical form. Science and fiction would have us believe that we operate independently of a Supreme Being. Science is clearly not yet fully compassionate when regarding our spiritual Source. Yet, scientists are realizing that we may actually already exist as a God-particle within a timeless dimension, although unknown to our present perception.

The higher reality is that we are invisible spirit-beings of consciousness with souls, temporarily inhabiting a celestially manifested physical form of a body; which is in itself our own little heavenly body, a highly organized system, a universe of coordinated multi-cellular organisms. This miraculous human form of ours is comprised of God-Conscious atoms, cells, elements living in an endless time-frame of activity, changing experiences and existences.

Our so-called soul is basically a marvelous recording device, that travels with our spirit through the eternities. It is the chronicling, the bookkeeping and accounting of all our daily bread spent in thought, word, and deed. The soul collects the details and keeps the record of every one of our activities, learning experiences, talents, emotions, and interactions throughout every sojourn of all our time, or more properly stated, our spiritual unfolding, through a timeless spirit's learning journey. It is an accumulation of all the personalities, including the various characteristics and idiosyncrasies we have ever portrayed.

Many find it difficult to distinguish between spirit and soul. I would say that my soul has characterized me differently from you while our spirit is one in the same—His Spirit.

OUR SOUL IS THAT WHICH DEFINES US, not our chronological age or physical stature. The soul records and keeps track of the entirety of lifetimes we may have experienced here or within the schoolrooms of other realms and planets, that we are requisitely unaware of, and yes, all this possibly before we were ever introduced to adventures on our earth.

"There is no remembrance of former things (lifetimes); neither shall there be any remembrance of things to come with those that shall come after."

—***Ecclesiastes 1:11***

Though we are consciously unaware, this soulful recording will continue with us throughout our experiences after earth as well. Therefore as God is never-ending, with or without the human concept of time, although for the most part we are unaware of this truism, we must be eternal too, forever growing and unfolding without an end. Amen.

What a splendid co-creative adventure we are experiencing!

If God hadn't divided up or apportioned Himself into an infinite number of individual consciousnesses, spirits with soul, then He would have had only His one experience, with One Soul.

What will be the end result of us in this earthly realm? How will we be judged by our One Source, the Creator, which has been individualized as our Christ-Self? Hopefully we will have earned the highest of marks. After all, in a fashion, we have been leasing or borrowing His Consciousness, His Body, His Spirit and Energy…for in essence, individually, albeit, in minute portions thereof, "God We Are," in His timeless eternity.

Gently transcending

If you were to dive into a pool of water, a lake, river or an ocean, you could explore and playfully swim to your heart's content. Eventually though you will have had your fill of snorkeling, scuba diving, and splashing fun. You will want to ascend the depths of the water and be about your business. The water is not who you are, it is only the element in which your adventurous experience takes place in that moment.

Similarly, you are currently immersed in the realm of the flesh, enamored with its concept of time, with its pleasures, trials, and triumphs, splashing about and playing your role in this beautiful earthly and artistic theater. Eventually it is going to be natural for you to want to mature, ascend out of the body, and give up all ties to this wonderful materialistic center for the arts; moving out of this world of the human experience, progressively and gradually transcending into the full reality of your Spiritual-Self, within "My Kingdom," as the Master called it.

As easily done as exiting the water, you will eventually discover that this body, our present physical form, is to be exited as well, although spiritually. And like the $H^{2}0$, the flesh and the framework of time in which your body abides is not defining or holding the real you.

When will we finally come to this enlightened conclusion concerning advancement out of the physical and expedite our spiritual journey on this eventual timeless celestial pathway? Then and only then can we truly be about our "Father's business," in our daily lives, while at the same time still enjoying, yet finishing up this wonderful and inspiring human experience.

It is highly liberating to live in a time-oriented society, yet at the same instant having dominion over it, feeling timeless—living in time, but not being of time.

Now hear this: If you and I have eyes to see and ears to hear, it is high time that we know the Master called the ONE SPIRIT "the Father within." He, the Spirit of you and the Spirit of myself, is that Father and lives all lives simultaneously, including the most minute of elements. He is me—He is you, so personally, "take no thought for yourself." In other words, put ego aside, take less thought about your mortal self, think from an exalted state without the pettiness, because in actuality it's not mine or yours—it is His Life, His Presence, His Body, the Eternal Being, being manifested, and which we should be honoring, every moment, irrespective of our human sense of identity.

You and I are the individual creative experiences of His Consciousness. So in tranquility, take thought instead, for having only divine consciousness. Not His Mind and your free willing mind, but be only the individualization of the One Infinite Consciousness.

To gain more the sense of a central stillness, the spiritual selfhood residing within you, is to develop the calmness of that mind which was also in Christ Jesus and is already inherent in the Christ of you and the Christ of me as well. This gives you a fuller realization of being in the timelessness of God-Consciousness, the stillness and dominion of the I Am.

God, the magnificent Source of all life, doesn't think mortal thoughts, nor does He think in reference to time. He knows no space or separation. And Jesus said, *"Verily, I say unto you, whatever you have done unto the least of my brethen ... you have done unto me."* (Matthew 25:40) Of course The Master is referring not just to himself, but to the One Father, Spirit within mankind and all of creation. You see now that the One Spirit is playing all the roles in this earthly theater.

Therefore, since time is not a factor to our spirit and we are all included in the same Oneness, whatever you do to another of my brethren, you are in effect doing unto yourself at the same moment. As they say in the East, "Everything I meet along the path is myself."

Central stillness

Have you ever had the feeling, the perspective, of being the center of your universe, perhaps the pivotal point in your galaxy? Our body, our physical form is comprised of more than 100 trillion cells, with each cell housing 100 trillion atoms, plus an infinite number of microscopic particles and each with consciousness, if you will, all intelligently orbiting around our heart center; each with its own particular task to be achieved. This system is much like a body of planets and moons revolving around their sun.

The poignant question here is: can you envision your human body being a universe within our galactic universe? Each of these elements is inherently listening to your directive to be either loving and forgiving, compassionate and happy; or angry and hateful, inharmonious, or uneasy.

The thought rising from our heart center is the axis of this personal universe and our body responds accordingly. As a matter of scientific fact, our body is continually rebuilding itself, moment by moment, very sensitive and responsive to our thoughts and feelings. It is in our best interest to keep them wholesome and healthy.

I can remember driving down a tree-lined highway for an extended period of time with my vision fixed on the road ahead. Suddenly my perspective changed. In my mind's eye I wasn't moving anymore, I was sitting still. The landscape on both sides of my car came rushing past me, the road disappearing quickly beneath me. I and my vehicle seemed to be at once stationary, yet the whole world seemed to be moving quickly past and swirling around me. After all, are there not occasions in our lives when we egotistically think the world revolves around us, our thoughts, our wishes and desires?

In that moment, time seemed to stand still, even thoughts came rushing toward me. I was remembering many years past when a very intuitive lady asked me the question, "If I was to be a portion of a wagon wheel and if I had a choice, which part would I like to be?" I immediately pictured a stagecoach in a western movie racing across the dusty plains. Before I could answer, she interrupted and said, "You should want to be the axle, the hub of the wheel—having everything in your world revolve around you.

"Be still, be the pivotal hub, don't waste your energy moving to and fro, going in circles, usually achieving not much more than being on a treadmill in a wearisome routine, wearing yourself down like the other parts of the wheel. Don't be like one of them—stressing yourself with worries and guilt, or concerning yourself with other's problems, your thoughts running amuck. You have more than enough on your own plate already."

I got the picture. In those few moments on the highway, I realized that we find ourselves anxiously orbiting within our own agenda. But at the same time I was now seeing the larger picture of each of us revolving around the nucleus of the I Am, which in truth is our center axle, our individual pivotal point.

Though this sensation of peaceful stillness had lasted only several minutes, I knew I wanted to feel more of this enlarged sense of Self, the true reality of myself. Maybe the final thought that came toward me in that small window of time was this: I must work daily to achieve more of these distilled spherical moments and turn these introspective minutes of quiet into hours.

The harried lifestyles we westerners have become accustomed to 24/7-365 must be reversed, for *"In quietness and confidence shall be your strength."* (Isaiah 30:15)

You should, *"Take therefore no thought for the morrow: for the morrow shall take thought for the things of itself."* (Matthew 6:34) Take on no worries about the past or the future, be the centerpiece, the hub, let this world continue swirling about you, with you being still, at peace, thinking out from a standpoint of compassion in 'My Kingdom,' and living in this moment, the now, over and over, the now. We would do well to abide by the wisdom in the statement: If we have time to worry, then we have time to be still and meditate in prayer.

Perfect order

Brilliant men have said there are no accidents in this world, that the universe works in perfect Divine order. It also works in perfect accord while balancing our own karmic creations, whether they be positive or negative, whether these human manifestations be heavenly or of a so-called sinful nature. So what are we to surmise regarding the time-honored belief in fate and destiny? Many, many occurrences seem to be predestined: like who I might have married, or whether or not to board a plane destined to crash.

There was no way in 1969 that the previous worst team in baseball, the New York Mets, could have won the World Series, but they did! That's why they are referred to as the "Miracle Mets."

In 1983, Jim Valvano and the N.C. State basketball team won the NCAA collegiate basketball championship. That was considered an absolute impossibility but fate had other ideas. I could go on and on recounting noteworthy occurrences, such as walking on the moon, or Berlin's East West Wall coming down, where fairy-tale endings have unexpectedly reshaped history; but I would rather contemplate time as it relates to destiny and fate.

Could the cosmos possibly be planning these miraculous-ending events and conclusions and also be overseeing the darker events of our human history? It can only give back whatever has been sown, individually or collectively. If you plant rose seeds, it will return to you roses, not tulips or daisies; if you have sown weeds, weeds you shall get in return.

Perhaps Cosmic Law presupposes events by working backwards from a predestined ending to a beginning already determined. How else could genuine clairvoyants see future events?

Maybe fate and time can work like a spinning wagon wheel. The faster it goes forward, the more the outward appearance of the wheel seems to our eye, to give the illusion of rotating backward. For instance, maybe in the case of the Lincoln and Kennedy assassinations, the end results were already set.

Then began the inertia, the motion of moving backwards in time toward its beginning—bringing about all the circumstances, plots, and involved characters that culminated in its eventual predisposed ending.

Could the predisposed dramatic conclusions of these historical events be the actual beginnings, the origination of how the events worked out in a sort of backward motion bringing it to completion?

Mind-bending of course, but perhaps we are always moving backward so fast from a predestined conclusion, which by all appearances of the speed and duration of action involved, like the spokes on a wheel, gives the perception of a forward-moving reality. Maybe this illusion has us believing that we are moving forward in time.

If by this same illustration, the spokes on a wheel were rapidly moving backward, wouldn't the opposite be true, would they not appear to the eye to be moving forward? It is possible that our human existence, our wheel of life, only appears to be moving forward. In other words, maybe we only imagine we are living in a forward time frame!

Can you explain time or timelessness? Again, if our life was moving at the speed of light, there would be virtually no time—no lapse of time, no forward, no back—and no aging to speak of. Could it be that the major events of our lives are already planned and we move toward their eventual completion? However we choose to define this human and relative sense of time, we can use it wisely or waste it foolishly.

We are hopefully bringing to fruition a bountiful destiny. Not just in major events but all along our path our free will is making choices, architecturally designing our future.

Even a person living a fate of karmic payback with its sometimes harsh and hellish consequences, believe it or not, does have the present creative capacity and the free will, the choice to alter his predestined endings. If this individual were to miraculously see the light, and change his zebra stripes, his life patterns of hostility, deceit and negativity, layered and imbedded, accrued over numerous sojourns, he could actually avert his impending doom. So would it even be possible for a human being to change his stripes? Unequivocally yes— in this instance time can be our friend and ally in the process of human transformation.

Canvas of life

Remember, great thinkers have also said that there are no accidents. Combining all of an individual's past and current accounts will lead him into every intersection of his life's interactions. His thoughts and actions predetermine the harmony or disharmony in the course of his future experiences.

The so-called major events in our lives are built not by spontaneously splashing paint onto a canvas, but by each repetitive action, brushstroke upon brushstroke, thought upon thought, lifetime after lifetime. Since our past behavioral characteristics and idiosyncrasies have helped develop our individual soulful human nature, then our personality DNA, so to speak, has been formed and set over many lifetimes.

Psychologists would have us believe that our first five or six years of childhood determine our personalities. Not exactly so. A child prodigy is no accident of nature, or merely a product of his family genes. His area of expertise may have been conceivably developed over unknown periods of time, many a lifetime as an artist, musician, mathematician, etc.

Fortunately, and at times unfortunately, we live in a material world of contrasts and attracting opposites. Although all is Godly, and all humans are spiritually and physically divinely endowed, we know of some people or sects of people who revel in hate and anger over many, many generations. They have developed a consistent behavioral pattern imprinted with intense hostility and aversion.

Even still, they are heavenly creatures, but over durations of existence their good minds have become warped and insensitive. They have become artists in the worst sense of the word; they have temporarily lost touch with their God-minds. Unfortunately, albeit occasionally, we all have anti-Christ thoughts.

Any thought or idea less than loving is anti-perfection; our daily bread, love-energy, turned upside down, time wasted.

This squandered, misspent energy might be pictured as invisible black clouds accumulating around us, our family, country, or our world. Just imagine all the negativity accruing from the masses of people who are creating anger, hate, violence, and outright "sinning." Thank heavens, love predominates and always prevails. And yes, as it turns out the zebra-stripes of negativity are not inherent to us as exalted earthly human beings, who are the epitome of Creation.

All men, even the "lost" can be saved from themselves, from their disillusioned image of themselves and their erred creations. Difficult to slow down, or bring to a halt, a Tasmanian devil? Absolutely! However, even tornadoes eventually come to a peaceful conclusion.

Since GOD is all there IS, and the negativity that exists is inextricably created by MAN and his earthly erroneous thinking, then it only stands to reason that in this world, evil's time, its days with its deleterious effects, are numbered. When humans mis-spend their personal bread, their daily energy, by fueling sin, then that too, like the tornado, will eventually burn itself out or implode from within.

The unreality of evil will always default, dissolve, transmute itself, back to its original energy-Love. Again, evils are in reality a man-made creation, invention, with no power, unless sustained by man"s erroneous thoughts and actions.. So if you and I and those artists of evil would come to a strictly harmonious place in our understanding, then and only then will sins and evils find no time or place to manifest in this time and space.

Time stands still when man rests within himself. When it comes to the universe of your personal heavenly body of molecules, atoms and cells, if you were to take less thought for this world and its clocks, calendars, and stresses, there would be no anger, or destructive forces.

By focusing on the now, your creative mind would be staying in alignment, clicking smoothly along, albeit one second at a time, in total harmony with your Source. In quietness and confidence would truly be your strength, and the speed of your vibratory Self would be approaching the rhythm of light. Hence no time, only eternity in motion. Then your daily bread—energy—given you would not be wasted or misused. But rather it would shine and rise, with the leaven of goodness every day.

Cease to inquire what the future has in store, and take as a gift whatever the day brings forth.

— ***Horace***

You would be creating a circuit of energy with no breakers or interruptions, expressing only goodness in the human realm, circulating and returning this timeless energy back to its Divine Source, completing a rhythmic vibratory circuitry. Identifying with this Love-Energy and having no ill thoughts or ill will toward your fellow man or negligence toward our eco-system or planet, you eventually would come to this enlightened conclusion: "Waste not, want not."

There would be no disease or deterioration of our atoms and cells. Eternal youth would be at your doorstep. The fountain of youth would be your new discovery. Too good to be true? Not for the mind that can stay focused within the highest understanding.

You would elevate your life out of involving yourself with the revolving status quo, and evolve in divine orbits of compassionate human activity.

It has been purported from the Far East that there are some sages who have overcome the "time factor" by staying in the moment, the now, over and over again, the now, in connection with the ultimate consciousness, their Higher-Self.

As they say down under, "no worries mate." That's right, take less thought for yourself, have no worries, no stresses, no evils, *"Be still and know that* (the) *I Am* (is) *God."* When you are at peace in prayer or meditation, with complete stillness of mind and body, you are in the now of the moment and touching the eternality which is the "Him" of the I Am of you and me, forever and ever. Amen.

All is the action of One Energy forever moving, circulating, ever evolving without end.

Just as flowers seek the sun … we ourselves are drawn to and magnatized by the Light as well.

Chapter 10

FOUNTAIN OF YOUTH

All that we are is the result
of what we have thought.
The mind is everything.
What we think, we become.

—***Buddha***

Have you ever wondered if the fabled Fountain of Youth was fictional or fact? And if true, where is it to be found? There are only a few people on this earth today with this most secret knowledge, and I myself happen to be one of the fortunate ones. So I shall, with all love and humility, share with you the hidden location of this very real Fountain of Youth.

If you were to search the world over, and then over again, you would never find it, because this treasure is placed in the very last location that a man would think to look. This most guarded secret is a treasure beyond measure which cannot be found in the oceans, beyond the mountains, or within the great gardens and vast earthly deserts. However, each and every man is capable of making this most wondrous discovery. For behold, this Fountain of Life is right at your own fingertips.

A person must begin his search for this great gift in earnest, holding himself in the highest regard. With respect and reverence, a state of homage must be reached. Only then, in total humility, can he begin this quest of finding the highest revelations that will lead him into his own soul, his own Higher-Self, which is the conduit to the source of this Fountain of Life. Here at last, the discovery is made! He has found the source of this miraculous gift. He is now in touch with eternal youth.

"Thou wouldest have asked of him, and he would have given thee living water... the water that I shall give him shall be a well of water springing up into everlasting life." (John 4:10) Eternal youth and beauty comes not from a spring in St. Augustine—or from a lotion or a potion in a jar, for that matter, but from within yourself. This wellspring of living waters is none other than your own personal Christ-Self.

This "living water" flows forth from the I Am, the Creator which sustains life. The qualities of youth and wholeness are attainable not only through moderation in diet, exercise and harmonious mental disciplines, but through the activity of the Christ-Consciousness within ourselves. Aging and physical decline result from a mental consent to negative thought-patterns of time, stress, deterioration, and uselessness.

Yes, this great treasure is buried deep within the temple, as the Master called it, the spiritually energized sacred structure of your very own body-church, the truest house of God. This is where the highest conscious awareness resides, far removed from the material world and above all senses. The real fount of youth where life springs eternal can only be reached by taking our human consciousness to its highest level, ascending into our Higher consciousness, which is the blending into our own divine Christ-Self.

Speaking of this heightened sense of awareness, Dr. Eben Alexander comments in his contemplative book, *Proof of Heaven*, that It, the Divine consciousness, was expressed under different names and through different world-views in earlier times... something known well and held close by pre-modern religions, but was lost to our secular Western culture as we became increasingly enamored with the power of modern science and technology.

He emphasized that knowing the deep and comforting truth that our eternal spiritual Christ-Self is even more real than anything we perceive in this physical realm, gives us the divine connection to the infinite love of our Source.

The very enlightened Alice Schutz also presents a few thoughts on what has been heretofore the most secretive of subjects concerning this conscious connection. Before the 20th century this sacred information was kept hidden. Only a select few enlightened ones were aware of this mystical knowledge.

Schutz writes:

"YOU CAN CHARGE THE BODY WITH YOUTH AND VIGOR. Your Christ-Consciousness wants perfection for you more than you could ever know.

"Remember, your Christ-Self (Higher Mental Body) knows your every requirement and brings forth your daily bread. This Self is a feeling Being as well as a mental Being. It is the silent watcher of the individual. It regulates the amount of energy (daily bread) flowing into your body through what could be envisioned as a silver chord or beam of living light, sustaining every life-stream.

"The increasing supply of Cosmic (Celestial) light is allowing the free will of every creative individuality, through the Christ-Self, to choose either for the Light or otherwise.

"The I Am Presence called into action compels selective discriminative activities of the Christ-Self. Alertness is the discriminative selective intelligence of this Self.

"Your Christ-Self will not stay close to you when there is discord in the feelings, but recedes. [I believe the thought Schutz is trying to convey here is that if we are thinking and acting without regard to our highest ethics, then we have distanced ourselves consciously from our Higher-Self—temporarily of course.]

"Your Presence, through your Christ-Self, is your only 'judge,' supervisor, evaluator, and is assessing your human performances. The Presence and Christ-Self are really one in action, and is or should be, your Divine Director.

"Have you ever thought where the blending line between God and man is? It is where the human and the Divine meet. It is the juncture where the human conscience blends with the Divine Consciousness—the human realizing its own Christ-Self."

Schutz continues, "Christ is a principle—Jesus was a man. The Christ-principle is that *youthful energy* that can no longer be contaminated by the human, mortal thinking.

"Your Christ-Self decides what can be done for you. It goes to the Presence on your behalf, talks to the I Am, and gets authority. This Higher-Self is the spokesman, and It acts through the direction of the I AM Presence.

"Ascended Master consciousness is that consciousness which has attained individual perfection. The Christ-Self calls to the Ascended Masters who project their consciousness—the Master's conscious feeling of having attained—into the feeling of the individual—the outer self or human. This gives the assistance the Higher-Self requires and It then can do what It wants done. Since the outer self, the person, has not yet made the Ascension, that particular Christ-Self does not yet have the feeling of attainment which of course, an Ascended Master has.

"The Ascended Master Consciousness should be the aspiration of every man.

"On retiring at night, charge your Christ-Self to take command and produce perfection while your body sleeps. YOU CAN CHARGE THE BODY WITH YOUTH AND BEAUTY."

Schutz reminds us, "You can cause your Christ-Self to demand certain things.

"It will render the service for which you have called when It sees there is no equivocation in you, no questioning in your confidence.

"However, there are times like during transition, at the time just before passing, when a person cannot speak an untruth, and no longer questions his eternality. This is so because his own Christ-Self has taken total command of his spirit.

"This Self wants PERFECTION for you more than you do—more than you can know in the outer human mind. It is the One who brings you in contact with instruction when you are seeking spiritual knowledge. With the assistance of the Ascended Ones who have gone before us, and they too, are wanting your perfection, this conscious loving Light draws you in a perfectly natural way in contact with this or some other teaching of Truth. Sometimes people do not accept these truths, but ridicule or criticize and go their own merry way. That is just like slamming the door on your Christ-Self—slamming the door in Its face, also in the face of the Master."

Schutz concludes, "CHRIST IS THE ACTION OF GOD. And the full power of Its manifestation will make you realize that the totality of you is Divine. While the presence of this Christ-Self hovers above us, it is also anchored within our human heart. The heart is divine. That pulsating spiritual organ in your body is the very activity of divinity."

We already have every capability within ourselves for "eternal youth," in fact to have eternal life requires that we first demonstrate the qualities of youthfulness, energy, vigor, and radiance.

However, somewhat like puppets on a string we listen to advertisements and admonitions to decide whether we should sometimes feel well or sick, energetic or tired, youthful or aged, instead of "charging our Christ-Self to take command and produce perfection." As the highly enlightened Dr. Wayne Dyer stated , "We came from perfection and we will return to it."

Jesus healed without drugs, without regard to time or incurability. He was able to hold an awareness, an altitude of consciousness that seemed distant and mystical to the materially-minded of his day; and which is still mythical and mystical to the unenlightened of today.

The Master knew that awareness and recognition of the personal I Am Presence "could do all things." The ascending progression of the Christ-Consciousness within himself proved that this precious and most valuable treasure, this "fountain of living waters," can neither be slain at its infancy or crucified in its maturity. It is the savior of all men in the world from the Herods of this day. The life-giving activity of the I Am is carried on through the Christ-Light within each of us, forever supplying youth and vigor.

Just as flowers seek the sun and follow it across the sky from morning till night, we ourselves are innately magnetized by Light as well.

With an ode to fall and the All-in-All
The sunflower blooms here and there,
By streams and fields alike.
One by one each face follows the sun,
Obedient to the light.
Like them, how I wish I might!

—***Diana Craun***

"Seek and ye shall find," (this mystical reservoir)... *"in quietness and confidence shall be your strength... knock and it shall be opened unto you."*

Now, since you have "ears to hear and eyes to see" what will you do with this secret treasure that will be found within yourself? Metaphorically speaking this magical Presence, this lamp, this Light mythically referred to as Aladdin's Lamp, is the I Am Presence, and your fountain of youth. Will you attempt to touch your own lamp of illumination? What will your three wishes be? Or will they be a spiritual zillion and three?

... we should be eliminating the stress in our lives through gratitude ... wake up every day—focusing on the beauty of our world, loving our Mother Earth.

Chapter 11

GOOD AND EVIL

It may surprise you, perhaps,
but I am not strictly opposed
to the spectacle of violence and crime.
It all depends on the lessons
you draw from it.

—***The Dalai Lama***

One Infinite

Whether you believe in God, Allah, a divine creator, an accidental or random Big Bang Theory or not, surely you must see we are each fundamentally the creation of goodness. However, almost every theology or God-philosophy in the world has molded within its teachings the premise of an ominous evil power with its satanic devil, as an opposing influence to this goodness, and promotes that man is a wretched, weak and sinful creature vulnerable to this enemy.

If you have accepted this medieval theology, you see yourself in a relentless battle between two forces, seemingly batted back and forth like a ping-pong ball between the powers of good and evil. One wonders how long must we vilify ourselves as per the misleading teachings of the early religious institution before we recognize and acknowledge our true righteous divinity, and the origin of one infinite Source, *that of good alone*!

We grow up hearing that there is evil both inherently inside of us and outside of us with influences beyond our control. We must advance beyond the repressive and demeaning mindset of this condemnation and unworthiness, this distortion which insists that we are born with a sinful nature.

It is imperative that we begin to leave behind those that have us proclaiming ourselves to be sinners, weak and lowly mortals. Instead, we should be embracing the exalted proclamation that we have never been anything less than Divine and in fact, made in His likeness, fully endowed with all His strength and goodness.

There is no such thing as an opposite to God, an absence of the All that Is, or a void, nothing to overpower or displace, erase, one iota of good. The spell of an illusory power of evil that has long been cast over mankind will soon be broken when we come to the learned conclusion of One single Power, His all-encompassing omniscience. Only this mental shift will bring the fundamental conscious change needed to end this perceived relentless battle between good and so-called evil.

No opposite

Almost since the beginning of man's time on earth he has been taught to envision an afterlife of heavenly pearly gates and streets of gold; or an opposite viewpoint, a hellish abode built for housing and punishing the evil-doers. These imaginings were greatly encouraged and reinforced by the Council of Nicea in their writings of the early 4th century A.D. in order to help keep the subjects of the Holy Roman empire restrained.

Here we are centuries later continuing to believe these fabricated fables, the reward of a celestial heaven in the clouds with a saintly figure of a man clothed in white judging us from afar; and somewhere down under, the punishment of a fiery furnace with a demented clown in a devil's costume, pitchfork in hand.

The archaic belief in an opposing power has marched on through the centuries gaining strength, until the young people, the millennials of the 21st century, along with a large portion of the baby-boomers, have said, "No more... we've had enough! It's high time we had a viable explanation for sin and evil, the dark side."

Dying into a heaven or hell for all eternity is as outdated and incongruous as the early church concept of the world being flat and the solar system orbiting around the earth.

It is absolutely beyond imagination and reason how fervent religious teachers of today can, in the same breath, espouse the omnipotence of God, all-powerful, almighty and supreme, then turn right around and speak of a devil and his opposing challenges as an evil secondary power.

So here we are, presented once again with the pagan belief in multiple gods and multiple powers, the ignorance and denial of the one and only allness of Good!

Our inheritance

So, where does *evil* come from?

All life consists of 100 percent goodness, Love-energy, yet, our free-willing human consciousness occasionally has an incorrect thought, hence the origin, and creation of sin and evil. However, please understand this: not even this incorrectness can be outside the Allness of the Divine.

This errant thinking by we co-creative divine beings may lead to errant words and actions. All the while, it is merely a small percentage of this pure 100 percent goodness, our God-given inheritance, our daily bread-energy, so to speak, taken and temporarily turned upside down, inside out, misused and badly spent, entirely by human consciousness. Even our attitudes can get turned upside down as well and we lose altitude of thought.

Creating evil is much like creating a mistake in mathematics, the principle of math remains inviolate, in spite of human error. We correct our mistakes, we are forgiven, lesson learned, we move on. See! All remains within Good. And a mind filled with the principle, power and presence of good cannot create a minefield of negative thinking. Remember, evil of itself has no power. It is a temporary human creation, mistake, and survives only by the energy man invests in his errors.

People excuse themselves for their erroneous thinking and their resultant deeds by saying, "The devil made me do it, I was influenced by demonic spirits," or "for a short time I lost my mind, I plead temporary insanity, I just couldn't control my rational thought processes." Even worse, "The wrath of God must have intended this misfortune." But who or what are these negative influences? It's time we realized they are nothing more than self-creations, man-made imagery manifested, played out and gone awry, yet soon to be erased and wiped clean from our blackboard of life-works.

Perhaps one of the greatest humanitarians in our world's history was the 20th century attorney Mahatma Gandhi, who had this to say about evil, in declaring to Muslims, Hindus, Christians and Jews alike: "The only devils in the world are those running around in our own hearts. And that is where all our battles ought to be fought"... instead of through endless conflicts between men, religions and countries."

Remember, until this time in our history, there has never in the world been a rational explanation for evil and sin. Therefore, the people cry out, "Why, and where does it come from?" In actuality, there is no such thing as evil or an evil man. Simply put, it is only we children acting up raucously, for God's Life excludes no lives.

There is however, or can be, a man who lives his divine life constantly delving in rage, antagonism and confrontation. This person's whole day is seemingly filled with negativity. Perhaps even his childhood environment, including his family, friends and neighborhood, were contributing to his hate and prejudice, forming his volatile nature.

His aura tainted to a black mist, a cloud of darkness, swirls about him, accruing and collecting more and more discoloration of Good-Energy. This now errant, fallen-in-consciousness soul is presently reveling in sin and attracting like-minded people of a hating nature. Our spirit cringes and is repulsed, when exposed to this type of individual's energy-field. We can't seem to move away from them fast enough. These men are the creators of evil. And every time a righteous person has a fit of anger, an antichrist type moment, the Love-Energy he misspends goes up in a puff of black smoke. Thusly, all of us at some point are unwittingly adding to the accumulation of darkness on a mass scale. The righteous man though, has enough positive credits of selfless compassion to hopefully override any stints of indisposition.

The bombardment of distracting media news may lead us to forget that there actually is more good going on in the world each day than there is so-called evil. We may unknowingly be in danger of perpetuating and fueling more and more negativity with our constant preoccupation with the ills of society, the bad news, the poor behavior. Hence, hurricanes, tornadoes, earthquakes, tsunamis, and our own personal unease respond to the negativity in collective mass thinking and seem to rule the day.

We need to constantly guard against being on the verge of stress and anger, possibly wasting our God-given inheritance. We must instead remain on the verge of tranquility and compassion. All the while we should be eliminating the anxiety in our lives through gratitude and being thankful for the graces already received.

Then we can wake up every day counting all our blessings, focusing our vision on the beauty of our world, contributing to the power of the positive, loving our Mother Earth and loving each and every one of our brothers and sisters, just as we should love ourselves.

Sowing and reaping

Universal Law requires that all goodness, even if erroneously spent, be returned to its perfect state. The out-of-order free will of persons, groups of individuals or a nation, must be righted in order to be reversed and transmuted; our dark and misty clouds reversed, and the non-power of evil is exposed and disappears!

This is perhaps why the Dalai Lama went so far as to say he was not totally opposed to the "spectacle of violence and crime." Being well aware of the lessons of karma, a reaping of what a person has sown, created, he knew that the perpetration of "violence and crime" had to return to its originator in like fashion in order to consummate the learning or correcting process. The definition of erroneous is: "not in conformity with truth"... and thus any error is not in conformity with the Universal Law Of Good.

If this same free will is not kept in check, it sometimes may seem as though it has taken us back to our own childhood of terrible twos. Our human free-wheeling wants to be the wild-child once again, like some of us experienced in our youth.

Evils and wrongs, however, are not part of our divine nature. They are, strictly speaking, humanly created and absolutely powerless until man bestows them with his own misused mental and physical energy. They are only inventions, the results of unbridled childish thinking, a lack of respect for oneself and others, and the ignorance of Truth, a mistake on our schoolroom's blackboard.

Once we fully understand that divinity is the Truth of our identity, then we can put away our childish ways—our errant and sinful behavior, the ego with its unruly pride, envy, and judgmental nature. *"When I was child I spake as a child, I understood as a child, I thought as a child; but when I became a man,* (spiritually mature and aware) *I put away childish things"* (willful wrongs). (I Corinthians 13:10) I no longer have need of nursery rhymes, fairy tales, or the clergy's threatening fables to keep me on the right path, in the straight and narrow.

No duality

If you were to glean only one supreme truth from the teachings of the Celestial Masters that are found in this book, let it be the following: *There is no duality.* God is One in quality and quantity. There cannot be God and something else, there cannot be God and evil, God and demons, or evil spirits. God and a devil. Nor can there be God and an evil man.

There is nothing, not anything outside of or in addition to Him, the All-in-All. Thus in reality it is impossible to have both good and evil. So-called sins, evils, are merely transitory, a temporal phenomenon of this earthly theater—conjured up by the imaginative, albeit sometimes ignorant co-creative mind of man and acted out.

This misspent energy will be transformed back into its crystallized goodness by that same errant creator of it, man. What we call evil, God would say is merely a learning experience, a child's misbehavior being corrected by a loving Father.

Identity of innocence

When your youngster comes to the door covered in mud, you don't accept the mud as being any part of the child. The young person only needs a good cleansing. Though it covered the child's cleanliness, the mud is not considered evil, nor is the kid for putting himself in this unsightly condition. Mud is actually a Godly and very worthwhile substance and has a wonderful building quality about it; it has its place of importance and usage. Its blemishing effect is merely a temporary condition.

From the apocryphal Book of Phillip, we read, *"The pearl which is thrown into the mud is not worth less than it was before. If it is anointed with balsam oil it is valued no higher. It is as valuable as its owner perceives it to be. So it is with the children of God. Whatever becomes of them, they are precious in their Father's eyes."* (Phillip:51)

Sin and evil, like the mud, are not a part of man's true identity. The person however, has the free will of choice to wallow in the mire and muddiness of wrong thought and deed. Yet when he tires of this futility, like the child, he still needs only to be washed clean, his mind that is, to be transformed.

Like the many skins of an onion, or the overlapping layers of mud, our Godly true nature may become hidden under overlapping layers of the seven sins.

We may find ourselves devolving, spiraling deeper into the physical world of the "natural man" and his senses, a multitude of sins. Yet our way up and out is forthcoming. Or, as some would have it, are we really now forever lost, destined to burn in a pit—Hi ho, hi ho, it it's off to hell I go?

Earning our way
I made the decision.
I'm accountable.

—***Janet Reno***

It is going to take much, much more than our family and friends praying or the clergy waving a crucifix over us to bring us to our spiritual senses. Once a person sinks into the depths or hits bottom, he alone is responsible for making the long trek back, earning his way to the top through his own steam and conviction. As he begins to forgive others for their hateful attitudes, sharp tongues and possibly the wrongs he believes they have inflicted upon him, then and only then can he too be forgiven, and start anew.

The weak can never forgive.
Forgiveness is the attribute
of the strong.

—***Mahatma Gandhi***

No man is capable of having fairy dust dropped upon his person to turn him righteous. Nor will his physical death miraculously change him back into his original blueprinted perfect person, that Higher-Self, his Christ-Self which is an individualization of the Father.

His death and consequent re-birth are very much like transferring himself from one train to the next, as he continues on his human and spiritual learning journeys. With full baggage, debts in hand, he travels on. His accumulation of deeds both good and bad, this accounting ledger, he carries within his soul until all his errant conceptions, creations, are eventually righted.

We don't call the muddied child or his deeds and wrong actions evil, we can see the problem as a temporary encumbrance. He is a child, for goodness sakes. So why then do we seem to put so much emphasis on the same word, evil, when it applies to a muddied or bloodied adult who has erred? In reality this grown person is no more evil and sinful than the young child.

We must learn how to separate the evil from the person, just as we separate the chaff from the wheat, as it has no value of substance. He may be in an adult body yet behaving more like a two-year old. And yes, if he has committed wrong, his errors would be on a much grander scale, and the proper human disciplines should be applied.

Whether supposedly known or unknown, these so-called adult sins will always be righted, corrected, either in this lifetime or the next or the next—his sins will be his own self-inflicted ultimate punisher, returning to him as lessons to be learned, the boomerang effect being very exact. Furthermore, we humans should judge not, as we all must yield to the disciplines of the Divine Will of correction.

Nothing lost

Once again, sin, evil, and negativity are nothing more than errant creative thinking—an image formed first in man's mind and then outwardly manifested.

There is also no such thing as a demonic spirit, just temporarily free-willed spiritually wayward souls. These sometimes are perceived as ghostly entities after their passing. In a very few cases, the spirit simply has not yet moved into the beckoning light. Hermes may have said, "As above, so below." But the opposite is true as well— as he was below, he will be the same above. If he had become wayward in the physical with a sinful nature, he could seem to be temporarily lost between worlds in the hereafter.

Yet we must remember this: "For there is nothing lost that may be found, if sought," said Edmund Spenser. And hopefully even these few confused, seemingly lost souls will see the light and soon return to its radiance. Jesus not only cast out the negative-thinking entities, so-called demons, he directed them back toward the light! This in fact had a positive healing effect in their consciousness.

Nothing is ever lost, whether perceived visibly or invisibly, because all can be redeemed, restored, washed clean and crystal clear. Again, only needing to be corrected and turned right side up like jig saw puzzle pieces thrown on a tabletop.

During the next lifetime in this world, this earthly plane, the errant soul may feel, by those same former transgressions of his own hand, his feet placed to the fire. Aha, here is our fabled and mystical hell. But what feels so painfully real to his consciousness is nothing more than the discomfort of his sins and evils returning to him. Guilt, remorse, and condemnation are portions of a lesson being learned by this self-serving creator of negativity. His karma can be a hell-of-a strict teacher!

Remember, as the Daila Lama suggested, negativity is not always a bad thing. This material world is formulated with positive and negative energies. Fire, for instance, is not an evil force just because it has been misused, destroyed a forest, a home, or burned someone's finger. Fire is a wondrous invention; it cooks our foods, warms our houses and shapes our metals. In like fashion, the fires of our misfortunes, in which original good-energy has been misused, can have a positive effect of reshaping and refining our character.

Refining process

When man's mind creates ideas and actions on the dark side of negativity, these evils will metaphorically speaking, place us into a fiery furnace to mold us consciously back into our straight and narrow righteous nature. We will experience a sort of hell on earth until we conform to the wishes and mandates of our own Higher-Self. This molding process is not much different than shaping iron and steel. Our Christ-Self, our better half is ever watching, even our most secret thoughts and actions, molding, reshaping and refining our character, the "precious metal" of our consciousness, back into its original perfect design.

When evils turn to purifying flames transmuting our transgressions, bending us to our knees, is this not a good thing? Shakespeare wrote that all is well that ends well. Shakespeare and the Dalai Lama may be saying that even though segments of the human experience encounter what we call sins and evils, these elements are not always a bad thing if they help lead us to a better ending and teach us good lessons, well-learned.

Whether we realize it or not, this is the Law of the Universe, the natural Law of our learning and perfecting, overriding the negative side-trips, the detours we have embarked upon. All our thoughts, actions, and experiences are always taking place within our Source, the Divine One, as we are never outside of His Allness and Goodness. Nothing is, or ever can be outside of God. Still, this learning process, in exercising control over our free will, is an essential step in reminding us of and returning us to our own divine sense of Self. For *"in Him we live and move and have our being."* (Acts 17:28)

One all-inclusive

The almighty power, God, is omnipotent. If a man believes in a secondary power per his religious teachings or various and asundery theologies, he *cannot* know God aright, as All-Power. In more than twenty languages, including the Saxon, the word for our Source, the All-there-Is, Allah, God, is the term "good." Thus *Goodness* is all there is. The higher intellectual understanding of this good fact will lead us to the ultimate spiritual knowing of this All-ness, which will soon supersede any of man's lesser learned perceptions and their deleterious effects.

Good is not exclusive to any one person, place or thing, religion, race, or country. When we sing *God Bless America* do we see all nations under God or perhaps—just our own? Do we consider praying for all nations? Are we allowing our universal sense of God, good, to flow to all our brothers and sisters around the globe regardless of their creed, race or gender? Do we perceive certain persons or groups as lesser quality human beings because of their beliefs or lack thereof?

Might we become more compassionate to all men? If so, evil or a so-called devil will not be found walking "to and fro on the earth." This phrase from the book of Job is just as well referring to humans walking to and fro in the flesh with the free will to promulgate negative energy; a so-called secondary power, conjured up, disgorged from their unbridled "to and fro" errant thought. Yet, we must remember, in spite of even this mortal miasma, man forever remains within the infinity of Love's omnipresence.

Evil unmasked

All wrongs will naturally, per Universal Law, right themselves, as with an invisible gyroscope, a compass returning to true north, or a GPS system recalculating, recalculating. The Christ within ourselves corrects, adjusts, and governs, recalculating our own personal journey. Remember, nothing can ever occur or exist outside of Him. No matter how much "mud" we have managed to accumulate or thrown.

Finally! We have arrived at a viable explanation for evil! It is both revolutionary and liberating to recognize that evil has no energy, power or origin of its own, only the energy that man has invested in his negative creation.

We have also learned that the inharmonious thought, word or action was Godly Love-Energy all the while, just temporarily reversed and turned upside down, like the aforementioned jigsaw puzzle pieces thrown on a table needing only to be righted and organized correctly.

And we are gradually beginning to see that there are no such things as transgressions in our own individual Higher mind; they originate, play out and transform all in the human. The Christ Mind, which is our spirit's true identity, forever remains crystal clear and unblemished, inviolate.

What exactly did the Master mean when he exhorted us to take no action against another who may not have our best interest at heart? He said that if they slap you in the face, then you should *"turn the other cheek,"* and sue not; take a different tack or approach.

Discipline yourself to make an unexpected reaction, a non-action of peace and calm, self-control and resolve. The reason he was telling us to live by a code of non-violence, was because his whole life's teachings were based upon "The Way" of love, peace and forgiveness. Jesus wanted us to end the self-created reverberations of negativity, especially where it involved retaliation. For Heaven sakes, if perhaps we all have lived hundreds of lifetimes—eternally, how could anyone ever know who threw the first stone?

An incident or an argument we might find ourselves now embroiled in, could be the result of an encounter during a past sojourn of which neither we nor our antagonist may even be aware.

Our deeds still travel
With us from afar,
And what we have been
Makes us what we are.

—***George Eliot***

Regardless the circumstances in which we find ourselves involved, instead of retaliation we should turn the other cheek, ask forgiveness for ourselves, and also turn our cheek to forgive our suspected perpetrator. We may unwittingly be the reason for this offensive occurrence or karmic boomerang that in some way, shape, or fashion has returned to bring its pay-back or drop its payload on us mentally, physically, or environmentally.

However, while we can't always know the origin of the discord, we can put an end to it by assuming a Christ-like posture of benevolence in dissolving the dark clouds of negativity. We would then be forgiving others as the Good Book requires of us, at the rate of *"seventy times seven."* Or, as Dr. Maya Angelou would suggest, forgiveness at the rate of "seventy times seventy" living our lives in the now, not in a past, or by stressing over a future that may never unfold. Thus we help to unmask, transmute evil in all its disguises, and only the clear energy of love remains.

Sometimes we may even sense, vaguely, the deja vu of a past circumstance. But frankly we are not meant to have full remembrances of past lives or past traumas. Rather those experiences bring lessons we should use to draw maturity from and live righteously in this moment with compassion and integrity; perhaps instead of repeating our egomaniacal mistakes lifetime after lifetime.

Blending our consciousness

When each individual is thinking rightly of himself and his brothers, and holding man, beast, and the elementals in the highest regard; he will not create a thought of anger, hate, retaliation, or any other action of sin. Once again, sin and evil can only originate or exist in a confused consciousness—they do not exist in the Divine— so if man thinks them not, nor believes them not, as a power, they will cease to exist in his mind or manifest in the material. Love will reign, because he, man, will then *"speak no evil, hear no evil, see no evil"* ...thinking them not. Nada!

In other words, do not give recognition or weight to another's wrong thought by reacting likewise. Forgive it, dematerialize it before it can accrue more negative energy from this world. It is imperative that we hold fast to the knowing that, in the Kingdom of God, the higher thought-world, where your Higher-Self reigns, there simply is no such thing as sin and negativity.

The accumulated effect of blending our consciousness with our own Christ-Consciousness brings ascension, a rising above confrontation. At this point in our history, hopefully we are dissolving all past and present negativities. This Love-energy that has been misspent is now being righted, transformed back to its original color and perfection of Goodness.

We must think outside the box regarding our own true identity which human misunderstandings and teachings have sealed us into over centuries of disinformation. No longer will we tolerate being called sinful sheep that are corralled and fenced within an antiquated mindset. *We are Godly beings, brothers and sisters of the One I Am, of Love.* Let us hold fast to the truism that there is only One Kingdom, One Power, with no opposing forces. None! Zero!

Standing forth

A wise Master once said, "By always standing in his high dominion, man is Spirit and that Spirit is God. This Higher-Self must be thought of, pondered over, worshipped, and blessed as being right within man."

First, there must be faith that it is there. This brings forth the knowing that it does exist in man; then the blessings and thanks given, bring it into visibility.

Man's Higher consciousness is this Higher-Self, and this is the way to the attainment of all knowledge.

How can man suffer discord, dissonance, sin, or sickness unless he idolizes, obsesses over them, helping to bring them into existence by continually holding them in thought? If he stands forth always and at all times, as the all-wise, intelligent Spirit and knows no other power than Love and its Goodness, he cannot be conscious of or manifest anything less. With this ideal always held in the crystal clear waters of man's intelligent thinking, he becomes God-Conscious. He is certain to be answered by this inner voice at all times.

Fruition

This same Godly-Consciousness will always bring truth to fruition. And it, the truth has now set us free, especially *free* from negativity. There is nothing for us to fear; not even fear itself is to be considered. There are no more arguments to be won, no incidents to be contested, because we are forgiving everyone, whether we suppose them to be right, wrong, or indifferent; including those who wish to continue in the fabled negative or hellish mindsets of old. We shall judge them not. Neither shall we see or hear any evil in others as real or permanent, for we are all the divine children of Goodness, and each one capable of total reformation.

Our new tack has returned us to our original course, the Celestial path, where we are tolerant of all opinions and beliefs, forbearing and mindful of every man's right to think his own thoughts, follow his own path. We no longer give recognition to the suggestion of so-called evil or a devil, demons, or any imagined opposing so-called "second power." They cannot enter our mental home-temple, as we think, act, and live in the divine order, of Good alone.

Others will see the change in us, because we will be able to say, "No more am I feeding evil beliefs or fueling negativity into my own soul or into my atmosphere. Hopefully people will be attracted to the inner light radiating from me, and the new freedom of consciousness that I have found.

"No longer am I judgmental, nor do I have to convince the world of a particular doctrine. I have found heaven on earth, the 'Middle Way,' of no extremes, as Guatama the Buddha taught. It is also 'The Way' of Jesus. The Master taught me to judge not, thus I no longer have the capacity for intolerance.

"I do however, wish to expand my capacity to love unconditionally. The Spirit, Father within all life-consciousness, from the smallest, yet intelligent particles of an atom, to the largest galaxies, which includes all mankind, are within the One Source, Goodness; and I am now recognizing them all to be, dare I make this divinely precious statement... ONE with myself."

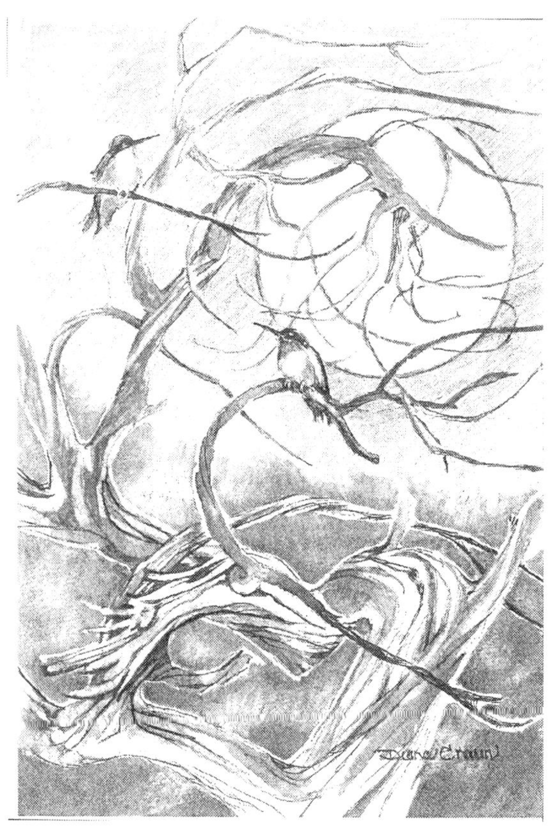

We no longer give recognition
to the suggestion of so-called evil
or a devil, demons,
or any imagined so-called second power.

I was seeing myself… as the spirit of the apple, one with the connectedness that threads throughout all things.

Chapter 12

APPLE OF HIS EYE

We must always change, renew, rejuvenate ourselves; otherwise we harden.

—***Goethe***

I'd like to share an allegorical story that I might tell my children or grandchildren. This story concerns a lone apple tree standing majestically atop a large hill.

The story begins:

Being an individual apple a' hanging on this majestic tree is one of my earliest memories. I was an apple swinging to and fro, gaily laughing and singing, socializing with all my apple friends. We had grown from a bud and a blossoming infancy to a ripe maturity, from green to finally a bright red. We talked, we played, delighting in the soft breezes, the scent of the flowers and clover, the refreshing showers, which we all enjoyed together.

At some point we each let go one by one, and fall, bouncing on the ground. As apple friends we compare our bruises. We frolic and play and eventually we roll all the way down the hill, well away from our creative host tree. As ripe apples we occasionally find ourselves looking back to the top of the hill, marveling at the grand tree which stands alone. At least from our point of view, way down here, we all see the tree as being the one and only tree.

Most of us are very busy entertaining ourselves, playing on solid ground, out of the mud and away from the sun, which tends to dry us out. I try to stay away from the petty teasing, the back and forth bantering about which of us is the shiniest, the shapeliest, the juiciest and most colorful, or who has more or less mud splashed upon their skin.

Instead of collecting together with all the others, I found myself growing contemplative and content to be alone. I was continually looking upward at the huge tree on the hill, wishing that I too, could be so large and gorgeous.

The others poked fun at me, calling me a joke, saying, you can't be a tree, there's only one apple tree, and it's at the top of the hill. But I constantly felt the compelling urge to see with my inner apple eye, and trusted that there was something greater awaiting me, a destiny of sorts.

They continued to laugh. "Ha ha... How could you ever be a tree?" "You haven't any of the characteristics of the one and only." "You don't even look like a tree." "You're an apple, silly, and a rotting apple at that!" "You're so unusual we even see you sometimes hanging out, meditating in the moisture and mud."

As time passed, the remaining apples began to shrivel up from the hard life they were living. Eventually they withered, dried up, and turned to dust. I stayed quietly to myself and relished listening to a mystical inner feeling, a still, small voice speaking to me from within. And at the same time, I rather enjoyed being away from the crowds. I just knew there had to be a higher purpose to my life. The dream of a more rewarding future surely must have been driving me forward. More than anything, I wanted to be like that majestic tree!

Though the other fruits laughed at me, I personally felt more comfortable digging in the damp, energizing soil and staying out of my friend's rotten scenario of one life, one death. Somehow, I just felt sure there was going to be an everlasting future for me. When I concentrated hard enough, I could faintly remember feeling the warm breezes of times gone by, swinging on a limb and seeing well off into the distance. Was I dreaming, or was I actually remembering the vision of other apple tree tops over the hills?

As the sun shined on my moist seed, I was nestling deep in the soft ground waiting for something to happen. I couldn't imagine what.

That's when I discovered deep down within me that I was beginning to take root and grow! Unlike all the rest, I hadn't disintegrated into dust. The more I turned my consciousness away from the daily activities, and took less thought for myself, the more I stayed focused on the job at hand, growing. I could feel something extraordinary was happening. Amazingly enough, I had no control over it. I found myself turning into a tiny tree, emerging and growing upward! Hallelujah, could. my dream be coming true?

As the maturing process continued, remembrances of formerly being a portion of a tree came more vividly. I stretched and dug my roots deeper and deeper for nourishment, and for the strength I knew it would take to survive and endure the storms of life that would inevitably come. I willingly let my true nature, my tree-nature take over, really sensing that my own purpose was being fulfilled.

I was being *still*, obedient, and listening, as there was work to be done. I came to understand my individual capacity to create within my own divine plan. I now was a co-creator, designing and manifesting limbs, branches, bark, leaves, and tiny buds. I seemed to intuitively know that with steadfast determination and focus I would eventually produce fruit! All I had to do was relax and let the Divine work through me.

An epiphany! When that day comes whereby I, as a tree, produce my first fruit, this apple of my eye will have its own blessings from "the I Am," the Spirit-Source of all trees, all life. And this I Am will then be placing a portion of Its Consciousness within *that* fruit. It too, will have the possibility to seed and grow and live its immediate existence as an apple with free will, to think for *itself*. It also, like myself, may find and know its magical and mystical purpose for which it is potentially destined.

And now I knew that this plan could only come about if this young fruit is not led too far astray, away from its creator's divine instruction, to *'Go and do likewise, to be fruitful, and multiply, and replenish the earth."* (Genesis 1:28) So many knowledgeable naysayers, doubters had shouted that I couldn't be like the one and only tree.

The person who says it cannot be done
should not interrupt the person doing it.

—Old Chinese proverb

My old apple friends were slowly but surely returning to dust. However, I intuited within my soul, that in spite of this transitioning senerio, their spirit-consciousness would be moving on, fully intact. I could almost hear these lost friends as each one spiritually returned to our Mother tree, telling the story of his or her prodigal journey, their life experiences as an apple and how they had ended up dead through no fault of their own.

Ha! They only *thought* they had died. Their spirit with soul had returned to the host tree and continued on once again as budding apples. Perhaps this next season, as a new crop, they will get it right. Maybe they will begin to feel their divine purpose sooner than later. Truth is, it may take them hundreds of prodigal sojourns through their own schoolroom of orchards, springs, summers, falls, and winters, eventually to find the next level, the next advancement in their Divine Plan of appledom.

As for myself, with serious contemplation and meditation, I have such joy in realizing how far I have come. I wasn't just an apple after all. In addition to that, neither was I just a seed or tree for that matter, nor the soil, grass or water, but was somehow a part of *all* the above; one with the Infinite Consciousness that is all forms simultaneously.

I was now seeing myself not merely as an apple anymore, but also as the *spirit* of the apple, hopefully to bring forth much fruit. I was one with the entirety of nature's connectedness that threads throughout all things. Wow! Along came the most profound realization, the understanding and knowing that my consciousness and the consciousness of the host tree were also one and the same.

I was no more looking longingly upwards toward the Spirit, Creator, within the magnificent host tree, no more feeling forlorn and separate; but was perceiving that my spirit was within His

Spirit, as an individual apple, just as an individualized drop of ocean water is one with the ocean.

Now I realized what I was feeling when I was sprouting and unfurling. It was the sublime joy of growth and enlightenment. I suddenly had the most wonderful sense that I was at the same time, not only looking toward my Father, Mother, tree, but was simultaneously *looking out* from the perspective of the tree itself. It was an affirmation of Oneness I had never felt before!

I wondered how many apple-lifetimes I had experienced before I came to this enlightened conclusion—guess I was a little slow—oh my, maybe I was once like one of them!

Oh well, I must be on my way, there is so much to be done. How will I share my story with all the others? And how might I convince them of their own special capabilities? To go and to focus, and to know that the dream of doing likewise is possible for us all.

THE END—NOT!

Now I ask you, dear reader, if the Creator had never divided, replicated Its Consciousness, or its seeds if you will, wouldn't there then have been only the one experience, one tree? What if the Creator has all this time been playing a game of hide and seek, hiding a part of His own consciousness into all forms?

So, realistically, all apples aside, in our universe there is only one material form that has the capacity and reasoning power to seek and know his own true origin and identity. Nary a rock, plant, tree, fish, foul, or lower animal has the capacity to seek its own Divine Source. Does a river ever question its source? Only a human animal has the wherewithal to seek and acknowledge his origin.

However, like the frolicking apples, it seems as though perhaps 95 percent of men do not question or seek to know their spiritual source. Because of busy agendas and their temporal ways of self-derived antics and carefree pleasures, humans seem to have little reason of inquiring as to their source, their purpose or plan.

Do they ever ask themselves, "Am I more than just the body? Do I even have a Divine source? What is my purpose? Could it be that I actually am a Divine Spiritual Being? Wow, I really like the sound of that! Maybe I too could be a light set on top of a hill that cannot be hidden. Then I might help others find their own luminosity, their own destiny."

Unfortunately, like the inhabitants of the mineral, plant, and animal kingdoms, or an apple kingdom for that matter, neither does the "natural man" think much outside his immediate existence, his form, body. Man does, however, have the capacity to think well beyond his physical makeup.

He simply doesn't care to spend much time contemplating the fact that his entire being, including his material configuration and his consciousness, is a spiritual energy. And that One Source, Creative-Energy, is the "All-there-Is," to himself and all creation. Furthermore, we seldom explore the fact that we actually live eternally, unimaginably and far, far beyond what we call our one earthly lifespan.

When we find ourselves hovering above the "apple core," hovering above our body at a car wreck, or floating over our deathbed, only then do we realize we were spirit all along, and that we simply will never die. We only transition, moving on, changing to our next form; or, as in the case of lower-life consciousnesses, their next planting, seeding, growing, maturing—transitioning again and again toward the light.

This is the secret to what seems to be like the ultimate "kick-the-can," hiding game, played by our very own Source, One Spirit-Energy, playing billions of individualities and personality roles. The one Creator plays all consciousnesses at the same time. Did not Shakespearian actors sometimes play multiple parts in all those plays of yesteryear?

We and all of creation are playing important parts individually designated to perform as *ourselves* at this point in time and space. And indeed we *all* are the *"apple of His eye."* (Deuteronomy 32:10)

Difficult to comprehend? Absolutely! But perhaps it's as simple as the Zen proverb that suggests, everything you meet along the path is yourself!

Awake, you sleepy children! Awake to acknowledge and know that the I Am is the Christ, the Spirit which abides within every man. Touch this Him who is you and I. It can grant your every spiritually-endowed dream.

Go now and bear much fruit!

(John 15:1-5)

1. *"I Am the true vine, and my Father is the husbandman."* (the gardener)

2. *"Every branch in me that beareth not fruit he taketh away: and every branch that beareth fruit, He purgeth it, that it may bring forth more fruit."* (He prunes it)

3. *"Now ye are clean through the word which I have spoken unto you."*

4. *"Abide in me, and I in you. As the branch cannot bear fruit of itself, except it abide in the vine; no more can ye, except ye abide in me."*

5. *"I am the vine, ye are the branches: he that abideth in me, and I in him, the same bringeth forth much fruit: for without me ye can do nothing."*

(Without the recognition of the I Am, your own Christ within, ye can do nothing.—And the Master said, *"of mine own self, I can do nothing."*)

"Now come along to some quiet place by yourselves, and rest awhile," said Jesus . . . his heart was touched with pity for them because they seemed to him like sheep without a shepherd."—Mark 6:31

Chapter 13

OUR DOMINION

When the power of love overcomes
the love of power,
then there will be true peace.

—**Sri Chinmoy**

"Now come along to some quiet place by yourselves, and rest for a while," said Jesus, for there were people coming and going incessantly so that they had not even time for meals. They went off in the boat to a quiet place by themselves, but a great many saw them go and recognized them, and people from all the towns hurried on foot to get there first. When Jesus disembarked he saw the large crowd and his heart was touched with pity for them because they seemed to him like sheep without a shepherd."

—***Mark 6:31***

The people of earth have always needed examples of good men and women to emulate, teachers to teach them, and a way of thought and action to follow. However it has also been proven over time that this follow the leader kind of mentality can sometimes work adversely, instead of for the good. It could set up a kind of vulnerability and gullibility.

Unless one has a strong sense of integrity and is well grounded with a firm sense of his own right to individual thought and expression, he may become passive and acquiesce to another's will. A good shepherd loves, guards and guides his flocks. But there is danger in blindly following or idolizing a wolf in sheep's clothing.

Jesus came on the scene at a time when men totally dominated and ruled the day. Women, not by choice, were kept very much in the background. One might wonder how many women, like a Mary Magdalene, who was said by some to have possibly been a disciple to the Master, not unlike the twelve, would have been drawn toward this new teacher of peace, forgiveness and equality, if they had only had the courage to step forth. In the midst of this male superiority, there surely must be something higher, better, holier than the role women had been dealt.

Century after century of man-made edicts, doctrines, legends, myths and fables have shaped our understanding concerning the truth of a Supreme Being. The "gullibles travel" only so far in their thinking as their leaders or instructors take them. Some tend to follow the rest of the flock with no reasoning, individual thought, or expressions of their own. At this particular point, Ayn Rand would say, and *The Atlas Shrugged*.

Either by idolizing leaders or by just giving in to the herd mentality and marching right into the stockyard; we sometimes inadvertently are led to the slaughter of our very own freedom of creativity, thought and speech.

At some point in man's early history he became intent on controlling the people around him. First of course, in his own household, or cave, as it were, then with his extended relatives, neighbors, and eventually exercising power over his tribe or townspeople. When he gained this much power, his ego became inflated, he wanted more and more control, so as to take in his state, his country. Wouldn't it be wonderful to dominate all the masses upon the earth?

The insistence upon male sovereignty helped set up the paradigm for manufacturing a manly-type God. This unreasonable so-called reasoning creates a man-like God, created in man's image and likeness, instead of a God-like man, created in God's image. This whole approach is extremely egotistical, lopsided and upside down.

Through physical strength the alpha-male could wield his power over the weaker. The dominance of the male over the female, one tribe dominating the next tribe, one pack leader over another, gained momentum until it became one country overpowering the next one. Better water supplies, a more fertile and superior soil for crops, wealth under the ground, oil and gas, mines with precious jewels or gold, made weaker nations susceptible to takeover.

The insatiable appetite for power and wealth, brought complications, such as the need to find ways to control the people. The alpha-male's mentality first used brawn to dominate, but as time progressed they needed more sophisticated methods for controlling their subjects.

Some mighty potentates used a psychological agenda,, in order to make people think of themselves as inferior, downtrodden, lesser beings. They looked upon their subjects as unworthy, uneducated, and lowly sinners. These serfs had no choice but to hold their masters in reverence. Eventually this alpha-male authority became the Roman Caesar with sword in hand.

Meanwhile, the undercurrents of a spiritual nature were growing within the masses. The oppression of the warlords was starting to be questioned by their subjects, as there was news of a different kind of king, a spiritual Master who had even walked among them. A new and challenging power was on the rise. Its strength mightier than the sword, its power mightier than that of the Roman legions or the Khans' pilfering hordes.

The few subjects who were fortunate enough to have had a small amount of education, in many instances, the spiritually-minded, were reading the tablets, scrolls, and some of the hidden Gospels that related to Jesus' teachings. It was now becoming evident that the pen could come to be mightier than the sword. This new wave of spirituality could not be deterred.

Some of the followers of Jesus happened to be women, and these women had caught glimpses of their own importance as they adhered to his teachings. It would eventually come to pass that females no longer could be silenced and hidden away.

Through the original revelations of Jesus, the literal and rigid interpretations of scripture were beginning to undergo a transformation to a higher and more enlightened understanding of Truth, Life, God. This newly inspired thought created a movement which placed a greater emphasis on an individual's spiritual value.

Eventually the Holy Roman Emperor and Pope would come to take advantage of these changing times. They would seize the grand opportunity to ride the momentum of this accelerating Christian movement, in controlling their people by creating their own new form of worship. And here we are, the remnants of the rest of the story.

If a rumor be told enough times, over and over again, eventually that rumor becomes accepted truth. Someone must have stated the opinion that "every word of the Bible is God's word, so every word must be taken literally." However, the original "Word" was based on a few men's swayed interpretation of only the four selected Gospels; and it would come to be learned that there may have been as many as fifty Gospels written, not just four. Many are being unearthed today; still others were suppressed from the beginning.

As Bart D. Ehrman references in his book, *Jesus Interrupted*... one can't help but wonder why seminarians who become pastors never bring this and other historical facts to the attention of their parishioners for their own perusal.

Strictly speaking, ladies, the Good Book says that women literally created the original sin...and, that women should be subservient to men. It is believed in some religions that even God must see women as lesser beings. Is all of this to be taken as the "Gospel truth," as many would have it?

Some men used their penmanship and their own translations of Scripture to exact an advantage over the physically weaker gender. As time marched on, these canonical rulers sought subservience to the church's rule not only of one particular gender but of all people. The dominance of the alpha-male was thriving in the form of a religious hierarchy, paralleling the offices of the Roman military rule.

Ruling men decided that women were not deserving of being educated. Females were not permitted to read or write. They were to be held further in bondage as they were not allowed to hold office, or own property. What's more they couldn't even have an opinion of their own. In the Julian Fellowes' television series, *Downton Abby*, the Dowager Duchess sets everyone straight when she remarks, that Sybil cannot have an opinion of her own until she is married. And at that point, "her husband will tell her what her opinions will be!"

Religions came to dominate the countryside and control their flocks, the masses, through the evolving proliferation of male dominance. Only a privileged few men were educated and these men were allowed to officiate in the churches. The higher church also mandated that male parishioners were required to be subordinate to their religious elders. Women, as second-class citizens, were to be subordinate to their husbands, and children obedient to their parents.

All had to follow strict doctrinal guidelines and responsibilities within their particular religious sect as well. Countless numbers of women were accused of heresy or witchery, burned at the stake or beheaded by the church for speaking their mind and their conscience involving religious matters.

After hundreds of years of this oppressive rule and thousands upon thousands of deaths attributed to repressive policies such as the Inquisition, intelligent men like Martin Luther and John Calvin had had enough. The teachings of Jesus magnified the message, that truth and dominion come to the individual from within, regardless of gender or class, and not from a priest or his doctrines.

It took innumerable Christian martyrs and the killing of many of the Master's followers to begin the revolt against this church-dominated tyrannical influence. It required the voices of the Gnostics, Cathars, Templars and many others who were speaking out for spiritual freedom. It required men such as Martin Luther to rise up against religious arrogance, rigidity and corruption. Inspired by his stand, reformers across Europe began to find the courage to question the authority and rule of the Vatican. This meant rebelling against and refuting the entire mindset of medieval society.

Luther's actions and Gutenberg's printing press led to the use of vernacular languages in addition to Latin, which finally allowed people to read the Bible in their own language. He also encouraged education for the peasants and poor, who until then had been excluded from schools by religious dictates. It became more and more apparent that each individual, not the church, was accountable for his or her own salvation. Luther's rallies for "personal thinking," thus ushered in a new era for the rights of women as well as men.

Value of the individual, his or her conduct, integrity and ethics, accountability for one's own thoughts and actions, along with great emphasis on love and forgiveness, were the cornerstones in the transforming teachings of this new Master, Jesus. His message was for all people regardless of gender; but women especially would have needed to take heed and realize their own equal place of importance, as they had been downtrodden for so very long. And unfortunately, today many still continue to be.

Until recent years, little was known about the role of women in Jesus' ministry; this written information was either suppressed, destroyed, or buried long ago. The newly discovered Gospel of Mary Magdalene reveals never before heard accounts of her close relationship to Jesus and her inclusion in the teachings and secrets given by the Master to his closest followers.

The suppression of women has continued to this day, in part because of centuries-old religious myths about Eve and Adam. Eve, of course, was presented in the book of Genesis as the perpetrator of wrong-doing that led to a long storyline of ills, rivalry, shame, family discord, and death. Seldom is it brought out that this could merely have been one creative writer's very imaginative and colorful way of depicting in Jewish story form how evil may have been invented.

Imagine, a centuries-old fable, albeit presenting a good learning message in what not to do, still setting the criteria for our modern attitudes toward women!

No one should allow themselves to be naïve or gullible or have their freedoms taken away, especially women. No longer should men, religions, or any organization hold women in suppression or bondage and keep them in the background. Nor should anyone be held in mental chains by the doctrines or edicts set forth by a group of men determined to dominate their brothers and sisters.

Education should be available to women as well as men all over the world. We might wonder what young ladies of today will think, when they hear for the first time that it was only a 100 years ago when men finally allowed the feminine gender to have equal rights of voting in elections. Now, in this day and time, females can even own property. Isn't that a hoot! Maybe in our lifetime we will see actual equal rights for women all over the world.

No one can make you feel inferior without your consent.

—***Eleanor Roosevelt***

Hopefully the day will come when the female gender will no longer be silenced and hidden away. They will be able to "uncover their faces, get an education," express themselves in every facet of life and career, and be able to serve in every capacity of church or government activity—if they so choose.

"The truth" knows no gender. The Christ-Self, the I Am, of every individual includes all the God-qualities, masculine and feminine, both strength and tenderness, wisdom and purpose. The Christ-Self resides equally in every man, woman and child as the very individuality and activity of God.

The Gospel of Mary Magdalene

"Although the text of the Gospel of Mary Magdalene is incomplete, the writings presented here, in part, serve to shake the very concept of our assumptions of early Christianity as well as Jesus' possible relationship to Mary of Magdala, whom we call Mary Magdalene." From *Banned from the Bible* by Joseph B. Lumkin:

Chapter 5

4) *"Mary's words turned their hearts to the Good, and they began to discuss the words of the Savior."*

5) *"Peter said to Mary, Sister we know that the Savior loved you more than all other women."*

6) *"Tell us the words of the Savior that you remember and know, but we have not heard and do not know."*

7) *"Mary answered him and said, I will tell you what he hid from you."*

8) *"And she began to speak these words to them: She said, I saw the Lord in a vision and I said to him, Lord I saw you today in a vision."*

9) *"He answered and said to me; You will be happy that you did not waver at the sight of Me. Where the mind is there is the treasure."*

10) *"I said to Him, Lord, does one see visions through the soul or through the spirit?"*

11) *"The Savior answered and said; He sees visions through neither the soul nor the spirit. It is through the mind that is between the two. That is what sees the vision and it is (there the vision exists.)"*

Chapter 9

1) *"When Mary had said this, she fell silent, since she had shared all the Savior had told her."*

2) *"But Andrew said to the other believers, Say what you want about what she has said, but I do not believe that the Savior said this. These teachings are very strange ideas."*

3) *"Peter answered him and spoke concerning these things."*

4) *"He questioned them about the Savior and asked, Did He really speak privately with a woman and not openly with us? Are we to turn around and all listen to her? Did He prefer her to us?"*

5) *"Then Mary sobbed and said to Peter, My brother Peter, what do you think? Do you think that I have made all of this up in my heart by myself? Do you think that I am lying about the Savior?"*

6) *"Levi said to Peter, Peter you have always had a hot temper."*

7) *"Now I see you fighting against this woman like she was your enemy."*

8) *"If the Savior made her worthy, who are you to reject her? What do you think you are doing? Surely the Savior knows her well."*

9) *"That is why He loved her more than us. Let us be ashamed of this and let us put on the perfect Man. Let us separate from each other as He commanded us to do so we can preach the gospel, not laying down any other rule or other law beyond what the Savior told us."*

10) *"And when they had heard this they began to go out and proclaim and preach."*

Let us all remember that we should not be duped into believing anything less of ourselves than the greatness that was taught by the Master. Yes, it will take hard work, perseverance, steadfastness, a renouncing of dominance, and a giving up of selfishness. Taking dominion over one's self means to emulate the Master!

We must learn to think with "that mind," an open mind, the mind that can be still, without thinking of itself first, thinking out from the Divine whole, instead of thinking from a portion of the whole. Then, and only then, are we truly being set free, free to be unlimited, free to "be like him." Freedom is a state of holiness. If it were not so He would never have said, *"Freely you have received, freely give."*

Heroes take journeys,
confront dragons, and discover
the treasure of their true selves.

—***Carol Pearson***

Freedom is a state of holiness.

The great need for individuals today is... to know and accept their own God-Presence... such acknowledgment is the open door... expanding the light of the world.

Chapter 14

THE OPEN DOOR

"I know your works.
Behold I have set before thee an open door,
and no man can shut it."

—***Revelation 3:8***

The brilliant and enlightened Albert Einstein once said, "We are in the position of a little child entering a huge library filled with books in many languages. The child knows someone must have written those books. He does not know how, neither does he understand the languages in which they are written. The child dimly suspects a mysterious order in the arrangement of the books but doesn't know what it is... we see the universe marvelously arranged and obeying certain laws but only dimly understand these laws."

The inherent Christ

Einstein's example of a child in a library unable to explain how the books came to be written or the order in which they may be organized might describe the point at which humanity stood before the coming of Jesus. The Master Jesus revealed hidden truth. One of the great laws of our universe is the revelation of "the Christ-identity" which heretofore had been dimly perceived. The Christ-Consciousness that dwells within each and everyone of us awaits recognition; and as we learn to align our conscious awareness with this innate power then *"greater works"* than these *"shall ye do."*

The ascended Masters are continually communicating this message to us:

- You can do it, you can comprehend this.
- You are a Divine Being, an individualized planet of God-Consciousness.
- Your spirit, including your heart and soul have a whole universe of conscious elements swirling about it comprising your physical body.
- Know ye not that you are a sun of God with zillions of conscious particles, divinely ordained, orbiting around your center, yet governed in part by your human consciousness.
- You have the free will to keep your heavenly body, your universe of atoms and cells at ease, in harmony; go forth and radiate your light to the entire world.
- Raise your consciousness as the Master taught, from "this world" into your Higher Christ-Consciousness, *"My Kingdom."*

Bodily universe

Of course, you can negate your good health and well-being by choosing to be dissonant and angry, filling your bodily universe with stress; the by-product of which is discord, discomfort, disease, and on a much larger scale than we yet realize, storms. But why would a divine being do that to himself? The kind of world you create to circulate about your heart center and allow to swirl and flow out into your experience is of your soul's own choosing. Choose wisely!

Our Christ-Self can be like a gravitational force within us, forever drawing only good to us. We draw in our energy, sustenance from the I Am Source, and in turn, completing the circuit, we send it back out. Know this:

God is at the same instant, the breather,
the breath,
and the air that is breathed.

—***C.S. McClintock***

Divine circuitry

The in-breath and out-breath, the taking in and giving back is the life-rhythm of the universe. If we don't continue the cycle, that of drawing good to us and letting goodness flow back out, circulating it, we cease to manifest health and harmony. We too often take in our daily goodness and return it into the ethers as stress, disorder and negativity, thereby closing the circuit of harmony, thus inviting upon ourselves premature aging, discomfort, disease.

It is as though "Scotty" has been waiting and waiting for us to come to our spiritual senses, which will lift us higher in our understanding of the dynamic principles of our own divine circuitry. We should be asking our own Higher-Self, our Christ-Self to "beam us up"— help our un-ascended worldly consciousness to arise, ascending the crossroads of time and space—just as our Master did.

Elevating the natural man

Hopefully, we are all grasping the idea of ourselves being individualized God-Consciousness, co-creators of ideas and images—our thinking makes us so. To quote Dustin, "We are builders. We are makers. We are explorers."

Unfortunately, our un-tethered human thinking makes error, sin, and evil seem so. But fear not, with a little payback of our debts and right thinking, we are on our way back to our normal, goodly human status—not yet great, but hopefully advancing. At this point, we may still be the "natural man" though now thinking correctly. However, that's exactly what The Master came to show us, that we can keep elevating correct consciousness in the so-called natural man, until it fully tethers and blends with this man's own Christ-Consciousness.

The original nature of all things is spiritual; first invisible to our mortal eye, but spiritually and indelibly blueprinted into the ethers, then clothed by the angels into visible bodily form in this world. With celestial energy, the elements of creation are fashioned into all forms—dust, stone, wood, water, flesh and blood— the clay of life so to speak. The highest manifestation of God-Consciousness within form is thinking man, who is the very activity of creativity, of God's creativity on this earthly plane.

The quickening

Worldly man's imperfect thoughts are devised through his imaginative free will. And this same free will can travel and create in any direction, positive or negative, Christ-like or anti-good, antichrist. The thoughts and ideas from this mortal mind, this natural man, unfortunately, are not always derived from his higher-minded Christ-nature. However, the good news is that man is more than capable of keeping his thoughts aligned with his Divine Plan.

Man cannot receive the gifts of the Spirit without consistently staying higher-minded. That takes strict discipline and a selfless air, just as the Master showed. This discipline includes one's willingness to serve his brothers and sisters by teaching, forgiving, and showing forth one's high moral character.

The natural man must come to the following realization: I may be in this world, but my spirit is not of this world. Furthermore, I must remember that my ultimate being is not the body, it is the spirit that "quickeneth" this human vehicle.

The proverbial natural man simply represents stagnated thinking—thinking stuck in a material and limited mindset, closeted as it were, to the further infinite possibilities of learned growth. It speaks to being unreceptive and unwilling to consider anything above or beyond the familiar established and programmed governmental and theological information, unreceptive to new ideas.

Behold, an open door

Perhaps it should be instinctive to stay independently open-minded, to think from a spiritual standpoint, or to listen from this more exalted state of mind. But that is not always so. As (Corinthians 2:14) says, *"The natural man receiveth not the things of the spirit of God, for they are foolishness unto him. Neither can he know them because they are spiritually discerned."* Yes, they must be discerned by the average man's higher consciousness—his higher mind. Our willingness to receive "the things of the spirit" provides an open doorway through which spiritual thoughts, truths, gifts of the spirit flow and may be freely received. This normal, ordinary man is now ascending his former status with a more elevated perspective.

The Universal Law of Life has rhythm and order. Our Source has a plan for every galaxy and every solar system. Now hear this!

There is what we call life-spirit, everywhere, in all universes; life-streams in varying forms on all planets. Wearing a different form, other life, extra-terrestrials for instance, may not look exactly like our human selves. However, sooner or later we must recognize that all beings, seen or unseen, familiar or not, are spiritual entities derived from the ONE God-Consciousness.

Are we open to seeing these galactic life-streams as our spirit ancestors, just as we do our own earthy brothers and sisters? Do we even begin to comprehend the fact that our Source may have a plan for every one of His infinitesimal or gigantic expressions, including planetary? Or are we seeing our earth as His only agenda?

Absolute harmony

Although we may yet perceive it dimly, like the child in Einstein's library, God-Consciousness resides in even the most infinitesimal of elements. Knowing that the One Spirit, Source lives all life simultaneously is paramount to enlightened understanding, as is perceiving that the underlying nature of this perfect "cause and effect" is absolute harmony in all things. Only with this perspective can we perceive the workings of perfect oneness in the unity of creation. All molecules, atoms and particles; all ethers, dimensions and planes, all shapes and designs, whether called spiritual or material, invisible or visible—everything is spiritual energy—and they were seen to be "very good." They are HIS Life, in varying form and expression. God is ALL things.

Listen with an open heart

There is a divine plan for our earth, as well as for our own individual lives. As in governments, this plan involves a system of order and structure. In structure there are offices with functions orchestrated by directors, managers and teachers. In the workings of the spiritual Universal Laws of Life many of these offices, roles, are held by those who have ascended before us, earthly graduates, such as the Master Jesus.

These enlightened ones continue communicating messages of help and assistance to us individually and collectively. In this reality, there is no failure to communicate. Truly, the only shortcoming lies within ourselves, in our failure to listen with an open heart and a stilled mind; and our failure to recognize the ever-presence of these enlightened helpers and teachers. While we may not see them with our three-dimensional comprehension, we can be sure that in every moment, they are seeing us.

If we accept this truism, we are no longer like the little child in our assimilation of truth, but mature in our reasoning, no matter the form in which it may present itself. There is a wealth of spiritual information waiting to speak to our receptive thought.

These highly evolved beings are right here beside us, vibrating at a more quickened pace, a higher frequency than ourselves, therefore invisible to our three-dimensional sight. They are operating in what we are now beginning to understand is a higher realm, a more elevated dimension. Ascended Masters and angels are forever beaming direction, guidance and encouragement from this more celestial level to our Higher Selves. We should be showing reverence and gratitude for their continued assistance, the tireless and loving patience that Jesus and all the Masters have shown us over countless centuries.

Spiritual assistance

Please consider with me the revelations found in the books written by Alice Schutz as she transcribed the enlightened messages given to her by Guy Ballard/Godfrey Ray King.

They received detailed information concerning God's plan for our earth, and our true identity, as given by Ascended

Masters. These Masters, or earthly graduates ascended the cycle of birth and rebirth. They, along with Master Jesus are still present, without need of physical form or human body. We should, at the very least, open the doors of our hearts and minds, being grateful and eager to drink in and ingest the highest truths these dear ones are presenting.

The Laws of Life

"Please engage your intuitive senses as you contemplate this Ascended Master instruction. This instruction is educational, not just religious: it is a science as well. It is no "ism" or "cult," written as it was given and in a manner to convey the feeling rather than to conform to literary standards. The information should give you a better understanding of life, for it is based in the law of energy and vibration. Statements, points of law, and bits of truth are compiled here so they will not be lost to the world. May they be of real worth to those interested!

"Our destiny is perfection. Jesus said, '*Be ye perfect.*' He manifested perfection through the same understanding that is again being given through these writings to mankind. He was Master over outer conditions, even death—the last enemy to be overcome. Most people have looked to their religion to give them understanding of the 'unknown' or 'other side' of life. The teaching set forth here gives an understanding of fundamental truths—universal laws and principles, with practical application and is not just dogma or creed.

"All that is asked of students is to accept their own God-Presence. One might consider this as a kind of special 'retreat' work, a study of the Ascended Masters, their services, and communications to mankind and the earth at this time; also how to invoke and draw forth their assistance that is so much needed.

"We have tried here to give enough on fundamentals, understanding and application to make it practical in a comprehensible way for beginners in this type of instruction, the Law of Life, as well as for students of the various teachings and those more advanced.

"The great need today is for individuals to know of and accept their own God-Presence and be one with It. Such acknowledgement is the open door, making the individual receptive for the instruction and expertise of these great ones to bless mankind with untold blessings, expanding the light of the world."

The I Am Presence

Schutz continues:

"When you call to the Presence, you are calling to the God Presence of everyone in the world. Even earnest students do not realize what a power their call to the Presence is.

"Contemplate life, where does it come from? From the Magic I AM Presence. Without that life, energy, flowing into you from this All Power you would have no intelligence, thought, feeling or action. Therefore you can see that it is the action of the Presence of God. The Presence is the doer in every way. So as to make the outer self accept the fact you can say to your Presence: 'It is my Magic I AM Presence making this call': it is the Presence acting and also answering it.

"Because mankind have turned away from the light, (although there is the eternal connection with their Presence through the ray or stream of light into the heart), each one must now again make a conscious connection with his Source: make contact with his own God Presence anchored in his heart. To go on into greater expansion and cosmic (spiritual) activities, it is one's own I AM

Presence he will progress in or through. No one can get away from this fact, no matter what teaching he is listening to.

"Each day, hold the attention definitely and unwaveringly on the Presence even if just for a short time.

"Try to realize when contemplating the Presence, that in It are the powers of the universe, given to you as a gift of Divine love.

"Attention to the God Presence is the most powerful thing in the universe, but the attention must be held unwavering for a time. Knowing the Presence, you now have a point of focus on which to anchor your attention.

"Give attention to and become acquainted with your individualized Presence of God—the Magic I AM Presence.

"Since we of our own free will have turned away from the awareness of God, It will not act in our world except by invitation. As you give attention to and call to your Presence It will expand more and more through you. And as less attention is given to discord and this Power expands and increases Its light in you, the shadows and limitations will decrease proportionately.

"Distance of the Presence—your consciousness determines that. Its closeness is according to your thought and feeling. It is not a matter of distance according to the human sense of space. In cosmic reality the Presence abides in a certain realm of light. If the I Am and Casual Body fully abided in the atmosphere of Earth, how could any discord or imperfection be here? It is a Being of a four dimensional, and even higher dimensional, action, but of course in radiance. It can be as great and as close as you accept it.

"It was said that if the recognition of the Christ Self was brought into the consciousness of the outer self, our light-body would be perceived as a blazing light.

"The Presence is constantly active at cosmic, celestial levels. The energy in the Casual body is not stagnate. This Power directs light rays through It and utilizes the accumulated good in cosmic creation. The Presence knows not of the human creation of the outer self, but the Christ Self does. Our I Am God Presence has projected us temporarily into this time and place in space. In turn, the Christ Self projects a large portion of Its Consciousness into the three dimensional world of spiritual energies we call matter. The God Presence doesn't see our human creations. It only knows and is Goodness. The Presence just Is—Love Energy.

"When one is purified and harmonized sufficiently, the accumulated good in the Casual body is released into one's three dimensional use.

"The Three-fold Flame in the heart is a projection of the I Am Presence, but the greater part is above, in our Christ Self. (A Flame is a concentration of a light ray; just as you can concentrate the sun's ray through a glass till a flame is produced. It is a ray of light condensed or concentrated sufficiently to make a flame. This flame comes from the invisible into the visible, and when extinguished, it returns to the invisible, the fourth dimensional.) More and more of this Power can be drawn forth and made manifest through the physical form.

"Even where the Presence is portrayed close to the physical body, It is still from without. The need is to get more of It in action through the physical body and that is done through consciousness and not through a concept of form in three-dimensional activity.

"The Three fold Flame in the heart of undeveloped mankind is but a spark. In an advanced student it becomes a small replica of the Presence, which is in some teachings referred to as the 'Golden Man in the heart.'

"Other teachings have a more abstract idea as to God and law, while this new instruction explains God as an Individualized Presence within and above and to which the physical form or body is connected. It gives one a sense of something more concrete. Most people have a concept of God as an abstract Principle only, instead of a focused Realty, an Individualized living Being—a Being to Whom you can talk and Who hears and answers your prayers or calls.

"Contemplate your Presence; try to get a feeling of Its reality—a living all-wise Being. Pour your love to It and it is possible to feel a response from It. Some people think they cannot love a Being unseen to them, or not tangible to their physical touch, yet when one thinks it through, he can generate a feeling of love when he thinks of a child or person he loves very, very much. In that same way, one can pour love to his own God Presence who has been sadly ignored and forgotten for a very long time, yet through the ages It has kept on giving you life and all by which you have had an existence.

"The spheres of colors around the Presence represent the powers of this I Am-ness. They are symbolized by blue which represents power and protection; yellow, illumination—the Christ in action; pink, love—divine compassion; white, purity; green, precipitating power—consecration; ruby, the color of the Sixth Ray, (instead of ruby, the color of gold is usually used at this present stage of development, as Jesus the Chohan the Sixth Ray has been working under the Christ activity); the action of ministration; violet (the violet flame) transmutation. The action of the Seventh Ray is not only that of transmutation, (on other planets where there is no discord they do not need purification as we do here on Earth) but also of invocation and radiation. The colors of the Casual body are tentative."

Schutz continues:

"We use one color for each ray although each ray is sevenfold, ranging from a very light tint to a very deep color. For example the violet: from a light orchid to a deep purple.

"This knowledge of the Individualized Presence gives one a definite focus of God, a power-house and active Intelligence from which to draw; while knowing God just as spirit does not give that. Spirit is the radiance or radiation of the focalized Presence of God. Spirit is the radiation, the aura or Casual body; but within that is the Individualized Presence. It is said, God is Spirit; God is Love—yes true, but those are only abstract ideas until fully understood.

"Here is a vital and important point in this understanding, not given in other teachings; that our Individualized Presences of God are simultaneouly in heaven (the higher Realms, dimensions), even while we as individuals are active in the human realm, dimension.

"The Presence is the highest activity, individually—the Presence of God Whose thought is flame, Whose desire is creation.

"Your Presence is the foundation of the universe; it is One with the Great I Am. God (the governor of the universe) has projected you—the light pattern (blueprint) upon which your human form is built, so you see, you are a part of the Great Perfection. Your Being is individualized, yet it is one with the Great I Am, which is one in quality so we can justly say that 'all'are ONE.

"The mankind of Earth were immortal beings before they came, and not only to evolve into immortals, but to expand their light and become greater outposts to render service to the universe. You are an individualized, outpost of the Divine. You are the focus of the Godhead at your particular point in the universe, within this time and place.

"Acceptance is a power of infinite activity within you. It is the Presence in action. You are the very activity of creativity individualized. The universal law of attraction governs all three-dimensional energy.

"According to your understanding and balancing of Its powers will you have the fullness of the Divine, or only part of It. When we call the Presence into action, It compels Divine Love, Wisdom and Power in balanced action. God in action ARE WE—think what that means! There is only one way—your acknowledgement of the Magic I Am Presence.

"The energy flowing through the stream of light, the 'Silver Chord,' as it is sometimes called, does not discriminate; but when you call to your I AM Source that becomes a wholly different matter. It is one thing to know the Presence is there, but to have Its action demonstrated here is the great command. That ray of light from this Power is continuous energy flowing.

"When one knows the Presence, then in the call to that Source it becomes Love, Wisdom and Power in balanced action right here on earth. One who does not know and accept his or her Magic I Am Presence cannot effectively have that action.

"Everything that is in the physical realm has come through the stream of light from the Presence. You must practice accepting Its use. Just to come into the knowledge of the Power is not enough. You know in your feelings that a ray of light from this Energy beats your heart and represents the Open Door.

"Remember, you are a Divine Being. Go forth and radiate your light to all the world. You are the focus of the Godhead at your particular point in the universe.

"Know in your feelings that a ray of light from the Presence beats your heart and represents the Open Door."

There is a divine plan for our earth,
as well as for our own individual lives.

We humans are slow to accept new discoveries.
The sky is not falling after all . . .
the earth is not flat.
It was round all the while.

Chapter 15

ALTERING MINDSETS

At the end of many births, the wise person takes refuge in Me . . . realizing that all things are the Self. Rare and wonderful is the soul that achieves this state of consciousness.

—***The Bhagavad Gita***

Our aged perceptions are almost immune to new ideas and are very slow to receive change. But we need the kind of change which advances us mentally and spiritually. In fact, being open and willing to grapple with new ideas is a requirement for advancing our level of thought and consequently our lives. It simply cannot happen otherwise. Being willing to modify our timeworn and inelastic mindsets leaves fertile ground for new and inspired study, an opening to our imagination; giving a whole new look to our formerly preconceived notions.

I have a very distinct memory of being an eleven year old. One of my best friends, Jimmy G. and I were riding our bicycles together on a sunny summer afternoon. I had recently come across some information, as children often do, that I knew would be of great interest to him. I proceeded to explain to him in great detail where babies come from. He immediately took offense, and began to argue with me. That's when I lowered the boom on him and said in so many words, "How do you think your parents conceived you?"

I remember it, just as if it had happened last week. He began to cry and cry. Through the tears, he angrily said, "My mom and daddy would never do something like that!" At that point, boys being boys and all, I probably said something to this effect, "Oh yeah, the stork must have dropped you off at your parents door, right? And while we're at it. let me tell you the truth about Santa Claus too!"

The remembrance of this humorous scenario came across my thought recently as I was contemplating how certain mind-sets are fashioned, sometimes in our youth, sometimes over long periods of time. Brick by brick, ideas are laid in the foundation of our beliefs. Through repetition, concepts are imprinted like an indelible dye upon the canvas of our mental make-up. Adults too, at times are rigid in their refusal, or their willingness to consider or accept new perceptions.

No one seems to care for change, or to be told that his version is mistaken, or could be improved upon, myself included! However, I've learned to become a much better listener and more patient in respect to where each one is in his learning journey. We are each finding our own way.

However, perceptions must and do change over time. Enlightened thought, the real truth, about a subject, especially where sacred writings are concerned, should demand our highest consideration. Newly uncovered knowledge cannot be hidden away or forever suppressed from spiritual seekers. The most elevated concepts about truth will eventually come to the surface. Even if it takes two thousand years.

We humans are slow to accept new discoveries. The sky is not falling after all. We didn't want to believe it, but the earth is not flat. It was round all the while. The early church argued vehemently against Newton, that there was no such thing as gravity. Voices of today say, I don't want to consider the discovery of a new planet. What's that got to do with me? Do I have to learn something new like moving into this computer age? Isn't texting just for the young people? I like things the way they were—its more comfortable to stay in the status quo. Simply put, I don't care for change.

The man who views the world at fifty the same as he did at twenty has wasted thirty years of his life.

—***Muhammad Ali***

A conversation

One day, after our family had completed Thanksgiving dinner, one of my sisters suggested she would like to have a private conversation with me."I'm very concerned about you," she said. "I read your book, *God We Are*, and while I was very impressed with your writing talents, I must tell you that some of your ideas differ from those of the Bible. Further, if you truly do not believe in hell, then I'm afraid you'll be damned and cast into the fire for all eternity."

"You've got to be kidding," I responded.

"No, I'm not kidding," Beverly said. "I am very serious, the Bible is the exact word of God, and you will be punished and sent to hell. Because you are a non-believer in the devil, you surely must be sent there."

I immediately asked her about the billions of people in the world that were not familiar with Jesus Christ. "Will they be condemned to your hell also?

"Oh yes," she quickly answered, "I feel sorry for them, but they will be lost forever. The Word is very specific."

"Yes," I said, "and Chicken Little was very explicit when she proclaimed the sky was falling too! I'm sorry, it's not my wish to poke fun at you. I have the greatest respect for the good intentions of every religion, and every individual spiritual quest.

"This is a very serious subject. I am just trying to point out that as a people we can sometimes be very gullible. The more I look into Bible history, I realize how the mainstream of religious thought has been dramatically influenced and swayed by a select few, who, for their own benefit, were intent on keeping their subjects in obeisance to rigid doctrines and literal translations.

"We have become skeptical concerning any other interpretations of truth, even where it relates to a substantial number of recently unearthed texts, un-tampered versions of the original Gospels."

At that point, I said, "Please, please, I love the Master. He is my ideal, and it is my fervent desire to be as much like Jesus as I possibly can. Don't you realize that human beings, mere mortals, translated the writings that make up the Bible?

"A few men with personal motives, one of whom had been a life-long pagan, decided which books would be chosen out of the many Gospels at hand, and then manufactured their own profitable version and translations of these same writings, before submitting them into this Good Book. The gospels of Matthew, Mark, Luke and John were not even written by their own hand. They were written in the names of these Apostles, in some cases, hundreds of years later from passed-down stories concerning the Master.

"For instance, did you know that this place called hell, was nothing more than the name given to a garbage dump set at the perimeter of a Jewish town or settlement? The Hebrew name for this burning trash dump was "sheol" or in Greek, "hades." When the Hebrew children would misbehave, the elders would threaten to throw them into the hellfire for not being good, telling them they would burn forever. Jesus knew full well his listeners would relate to this figure of speech."

My sister responded by saying, "Hell must be real though—do you realize how many times the words 'hell,' 'demons' and 'devils' are mentioned in the Bible?"

"Yes, but these words are symbolic of the torment we are creating within ourselves. Jesus simply used this word 'hell' to describe the self-inflicted repercussions we incur, the boomerang effect generated from our less than perfect thoughts and actions; the so-called sins and evils we have ourselves created."

Since that day, my sister and I often exchange differing opinions about religious theology. We have loving exchanges, and know that we are each headed in the same direction, though she takes a literal path and I the more metaphysical, in interpreting the Scriptures. And I let her know that I too, have great respect for this Good Book and all we can learn from its message.

Saved?

I remember several years ago giving an inspirational talk to a group of people. I had addressed several questions, when a lady in the audience stood up and asked "Have you been saved?"

I thought to myself, oh no, here we go again. I must have accidentally stepped on her toes or tread upon the foundation of her religious convictions, the brainwashing we all seem to have received.

No, no, I'm sorry, that word sounds too militant. I really meant the belief structure impressed upon her from the teachings actually handed down over the centuries by the early church, and early religions.

Don't get me wrong. I love to stir the imagination of my listeners, but it is never my intention to debate religions or politics. However, I know my audience is really listening when their thought is challenged. I quietly thought of one of my mother's clever church sayings, mimicking a nervous usher from the old days, whose tongue got in the way of his words: "Mardon me padom, but I think you are occ-u-pew-ing the wrong py!"

My response was, "Pardon me ma'am, but 'saved' from what? I don't happen to believe in your hell as a destination in some fabricated, medieval afterlife. To me, hell is an experience in our life on earth right here and now, if we have unfortunately earned it. Simply put, it is the reaping of what we have planted. Hell is not a location or a destination, but rather an unfortunate set of consequences, the discomforting circumstances we bring upon ourselves.

"The only things we need to be 'saved' from are the false teachers, false teachings, and religious fanatics, whose agenda is to do away with anyone or any group who have differing philosophies or beliefs, other than their own. In the name of religion, most have been taught that their way, is the only way. Intolerance of another's spiritual journey, their individual beliefs and opinions, just breeds more intolerance.

"The Master's entire philosophy was to judge not. Jesus was an advocate of independent thinking with compassion. When he cried out and spoke strongly, he was just upset, actually angry, with rigid doctrines, formality, and their judgmental nature."

I couldn't help but think at that moment how eerily similar the past is repeating itself. For these very reasons, I too feel a bit angry. I can think of one of our great presidents who felt as though religions seem to be stifling man's own independent thinking with their rigidity of doctrine, tenant and creed.

President Abe Lincoln, an avid reader, even questioned the divinity of the Bible, since for the most part, the original texts had been translated and transposed by men who were driven by their own personal agendas, i.e. a Roman emperor and his Pope.

Fortunately, many today are breaking free from outdated religious rhetoric.

Loyalty to petrified opinion never yet broke a chain or freed a human soul.

—***Mark Twain***

Redeeming grace

Much to my consternation, I recently watched a television evangelist, one of many ardent, yet misinformed speakers, explaining to his viewers how our Master Jesus has paid for ALL their past sinning, ALL their present transgressions, and ALL of their future sinful mistakes. How is this bit of theology working out for us? Wow, is it any wonder that the unenlightened are out there raising hell, our prisons are bursting at the seams, and the U. S. has more inmates than any country in the world?

Some preachers are inadvertently teaching the blank-check theory—they say "Not to worry, you don't have to be personally accountable for your erroneous thoughts and actions, someone else will pay your debts. Just be sure that on your deathbed you confess, and ask a priest for forgiveness, and all will be well, your transgressions forgiven!"

Please, where is the accountability?

Do we actually believe that a human being, with the wistful wave of a hand, has the divine power to forgive another person's debts? Does this priest have the ability to reach out and snare the boomerang that will most assuredly land on its sinning creator? This ruse of an application of "white-out" can in no wise blot out every jot and tittle and transform one's character. The world needs true enlightenment instead of a sense of entitlement!

This senseless assumption flies in the face of cosmic law, the law of accountability and adjustment, the reaping of what one has sown. And in fact it bears no resemblance to the grace that Jesus taught. By planting negative seeds, you and only you, will reap their harvest, their repercussions and entwinements.

Only through your own suffering and reformation may you become untangled. "Vengeance is mine" saith your own Christ-Consciousness. Like a good parent, God does not recognize evil, only the need to better learn. Again, sin is its own punisher. Evil by any name is a human's own temporary creation of entwinement. When the lesson is finally gained, evil is no more. Only then, is it what we call forgiven, forgotten, done away with, transmuted and dissolved! We are finally freed, saved from our negative thinking. Maybe someday we will also be saved from centuries of religious misconceptions!

In the history of the world, has there ever been a farmer who actually believed another would benevolently do his harvesting for him?

Widening perspective

A friend once asked me why the "stretch of the imagination and a vibrant expectation of the future and unknown" was so important in spiritual enlightenment. I answered, "It is a well-known fact that artists, musicians, inventors, scientists, spiritual seekers, and people in all fields have used their minds and imagination in projecting ahead to what 'could be,' as well as what is already known." I then explained to him one of my favorite scenarios:

"As we advance through spiritual understanding, we could find ourselves entering a future universe, ever evolving, exploring, ascending the grades in a new lifetime of sojourns. Perhaps in that next schoolhouse, our next plane of existence, we would be living in a progressive civilization with no discord or sin, where no forgiveness or being 'saved' is required.

"In this Perfect Society, a type of Utopia, as Thomas More calls it, with no inhabitants thinking negativity, there would be no manifestation of disharmony or disease. We might even be so technologically advanced that we could travel across universes in our flying saucers. Maybe we would be visiting other solar systems, checking out the different types of life-forms; communicating amicably with others of differing look and nature, with no judgment whatsoever, no matter what body-form the Spirit was required to wear on that particular celestial sphere.

"We would then realize how utterly ridiculous it was to think, with all the differing global environments 'out there,' that another spirit's life would be required to look exactly like us! How narrow-minded and arrogant that would be."

In order to stretch my friend's imagination a little further, I said, "Think about it! Open your thought and envision this. One day, we will all finally graduate this schoolroom called earth. We will then have the choice to ascend out of this world or not, readying ourselves to move on to our next realm or our next possible solar system, the choice many others before us have already made, including the Master.

"Thanks be to Jesus and other ascended Masters who, after their earthly graduation, chose to postpone their future planetary excursion for their elect mission of staying behind in their continuing 'professorship role' and remaining in our earthly realm, doing their spiritual work. In this compassionate mission as helpers and teachers, they are determined to raise the consciousness and 'stretch the imagination' of all humanity, to help lift earthlings above their material thinking into a more ascending pathway, and leaving the five-senses behind."

'I appreciate your challenging story,' he remarked, 'but how does this opening up and expanding of my imagination help me in the here and now?'

As we were enjoying lunch together, I replied, "Look around. What do you see?"

He quickly answered, 'Well, I see a large room full of tables and chairs, people dining together, and waiters and waitresses bustling about.'

"Yes," I said, "that's the surface view, but what if you could see that there was nothing but God going on here? Can you not perceive with me, the One Source manifesting Itself as everything you see, including the plants, the food, the air we are breathing? Can you see that every individual is God-Presence, materially manifested, every activity is moving with His energy, everything, everyone is Him and His experience?

"You must first be able to *imagine* it, then move on to knowing in your heart the pure truth that God is All-in-All, *All* there is."

'Whoa,' he said, 'I think I am beginning to understand what you mean. I feel a change in my thought already. I now realize that spiritual enlightenment involves much more than stretching the imagination; it requires being willing to expand one's conscious awareness beyond the physical, beyond the normal limits of human thinking.'

I went on to recount a personal experience to him from some years past. I had exchanged friendly conversation with a waitress, during which time she shared a health concern. Her doctor was readying her for a costly knee surgery. As she walked away with a noticeable limp, I quietly held to my conscious view of her spiritual perfection.

At this point it was more than just imagining, envisioning or projecting thought toward something. I was knowing her perfection as present fact, both spiritually and physically. For the moment I had placed my consciousness within the Allness of the Divine.

While leaving the restaurant that day, I promised that I would continue to pray for her. She responded, "I would very much appreciate that," and gave me a hug.

And I did pray for her, but not in the way the world prays, not in petition, but in declaration. I periodically meditated to see her in her original, perfect Godly form with no encumbrances. I knew that the Father within me was the same Father, Spirit, within her and that her own Christ-Self within could manifest the healing.

Several weeks later, when I returned, she rushed over to my table and excitedly said, "I don't know what you did, I knew you were praying for me. I no longer require knee surgery, and as you can see, I am walking normally again. I have no limp, and my pain is gone!" With a huge hug, the waitress said, "Thank you, thank you, thank you!"

After sharing this story with my friend, he wanted to know more. I then tried gently to convey the concept of One God, One Power, the One Father, Spirit living all lives simultaneously. I opened my arms and gestured toward the restaurant full of people as I said, "How this understanding could change the world, if we each saw God in, and as, everyone, everything!"

My friend was left with much to contemplate.

Recognition

I'd like to share an uplifting event that happened in my life not so long ago. While exchanging departing pleasantries with folks leaving one of my recent talks, I couldn't help but notice a lady waiting patiently so that she might be the last to shake my hand. As I finished with the others, she approached and asked if I could take a few extra minutes to visit with her. I promptly agreed.

The sparkle in her eye was evident as she began to speak. She was eager to tell me about a beautiful day in early April. In the previous few weeks, the weather had been rather inconsistent. This particular day, however, was bright, sunny, and 85 degrees. An afternoon off from work was a foregone conclusion, because she needed more time to worry and think about her depression. Living alone had become more and more difficult.

She was now living on the east coast after having relocated from California, where, after falling asleep at the wheel she had been responsible for a major automobile accident. She had been trying desperately to leave her past behind. I didn't presume to ask for details.

Feeling settled, yet still trying to find solace in her new life, she went on to tell me that on this day she had placed her beach chair down within a few feet of the outgoing breaking tide. She breathed in the ocean air. The panoramic view of the aqua blues and greens was scintillating, as she listened to the gentle rhythm of the lapping waves. The pelicans were working near the surf, and seagulls were dancing in the sand looking for handouts.

She painted quite a picture of her day, and mentioned that she knew a little about meditation, and had finally relaxed enough to become very still. Once she became comfortable in her lounge chair, she began reading the new book a friend had gifted to her.

Time became irrelevant, a few hours had drifted by, when she came to the realization that the book in her hands, my book, *God We Are*, was the answer to her prayers!

This new friend said that she had now read the book cover to cover three times, and it had given her a new perspective for living her life. It seemed as though the weight of the world had been lifted from her shoulders, and her longstanding depression was finally gone. She was truly sensing her spiritual nature.

She had admitted that, at first, it wasn't easy trying to see herself as a "Divine Being." It was very difficult, but as she continued to read, everything fell into place, and the possibilities began to make sense. Not only that, but she rewound her whole life's history, reflecting on, and forgiving, everyone from her past; everyone, whether she thought them to be right or wrong. A monumental step forward, and now all were forgiven. *"It is finished."* (John 17:4)

This act of forgiveness, and letting go of the past, was the key to unlocking her future. As the Lord's Prayer graciously requests, forgive me, just as I have forgiven; And *"forgive us our trespasses, debts, as we forgive those who trespass against us."* (Matthew 6:9-13) Indeed, having said the Lord's Prayer hundreds of times, she asked herself if she actually had ever pardoned anyone? Or had she previously just been mouthing the prayer? She realized she never had fully understood this illustrious Truth concerning FORGIVENESS. Up to that point in her life, not only had she never pardoned others, but she had not even been able to forgive herself.

One last thing she wanted to share with me was that even before the accident, she very often cried herself to sleep at night, beseeching God for answers to her deepest questions. What was her purpose on this earth, and why was she here?

"This is going to sound really strange, but I'm going to share it with you anyway," she said. During the past Christmas holiday, she was awakened in the middle of the night by the radiance of an angelic-looking lady standing at the foot of her bed. For some reason she wasn't startled or afraid. Perhaps it was because she could see that the heavenly being was a figure of light, with a very loving countenance. The lady never spoke, but my new friend said she could hear the angel's words in her head. "Do not fret dear one, your answers will be coming in the very near future; be patient, all your questions will be answered soon," the angel had said.

Less than four months later she found what she described as "your wonderful words" in *God We Are*. She concluded by saying, "thank you so much for helping to lift me up on my pathway." She was now in touch with the spiritual side of herself, seeing herself as a divine individuality, a co-creator, writing her own script, directing her life with love, forgiveness and harmony. And yes, now she was finally able to forgive herself. She was truly feeling "the peace which passeth all human understanding," and continuing along her journey.

She breathed in the ocean air... This act of forgiveness and letting go of the past was the key to unlocking the future.

There is no best way except to listen,
Allow fear and anxiety to drop away…
the FORCE, energy,
your I AM Presence, which IS GOD,
is with you.

Chapter 16

A CHRISTIAN MYSTIC

I count him braver who overcomes his desires than him who conquers his enemies;

The hardest victory is the victory over self.

—***Aristotle***

A new acquaintance and friend of mine, Dr. Jack Bruns, tells an intriguing story in his book, a *Diary of a Christian Mystic*. His early life includes many years spent as a Baptist Minister.

He says, "By 'mystical' I mean those occurrences wherein one makes contact with a power and consciousness that transcends who we are but which is a part of our very being. Mysticism is the work of the Holy Spirit and was the primary emphasis for hundreds of years in the early Christian fellowships.

"We come from the realm of divine power and consciousness and are intended to function in the spiritual and physical realms at the same time. Young children often speak of their awareness of the spiritual realm in dreams, fantasy and daydreams. This spiritual awareness usually recedes as they age.

"It is no surprise when I say to the reader that becoming a human is a very tough job. It takes so much of our concentration that we have little strength to focus inward where the bridge to the spiritual realm lies dormant. Learning to function in the physical arena dominates the surface, or earthly consciousness.

"Before long we assume that the only mind worth developing is the conscious mind. This is what we are told by our parents, teachers and friends. Young people are discouraged from talking about their inner perceptions and are often instructed to be fearful of the inner mind. Regularly in church I was told that nothing good dwells within me.

"My early pastor often quoted this scripture, *'I know that nothing good lives in me, that is, in my sinful nature. For I have the desire to do what is good, but I cannot carry it out.'* (Romans 7:18 NIV) We were told not to trust our emotions but to follow the rules and laws of the adult and church world.

"However, this leaves humans with a major problem. We are incapable of deriving complete satisfaction from the physical world. This inner emptiness exhibits itself in numerous ways. We develop cravings in an attempt to fill the inner itch. Through substance abuse we seek to deaden the inner pain. The phrase 'The grass is always greener on the other side of the fence,' speaks to this.

"Changing jobs or mates is another example of trying to ease our dissatisfaction through acquisition. We cannot even meet this need with the trapping and rituals of religion. This external religion can become so great an empty burden that spiritually discerning people flee and leave it behind. A religion that does not enable a person to establish a bridge to the inner Kingdom of GOD may cause many to become ill.

"I believe that when we sin, miss the mark, we enter into what is clearly spiritual mental illness. We are created to walk with GOD and HIS Holy Spirit within us. When we consciously disconnect ourselves from this communion, we live in a state of separateness and emptiness— being forgiven for our sin is only the first step towards full reconciliation.

"...the word 'salvation' translated reveals the necessity of this continuing process. The word salvation in the Old Testament means to be expanded from within. David prayed for reconciliation (in Psalms 51:10.) *'Create in me a pure heart, oh, God, and renew a steadfast spirit within me.'*

"The New Testament word in Greek for salvation, means 'to become healed and whole.' We erroneously treat the meaning as being 'saved *from* our sin,' whereas, the force of the word deals with being healed *into* a new and whole state of being. The process of 'salvation' is in actuality being healed of our mental *spiritual* illness.

"I believe it was the central goal of Jesus on earth to awaken us to the presence of the Holy Spirit within ourselves. It does not take much reading of the scriptures to detect that Jesus condemned external forms of religion. To the woman at the well he said, *'GOD is spirit, and his worshipper must worship in spirit and in truth.'* (John 4:23)

"The temple in Jerusalem was destroyed in 70 AD and the followers of Jesus worshipped without buildings and most of our current established forms and rituals were not developed for almost five hundred years. And, during that period, without universal form and rituals, the living faith covered the known world.

Dr Bruns further states: "Humans are dying for lack of a mystical faith. A church is a servant of GOD only when it aids people in releasing the consciousness of God within themselves. If the church does not do this it is a foe of GOD. Most churches work mightily and expend enormous human effort to provide 'fool's gold' rather than the real thing.

"So how do we open the 'mine' to the gold within? There are two ways in which we make contact with that higher consciousness. The first is when we become aware that God is speaking to us constantly and we respond to the inner prompting and message, especially in light of the teachings of Jesus and the many examples within the scripture of individuals hearing GOD speak directly to them in words and through dreams and visions.

"It is astounding that a Christian today is afraid to believe in such direct contact or to admit it when it happens to themselves. How can GOD (our own I AM Presence) speak to us when we are reluctant to listen or to admit that it is even possible. Let alone share it with others when it does happen.

"The second way to make contact with the higher consciousness of GOD is to admit we are starved for it and seek it. Many are those who mumble reiterative prayers to God but then do not take time to listen. I was flying back from Houston, Texas after holding a meditation workshop when I noticed my seatmate had a book on meditation. She allowed me to scan the book and I noticed that nowhere did it speak of listening to GOD.

"When I pointed out this lack my seatmate became offended. She quickly withdrew from our conversation when I talked of people hearing the voice of GOD in words, allegories, dreams and visions. I could tell the very idea scared her severely.

"I was very lucky that when GOD spoke to me it was forceful enough that I could not deny what was happening. The more often it happened the hungrier I became for more of that voice. But I had no instruction on how to seek that communion. I felt I had to wait until GOD was ready to reveal Himself to me. There were many long dry spells where, if I had been taught how to listen, the water of the spirit would have broken through much more often.

"Possibly I had to follow a hard path to where I am today in order to relate to others who are hungry and are traveling through the desert. I was fortunate in that GOD sent me teachers who instructed me. I am able to live most days expecting GOD to speak and thus am aware when He does. There are many days where I content myself with walking the dry path. But I am grateful that it does not take long for the joy to drain from my life until I return to the well."

Dr. Bruns relates an instance in 1969, "I was about to close out my ministry as an active pastor of a church. Within my sermons I often used my mystical experiences as sermon illustrations. One Sunday Danny and Sandy, a young married couple, asked if they could see me... When they came in my office they began to relate how much my sharing meant to them. I was pleased. Then they dropped a bomb on me. They said, 'Will you help us to have the same type of communication with GOD?'

"I was stunned and stumped. I had to admit I did not know how to instruct them. I made a feeble suggestion that they spend time in prayer but prayer in our church context was speaking to GOD with little, if any, listening to GOD. When they left the office, my heart was deeply bruised and broken for them. How dare I share the times when I had drunk from the well of life without being ready to help others to have the same communication.

"I realized that as a pastor in a denominational church I was more of a hindrance to GOD than a servant. I had to shed many aspects of orthodox religion and this took several years. My attraction to the presence of the Holy Spirit led me on. I am sure my journey is not complete.

"My hope for you, dear reader, who wish for more mystical happenings, is for you to know that the transcendent Spirit is already within you. You need do nothing but hunger for it, and expect it to reveal itself through prayer and meditation, 'listening.'

"At each phase of my life, fellowship in a traditional Baptist church, my being a Baptist minister, experiencing the charismatic revival, and leading the church, this Spirit of God was active at each level.

"At each stage I was tempted to tell anyone who would listen what to do to advance to where I was. I wanted everyone to experience what had been given to me. At each progressive level I thought I had achieved wisdom.

"However, now all has changed. Every phase brings the knowledge that it is correct that each person has the right to grow from where they are without being told what they should achieve. I have found it easy to relate to individuals right where they are. If I sense when they are ready for a hint to move on, I am free to supply it. But I know now that GOD works with each individual without my help. I learned I could drop my conditioned inheritance and be free to make decisions without bias."

My friend, Dr. Bruns, remembers another situation where he was reluctant to write a particular letter to a female friend he had grown up with. She knew very well that his religious quest had led him into the Baptist ministry. In fact, she had married a Baptist minister herself. After writing and rewriting the letter several times, he finally mailed his correspondence in December 1991. Dr. Bruns says, "I began the message speaking of my having left the institutional church, to work in a small group ministry."

He went on to say that he could no longer minister shackled by the orthodox doctrines in which he had been raised. Of course he wondered if she was still steeped in traditional views, which could be a communications breaker, hence his reluctance to mail the letter.

He wrote, in part: "During my years in the seminary (1954-1965), having gained three theological degrees, I came to realize through my study of the Scriptures that the Christian message I had been raised with missed the mark, in very important aspects and lacked some initial elements which produced the healthy and joyous transformations experienced in the church of the first century.

"As I tried to minister as a Baptist pastor for twelve years, I was continually confronted with the truth that I could no longer continue within the orthodox framework.

"Through my study of the scriptures, including both Greek and Hebrew versions, I became convinced that one of the key doctrines that was taught by the church for the first five hundred years, but which was later declared a heresy, largely for political reasons, was essential for the full understanding of the early and primary Christian message. Its elimination warped the perspective of the effect that redemption and salvation should have had within the human life. That doctrine is the principle of reincarnation.

"I knew from my study of church history that the belief in reincarnation had existed for over five hundred years AD. Origen, the great scholar who translated the scriptures into Latin for the church, was a steadfast believer in reincarnation. In fact, even after he had died, the church condemned Origen for this belief—anyone who expressed a belief in rebirth was condemned. Those independent thinkers who were not willing to become strict followers of the church's new doctrine had to be killed."

Over the following centuries, the Catholic church eliminated by death thousands upon thousands of an enclave of believers which held to this rebirthing concept. The concept contradicted and threatened the Church platform of salvation, which worked exclusively through their priesthood. And it eliminated the need for outward confessions. Not to mention the fact that the early church had built its entire Christian theology on the finality of one life, one death, one heaven and one hell.

His letter to his long-time friend continues, "This brings me to the reason I am writing to you. In 1981 I was convinced intellectually that the doctrine of reincarnation was believed and practiced by the early believers and is necessary today if the same type of personality transformations through individual redemption and accountability are to take place. But there was a part of my mind which was still skeptical, or at least unconvinced. After talking with numerous individuals who professed to having past life regressions, I decided to put the belief to a personal test and explore the possibility that I might be able to experience my own regression. When I allowed myself to be open to, and desired past life memories to come, to my astonishment, they did.

"You, Ruth, were a part of one of those memories. In an early life in Palestine, you were my twin sister. Twin, it does not surprise me that we may have been connected previously as brother and sister."

Dr. Bruns went on to say that in her return letter, she mentioned to him a reading *she* had previously experienced. The reading itself was a bit vague but here is what she was told:

It was suggested that a staff person within her congregation was being dishonest with church funds. It was later determined to be so. As Ruth mentioned her children's names, the prophet said that all was well with them; and that one son was tied closely to home. Ruth confirmed this was true as well.

Ruth was told that she had lived approximately eighty past sojourns on this earth, and among the many lives mentioned, some of them were in China, others were lived as nuns, etc. and interestingly enough, Ruth revealed to Dr. Bruns that as a teenager she had felt a calling to be a missionary to China.

This was music to his ears. When he found that she had been on a similar pathway to his own, it was very inspiring to him how their lives had paralleled one another's seeking journeys. This confirmed again to him how marvelously the spirit works within each individual to further their continued understanding and enlightenment, even outside the constraints of organized religion.

"Elohim" is the Hebrew word for GOD, meaning "energy" or "force." He tells us, *"We have many lifetimes to grow and advance.* When I recently addressed a college class I began with these words: 'Relax, the FORCE is with you.' I often told trekkies that a good translation of the Old Testament word for God, would be 'The force.'"

As Dr. Bruns has given us much to contemplate, I would say the same to you dear reader. There is no best way except to listen, allow fear and anxiety to drop away, and know that the FORCE, Energy, your I Am Presence which IS GOD… is with you. And yes, how marvelously this Spirit works within each of us.

Do we realize how spiritually *inspired Jesus was in turning water into wine, changing a raging storm into calm, disease into health ...*

Chapter 17

THE GENIUS WITHIN

Whatever you can do, or dream you can, begin it.
Boldness has genius, power and magic in it.

—***Goethe***

Creative forces

How we marvel at creative imagination, especially when it comes from great inventors like Marconi, da Vinci, Fulton, Edison, Tesla, Bell, Franklin and Carver. It moves one to wonder where such inspiration springs from. That same intuitive imagination helped bring forth the works of Dr. Oppenheimer and his group of brilliant men who split the atom and discovered atomic power; and Dr. Von Braun, with his German scientists who developed rocket propulsion.

In the field of literary art, there are only a few qualified to debate whether or not Shakespeare actually authored his plays. Whether the answer is yes or no, it doesn't change the intrinsic value of the subject matter. Regardless of the source, there is literary genius in the writings of this greatest of authors. The brilliance in these inventions and written works will forever be inspiring man to forge forth toward the imaginative and unthinkable.

Man is the outpost in time and space where the very activity of *God's creativity* takes place. Research shows that some great inventors, artists and musicians were given their inspired revelations while they meditated or even slept. These great thinkers were conduits for receiving above the norm out-of-this-world intelligence. Einstein remembered vivid formulas of numbers from his dreams, and da Vinci retreated to a cave many hours at a time for silent meditation and enlightenment.

Leonardo even spoke of being taken up into the heavens, the skies, by flying machines. And like Edgar Cayce, Michelangelo would go into a sleep state while on a scaffold near the top of the ceiling of the Sistine Chapel, where he would receive through dreams the beautiful angelic images he would portray with his brush.

Mozart experienced in his subconscious far more than he was able to express with his pen. The rapture of his grandest symphonies may never have been written or heard. His musical talents reached beyond what this world knew. Amazingly, Ludwig van Beethoven spent much of his adult life totally deaf. The sweet strains of melodies these magnificent artists received mentally, far superseded what they were able to produce through conscious sound.

The man who has no imagination has no wings.

—***Muhammad Ali***

Genius however, is not always appreciated. For example, early on, Robert Fulton's steam engine was called "Fulton's folly."

Sometimes human nature is quick to resist change or new discoveries; then over time society gradually accepts that which proves to be practical or best suited for humanity's advancement.

Dubious attitudes about the unfamiliar are continuously presenting themselves. Did you know there are hieroglyphic paintings of extraterrestrials and their flying machines on the walls in caves from millenniums past? In recent years as well as the past, thousands of people have sighted saucers in our skies. Through hypnosis, large numbers have recalled their own abductions by these alien ET's. Yet our government in some strange protective way continues to resist and deny these facts. Like the early Church, ruling authorities insist that our ignorance is bliss.

New and perhaps very significant information, whether it be communication from ancient Gospel texts recently unearthed or sightings and encounters of a celestial nature are sometimes deemed so far-reaching and controversial that political and religious leaders choose to downplay them. The essential value of much information thus becomes denied, lost, or forgotten. Not all that is newly perceived is readily received.

"To everything there is a season, and a time for every purpose under the heaven." (Ecclesiastes 3:1) Whatever we need in the way of intuitive invention, discovery, and artistic expression may come in the form of new creation needed to meet the demand at the time. This is especially true in the field of spiritual exploration. Such a wealth of inspiration has already been gleaned from the four standard Gospels. Possibly we are at the point in our spiritual history where we should be ready to consider scriptural discoveries more recently unearthed.

There may have been as many as fifty Gospel texts written, and perhaps even more yet to be found. Why are we not clamoring for the "rest of the story," unabridged, not shortened by omission of parts? Perhaps it would be music to our ears. Creative and inspired answers to many of life's questions concerning spiritual matters, such as the afterlife, could be waiting for our hearts and minds to consider at this time. These newly found ancient texts could add even more insight into the treasure trove of inspiration already found in the Scriptures.

Communicative efforts

"What we have here is failure to communicate," said Strother Martin in the Paul Newman movie, *Cool Hand Luke*. No matter what its motives, the Church traditionally has fallen short of fully communicating the Master's message. A large portion of his words have either been suppressed, misinterpreted, locked away, or crucified.

History shows that a large amount of the original Gospels were hidden; some were buried by monks, to protect them from destruction by religious officials who felt Jesus' true message might usurp their power. Some people secretly shared original texts, but they feared for their lives because the hierarchy of the church, including the bishops and priests, prohibited the circulation of these documents. Hence, a failure to communicate more of the genius within the Master's teachings.

Do we fully realize how spiritually inspired Jesus was, in turning water into wine, changing a raging storm into calm, disease into health, as he listened to the Father for needed solutions? Jesus was showing us that everything good that we can possibly envision in the way of supply and answers to human needs, is already present in the blueprint of the Infinite Source. The omniscient All-in-All, the I Am… *"the Father that dwellth in me, he doeth the works."* (John 14:10)

Perhaps we will never be able to trace exactly when and where the suppression began. It may have taken place during the early years of Christianity when the role of individuality was rejected by potentates and priests. Whatever the reason, there has been a failure to illuminate and communicate the natural gift inherent in all of us, the *co-creative* quality of our own Divinity.

The fact remains, Jesus came to show us The Way. The enlightened and inspired stories of his footsteps are indelibly imprinted to guide us onto the pathway leading ever upwards toward our mastery and ultimate graduation from this schoolroom we call earth. And this task should not be ignored or taken lightly. His teachings of ethics, morals, and conduct in this educational process are meant to show us how our talents in this ultimate school of the arts, we call earth, should be utilized and played out.

We are the actors projected into this magnificent earthly garden, in a temporal theatrical production provided for the expressive creative abilities of the individual Self. We should be following his lead for inspiration and guidance.

Jesus' parable of the unused talent, had a more far-reaching message than the value of silver and gold. Our God-given talents developed over our personal eternities are not to be taken for granted, wasted, or hidden away. Spiritual individuality and outward creative expression work hand in hand. Life is art and art is life, to which every individual soul presents his own special contribution. We each bring unique brushstrokes to the canvas of our everyday experiences, as we paint our future. As Sly and his Family Stone sang, *Different strokes for different folks.*

"The whole world is a stage, and we are but the players," wrote Shakespeare. We may have temporarily turned our individual script, our pathway, into a Prodigal journey, but this play, this earthly movie is our own production.

As we listen to The Master's loving communication, let's make our divinely creative trip a heavenly excursion. We should be enjoying all that this wonderful Eden has to offer as we travel along our learning journey, particularly in the area of overcoming the senses; bringing dominion, moderation, wholeness, and inspiration to every facet of the physical world. This material backdrop, stage, and all temporal formations, including the body, must eventually be brought into conformity with our original spiritual blueprint, in harmony with our original perfection.

Purposeful pursuits

Now is the season to realize that we are overcoming the obsession for attachments or the affinity we have developed toward materiality and all of its beautiful creations. With our development of strong will-power and dominon, we are beginning to see that everything is spiritual. Whether visible or invisible, all forms are Godly. Presently our consciousness is elevating. To blend or not to blend, is the question. To be or not to be one with our individual Christ. Do we stay behind, continuing our repetitive patterns, wasting our higher talents? Or should we raise our consciousness blending into our Higher Christ-Self, our "genius within?" This is the magical genie from which springs our most inspired thoughts and our creative imagination. And this same genie may grant our wishes, if they be of a selfless nature.

The life of our individual expression is eternal, no matter how multiple the sojourns we might experience, all the roles we may endeavor to play throughout our individual lifetimes This prodigal pathway could be likened to the ultimate Broadway or Hollywood production. But all the players must understand that greed, hate, anger, fear, and resentment, like outworn props, must be laid aside. The love energy spent on such negative pursuits can be reversed and ultimately transformed. It is time to exit stage right and return to our Father's House, leaving the limited role-playing personality behind as we ascend gracefully to our higher individual consciousness.

We can do this in the here and now of our daily round of activities—including our creativities—live our higher Self, the Christ-Self, bringing to our human role the greatest degree of quality and character, self esteem and integrity. In other words, actuating Heaven on earth. The fact that we are involved in a material world and framework by no means restricts or hinders the flow of creative forces in our consciousness. We simply will be drawn to our own area of expertise, be it sports, painting, writing, music, building a skyscraper, or inventing a better computer. And we are simultaneously always being magnetically drawn toward our ascending steps.

It is absolutely imperative that we begin this holiest of quests immediately if not sooner. Each person must spark the fire within, the flame of spiritual inspiration, in order to fulfill the sacred mission, to be like the Master. It is possible to think with that *"mind which was also in Christ Jesus."* (1st Corinthians 2:16) Through our innate divine talents of giving and forgiving we will be living in grace.

Perhaps after the final graduation of all our earthly sojourns, we will be prepared to move on to a different planet or world, a higher plane where there is no negativity. Our next planetary experience or realm of existence, could very well be a graduate schoolroom, where we too, would be working on our own Master's degree.

Present understanding suggests that earth is our final destination, our last stop. It predicts a future celestial existence of floating aimlessly in the clouds, regaled in white robes and sandals, harps in hand. Not so! With passionate emotion and feeling we should, instead, fill our thoughts and imagination with the concept of a continuing eternal life, pursuant to a more elevated and inspired understanding and existence than we can even conceive of today.

Can we not use our present creative imagination to envision grander opportunities? Our next world-planet-universe with lifetimes of discovery to follow, should be filled with extended purpose, grandiose activities, mas creativity, and talents, and certainly, a continual rising of vibration within our spirit, and soul.

Imagination has always had powers of resurrection that no science can match.

—***Ingrid Bengis***

Dimensions of expression

Great thinkers from our past were open-minded to higher dimensions of thought where they gathered new ideas for building, shaping material invention and the creative arts such as music, painting, writing, sculpting, or architecture. They filled our world with their beautiful works. Just think of it— George Washington Carver, for instance, opened his mind, the powers of intuition, which broadened his perspective, and in a "Jiffy" he discovered over three hundred uses for the peanut! Thankfully, still others were receptive to spiritual revelation, and put it into print, leaving us a rich legacy of eternal truths.

Over and over, the requirements for great accomplishment echo a timeless pattern:

- a quiet mind
- receptivity
- intuition
- creativity... with feeling
- and expression!

Artists in all fields of endeavor have extended their consciousness to receive enlightened ideas from the realm above. In this same manner we too, can become creators in music, art, literature, architecture, invention, business, and commerce. Wherever our interest lies, or our longings and feelings take us, when the student is ready, the teacher or the revelation will appear. The key is to be ready, with our consciousness fertile and prepared. We should be still, stay at peace, meditate and listen receptively, then we too, can receive genius, go forth and bring our creative thought into manifestation.

True genius doesn't fulfill expectations, it shatters them.

—***Arlene Croce***

Look around and you will see God's creativity expressing itself through the genius of man's attentive listening power. Once again, man is the outpost in time and space generating, receiving, and projecting the activity of the One Intelligence. This is manifested in bridges and buildings, cars, planes, boats, new technology, space travel and all the fine arts, not to mention possibly the most important formation of all, the creation and building of human relationships.

From our own thoughts, feelings and actions of sowing we create our own personal circumstances—with their ultimate residual effects, karma, both the good and the bad reapings. However, the master within ourselves doesn't complain about challenges. Adversity can be a stern instructor. Our so-called sins and evils could be viewed as a part of this ongoing learning process. They are opportunities for our own evolvement.

One of the effects of enlightened thought is to bring problems to the surface to be resolved with an innovative and creative mind—so we can then say, *"behold, it was very good."* (Genesis 1:31)—to weather and calm the storms we have created. We now have triumphed through the experiences of the negative and the positive!

Progressive components

Creativity is a necessary progressive component of spirituality. If we are not increasing our innovative creative talents, we are not perceiving the energies lying dormant within ourselves. The mathematician does not learn his craft to keep it stored in his head. He uses his numerical expertise in countless ways, including solving problems.

Artists and writers use their inspiration to bless us with beautiful works. Necessity, being the mother of invention, inspires inventors to bring forth more ease and convenience to our lives.

But the contractor does not continue building a foundation forever. When his base is finally strong enough, he goes up with the building. Likewise, the spiritual seeker need not seek the foundation of his understanding forever, before he is qualified to "go up" and make use of his enlightened creative talents, or possibly have his greater works evidenced! To everything there truly is a season.

> *Man is the outpost in time and space*
> *where the very activity of God's creativity*
> *takes place.*
>
> —***C. S. McClintock***

Creative birthright

The following is paraphrased from the works of Dr. Barbara Condrin's *Kundalini Rising*. In her book, she addresses creative energy:

To begin conceiving the essence of creative energy, is to appreciate its expression in our everyday lives. Most take their own and others' creativity for granted and for this reason settle for much less than they are capable of producing. Bound by habit, we become mentally lazy, causing our minds to dwell in the mediocrity of normalcy, thus perpetuating the ills of mankind.

In truth, it is easier to create than to destroy, to love, than to hate, to trust than to fear, to evolve than to stagnate. To become free of self-imposed limitations, you must break free from compulsion by becoming aware of the freedom inherit in your ability to think. Thinking frees you to see, to hear, to feel, to taste, to smell, and most importantly to perceive.

As reasoning is understood and utilized, creativity flourishes. Wherever you experience expressions of man's creativity, you will find the action of creative energy. When this creativity is used by an evolved soul with the highest ideals and purposes in mind, you will find the use of this energy is an innate *action of attraction*. Where your vision is, there you are, mentally and physically. You and your whole experience move toward that which you love and adore. As this energy is used in the highest type of expression, all of humanity benefits.

Genius is one percent inspiration,
and ninety-nine percent perspiration.

—***Thomas Alva Edison***

The utilization of this energy has been taught in the East for thousands of years, they call it the "Kundalini." It should be each person's pleasure to pursue this advanced, yet secretive knowledge. It is well that we examine the lives of those possessing expanded awareness of this action of attraction. In their thoughts we find the Universal Truth, and Universal Truth can be applied in any one's life at any time. The thinking of these evolved souls rises above the normal, challenging limitations accepted by the masses, paving the way for the advancement of all.

Those displaying this expanded consciousness are often described as living before their time. Yet it is their willingness to stimulate others, even in the face of severe opposition—toward the attainment of the visions they conceive that propel them to a place reserved for history's greats. As it has been said, "Talent does what it can, genius does what it must." By investigating and putting to use the talent you posses, you can become known for your creativity. By expanding your consciousness to include all of mankind, you can become known for your genius too. The creative genius' thinking includes the world and all of humanity, for this reason, in time he is revered and remembered.

Creativity is abundant in man's search for Self expression. From a piece of art that captures the soul to the preparation of a meal that delights the senses, from the ability to explore outer space, to the composition of a letter, every day the mind is used for creative endeavors. Yet many are truly restless in the accepted limitations of complacency. They desire to soar beyond what is considered normal and expand their consciousness to ever evolving states of imagination.

By exposing ourselves to the quality of thinking of those remembered in our history as masters of reasoning, we can begin to align our thoughts with our own inner urge to create. What faculties does the individual who comes to be known as a genius posses that elevates his status to a master of creativity? What thoughts fill the consciousness of the creative genius?

History is filled with evidence of great thinkers. These individuals have furthered our progress in societies, and as a race known as mankind. Their lives are varied. The consequences of birth hold no limitation for these individuals, for we find the complete range, master or peasant, rich or poor, educated or not, with the experiences represented by their lives.

From the early thinkers who learned to harness the four basic elements of air, fire, water, and earth to make physical life easier, to more recent thinkers who use the same thought processes to enhance the mental and spiritual evolution of man, we find advanced inspiration in the lives of these thinkers. They embody some of the finest we can become and the wisdom in their thoughts enables us to share their vision of the spiritual unfoldment that is our destiny.

To become acquainted with these thinkers is to witness the benefits of the awakening of this attracting energy and make it available to man. Their lives are evidence of the "Kundalini" in action for the benefit of all and their conclusions reflect the awareness of a consciousness expanded, Condrin concluded.

Spiritual gifts

The willingness to extend the boundaries of our thinking is well described in this quote:

> *A man's mind stretched to a new idea,*
> *never goes back to its original dimension.*
>
> —***Oliver Wendell Holmes***

Embracing new ideas strengthens our ability to move beyond limitations, no longer dependent upon someone or something outside of ourselves for spiritual salvation, mental guidance, emotional balance or physical stability.

Man seems stuck in a kind of 'paint-by-number' stage when it comes to realizing his potential for creativity. He believes it to be a talent that just a special few are born with. But if he was to realize by his own spiritual graces that he already is an artist of sorts, able to be inventive, innovative, inspired; he would be able to bring beauty, worth, and value to every aspect of his experience.

We profess to love, because God is Love. We have a spirit because God is Spirit. But we fall short of claiming that we are in a small way co-creators, because God is Creative. *"Every good gift and every perfect gift, is from above, and cometh down from the Father of lights."* (James 1:17) What God is, we are. What talents and attributes He has, we have as well, for the employment of His good works.

Innate capacity

Again, I would like to share more insights on creativity given by Dr. Barbara Condrin. Here Dr. Condrin presents a new twist on a familiar cast of characters:

"In Mind First: Everything in our physical existence first began in the inner levels of spiritual consciousness, guided by the Universal Law of contrasts, positive and negative energies used to make up the physical realm. In the third dimension, the earthly, the more forceful and assertive receptive principles are called into action. When they cooperate and harmonize creation occurs. Through spontaneous awakenings of Kundalini energies man enters realms of conscious thought and existence previously alien to his view of life. Only by experience in the inner realms of existence can man expect to reveal the true nature of his own creativity. Through acts of creation, he comes to know him-Self as the Individualized creative capacity of God, a co-creator. This is the enlightenment we seek.

"...To more fully understand the importance of 'enlightened energy' in the dawning of a new and expansive consciousness, let us explore creation from the beginning of our existence. Whether we explore creation philosophically or scientifically, we find the essence of creation is light. Spiritually light is the building block of consciousness because it represents awareness.

"Scientifically light, known as the photon, is the building block for all physical forms.

"Since the universe is filled with order and structure, there are no accidents or coincidences. From the first creation of light, evolution begins as a result of the needs and desires of an individual thinker. Man's needs become apparent to the conscious mind, thus stimulating the visualization process. The same principles hold true throughout every stage of creation for this is the inherent and innate urge of the thinker—to be like the Creator through progressive acts of creation.

"Throughout material creation we find the expression of balance and imbalance. When one's balance is achieved another imbalance will become apparent because the inner urge of the thinker is to evolve and mature.

"...The creative power is a spiritual energy effective in the physical— Lower forms of creation, such as minerals, plants, and animals, enjoy this flow of creative energy which enables physical procreation to occur, but they lack the necessary experience and understanding to harness their spiritual powers. By the time reasoning is developed, the human thinker can realize his individual ability to guide his evolutionary development through the choices he makes.

"The acceptance of the responsibility for volition elevates man's awareness to consider his purpose for existence and awaken to his need for spiritual progression. This prepares his consciousness for the conscious use of the highest Spiritual Energies.

"One who has sufficiently expanded his consciousness, realizes the duality or two-fold nature of his existence. He knows there are seemingly two worlds of existence: the physical world, the third dimension as we know it, would be experienced through the five physical senses of the body, and the fourth dimension or spiritual world would be experienced through mental attention and perception. This heightens his ability to function in more levels of consciousness, opening his awareness of time as a measurement of progression.

"He realizes time is dual in nature. He knows horizontal time is measured by his experiences and vertical time is measured by his understanding of those experiences. The first, time, is registered in the brain, the latter is time registered in the soul. The first is the time required to live a full lifetime in the physical plane, the latter is the time invested in making Universal Truth a permanent part of the Eternal Self.

"A metaphysician understands the origin of what is perceived with the five physical senses of sight, sound, taste, touch and smell. While with the Greek word meta meaning 'after' and physikos meaning 'nature,'—beyond the physical— metaphysics can be described as the exploration and knowledge of the invisible Universal Laws which govern our existence. This knowledge frees man's consciousness to learn from, abide with, and make use of all creation. It is interesting to note that the word 'physics' is also akin to the Greek phyo meaning 'to bring forth,' and phyo has its origin in the Sanskrit bhu meaning "to be." Thus, to be a metaphysician means bringing awareness of the universe to one's Self by becoming a co-creator in your own right.

"In the world's Holy scriptures, man's origin is described as being divine, as being from a Creator, and his purpose for existing is to be like the Creator which brought him into existence. For millenniums, the Creator's offspring has evolved in consciousness to reach the point of awareness embodied as Reasoning Man. The continuing spiritual evolution of Reasoning Man is the foundation for seeking the rise of consciousness within one's Self.

"The world's spiritual literature is given to us largely in the form of metaphorical stories conveying the spiritual potential of man. Parables, myths and legends were intended to put us in touch with our spiritual life. The goal of man's early existence was to live in constant awareness of Spiritual Principles. Some of these Principles have been lost in the material existence of recent centuries and remain lost to this day. The awakening of our Higher Self and our Kundalini energy beckons us and indeed commands that man rekindle his desire for Spiritual knowledge, experience and understanding.

"...The account of the man, the woman, and the serpent in the Garden of Eden is a Hebrew myth borrowed from an earlier Babylonian legend revealing the nature of consciousness. To those who think in linear, physical ways, this passage appears to be an account of what is commonly called the 'fall of man' complete with malevolent evil, damning temptation, blame and regret. For those who think physically, this story becomes a deceptive illusion to explain the difficulties in their lives offering a scapegoat as the cause of man's misery. However, for those willing to remove the shackles of limitation bred by complacent yielding to inaccurate interpretation and ignorance, what has been kept secret for centuries can finally become known.

"When we examine this Biblical passage with keen discernment and open- minded study, we can decipher the universal symbols used to reveal the relationships that compose man's inner consciousness and his urge to be like his Creator. In this way, we can learn about the structure of inner and outer balancing of the physical and the spiritual resources in the consciousness of Reasoning Man.

"The Lord God implies a singular experience of creation. If we are to understand spiritual literature as revelatory of our inner condition, this would represent our true individuality, a recognition of existence that can be termed 'I Am.' I Am says I exist. It is a state of being at a point of origin where there is awareness of a Creator.

".... The story begins by describing the serpent as 'the most cunning of all the animals that the Lord God had made.' Animals function from instinct or compulsion, so this would be an image indicating instinctive patterns of thinking. The serpent however, is distinguished from all other forms of compulsive thinking because it is described as the most cunning. The word cunning comes from the Gothic kunnan meaning to know. Thus the serpent is an image used repeatedly in Eastern spiritual literature to describe the Kundalini energy; this energy spirit has been placed in the physical person by our Christ Self. This healing energy is symbolically placed curling at the base of our spine. It is prevalently portrayed on the Medical Doctor's logo as serpent and staff—kunnan, cunning, kundalini."

Dr. Condron continues: "In the story of creation, man is created in the image and after the likeness of his Creator. This indicates the birth of an intelligence, assertive, or male in quality, which is created from thought and contains similar attributes to its Creator. Spiritually we are all our Father's son. And woman is also created in the same image, with feminine qualities, such as tenderness and love.

"The interchange that ensues between the serpent and the woman actually represents the stimulation of the desire for knowledge and wisdom. The awareness of choice, free will, is awakened and the motivational force goes on to propel the aspect of discovery that the conscious mind begins to reach. By stimulating the conscious mind to use information already gathered, the serpent becomes the expression of our individual desire to grow. We experience this as ego. The ego then motivates the conscious mind into action and the resultant effects are experienced. Rather than being instinctual, the result is awareness of choice. This becomes the pattern for the relationship between the conscious mind and the conscious expression of ego.

"The story continues describing how the woman eats of the fruit of the tree and gives some to her husband and illustrates the learning process of this earthly life….'the ego' led to self-consciousness and the need for loincloths evolved. Man and woman, the masculine and feminine, are discovered to be creative in nature.

"The serpent, the apple, the self-consciousness and shame are all part of the reasoning process. Each experience indicates either a temporary sense of separation from their Maker, or a fervent desire to set things straight and return to their native purity and goodness. Their resultant experiences of tasting, feeling, and being self-aware, teach valuable lessons….their eyes were both opened, and most importantly, they realized the ability to produce experiences and to reason.

"Our true individuality, the I Am, guides the evolutionary development of the thinker. Here we find the seat of the desire to 'be like,' to mature as a creator. Unlike an animal, man's conscious identity is not based upon instinct, rather it is based upon the conscious ego and the conscious mind. The purpose of the ego, free will, will be to form the identity through the *expanding old ideas of Self into new ideas of still Higher Consciousness.* It will bring constant stimulation of the desire 'to be like' to the conscious mind until full maturity of the reasoning ability is achieved.

"As reasoning produces experiences for the conscious mind, the opportunity for understanding is made available thus giving the conscious mind its purpose. The understandings gained are given to the subconscious mind to be recorded and stored in the permanent memory of the soul. In this way, these understood experiences become a permanent part of the prodigal journey of our eternal identity.

"We know good from evil, right from wrong, what will produce harmony and balance with Universal Law, and what will not. This is the message of discernment in eating from the tree of good and evil. Far from being an act of unworthiness, a reason for disgrace, or blaming the feminine, the activity described in the Garden of Eden reveals the inner spiritual connections that give man the ability to reason and the power of creative discovery.

"The Garden of Eden represents a place of unity, a place where man shows power, strength, discipline, and wise discernment, and woman the 'feminine,' shows gentleness, tenderness, compassion and love. It symbolizes the place of origin and the place of destination in man's spiritual journey, for it is also where the tree of Life exists. The tree of Life gives knowledge of immortality. The real knowledge of the inner Self begins with the tree of Life.

"When our inner spiritual energy is awakened we come to know enlightenment as reflected in the statement 'I and the Father are one.' Here we transcend the boundaries of mortal thinking and enter into the omnipresence of continual existence.

"When the conscious mind reaches to develop its innate creative ability, discovery occurs. The more expansive the conscious thinking, the more far-reaching are the effects of its creations. The more we exercise a willingness to birth new ideas, the more we advance and accelerate our own and other's human and spiritual evolution."

Let the beauty
of what you love
be what you do.

—***Rumi***

"When Yahweh, or the Lord God expels the man and woman from the Garden, he places at its entrance two cherubim and a flaming sword. This represents the challenge of raising our Kundalini energy up the spinal column to produce revelation in consciousness. Man must expand his consciousness of Spirit to become more free from the earthly plane of mortal thinking and the five senses, resolving his karmic indebtedness, as represented by the flaming sword. And now he becomes a receptive vessel for creative ideas.

"Only your own unresolved fears and material desires can keep you from entering your own temple of thought, knowing, and reasoning, and experiencing the surety of your immortality. Your Spirit is ever-present, awaiting the moment when you will transcend limitation and enter into the enlightened state of being, described by all the great masters of our history!"

Inspired evolvement

This candid overview of a familiar Jewish story-form reminds us that Bible stories are colorful and poignant treasures to be unlocked through spiritual discernment, showing us the way of conscious knowing and learning, stirring the desire for spiritual discovery and higher enlightenment. These stories were never meant to be held in the bonds of literal interpretation, limitation or condemnation, thus stifling the innate urge to rise above the mortal and mundane sense of materiality.

There are a myriad of theories as to the creation of the universe and the evolution of man—from the big bang theory to the possibility of our living within eleven dimensions simultaneously— and everything thrown in between. However, the fact remains that the one "evolution" that relates most to our progress is not physical, not psychological, but rather is an inspired spiritual evolvement. If we would open our eyes and ears there is much to be learned from the ancient sages and philosophers. Not to mention the modern-day earthly spiritual Masters, who, not wishing to be praised, or idolized, live their esoteric lifestyles secluded in the Tibetan Mountains of the far East.

Creativity is your birthright. The genius of your life's work evolves according to your realization and utilization of this marvelous gift!

Lives of great men all remind us
we can make our lives sublime;
and, departing, leave behind us,
footprints on the sands of time.

—***Henry Wadsworth Longfellow***

Man is the outpost in time and space where the very activity of ***God's creativity*** *takes place.*

We can't block the light of ever-present Love and Truth from coming in to us. It is ever forthcoming.

Chapter 18

ILLUMINATION

"Know ye not that ye are gods,
I said you are gods, you are all sons
(suns, or individualizations)
of the Most High."

—***Psalms 82:6***

Jesus said to Thomas, "It is not fitting for you to be ignorant of yourself. So while you accompany me, although you do not yet understand it, you have already come to know, and you will be called, 'The one who knows himself.' For whoever has not known himself knows nothing, but he who has known himself has already understood the depth of all things." The Master was actually giving Thomas high praise for recognizing the light within himself which in fact is the I-Am-Presence, in all life.

Indulge me for a moment while I converse with a proverbial light bulb. I would say emphatically to this apparatus, that you are the light of the room, porch, street, etc.

The bulb may in response say, "No, no, I am only an empty glass bulb, too lowly, insignificant, and dusty to be noticed."

I would then reply, "Yes, but with my help all this will change. You are destined to have an illuminating purpose and presence about yourself and consequently do the job you were meant to perform."

I flip the switch, the electricity runs and the miracle happens. The glass bulb becomes a brilliant light! Yet, unknown to itself, it was a potential light all the while. But, like many of us, it was unaware of its divinely intended mission.

When Jesus and other Masters say to us, we are the light of the world, or when our understanding of ourselves reaches oneness with God, our light source, then we too, like Thomas, truly are an active beaming and radiant portion of Him.

What good is a light bulb if it hasn't been turned on? What good are we, as men, if we have not been turned on to our spiritual radiance? You already are a "Sun" of God, a light unto our world, but your brilliance goes unnoticed until your inner switch of awareness is activated. Perhaps you are too accustomed to being denigrated and told how lowly and unworthy we sinners are. You must become aware of the great potential that lies within you. You are a Godly Divine Being. Wake up out of the deep sleep into which you have been lulled by false theologies.

The Irish author, James Joyce, wrote that "History is a nightmare from which I am trying to awake." Having lived through portions of two world wars, and civil strife in his native country, Joyce's life may have seemed more like a nightmare than a fairytale. It doesn't have to be this way, no matter what our earthly plight. Our own individual life's history, along with our Earth's history, is what we have created and gathered from the sojourns of our past experiences. However, we have the wherewithal to escape our apocalyptic nightmare, and possible Armageddon, and choose to turn our future into heaven on earth.

We can't block the light of ever-present Love and Truth from coming in to us. It is ever forthcoming. However we do tend to block it from emanating out, shining forth from us. Taking too much thought for the outside world, what we shall eat, how we shall be clothed, and how our own ego is going to solve a problem, is like a lampshade over our inner illumination. The more negative lampshades we add, the less light we emit.

Go now. Rise n' shine! Tell all of the people that they are lights. Turn yourself on to this fact, hold to it, and others will feel your illumination. The current of celestial energy has to run through your consciousness for your divine light to be activated. Thus, nothing changes or improves if you proceed in the currents of everyday mental dimness in the worldly living of the status quo. You too, might remain a dusty bulb with no particular purpose or brilliance to your animation.

When we go to church on Sunday or say our prayers, we may at that point feel a small flicker of that mighty current running through us to quicken the brilliant light within our being. This tiny bit of juice may not seem to have much effect on our candlepower; much less show us that we on earth are a descendent of God, the light of this world. But regardless of our temporary opacity, something marvelous is taking place! It is a starting point. These small glimmers are a spark, a flicker of our luminosity to come, our true resplendence. You should be able to feel the flicker of this "lightening-bug- effect," without having to catch it in a jar!

Consider the lowliest man on this planet. He may be on his way to permanent incarceration, a man already living his life in solitary confinement inside a prison, or perhaps an individual chained by mental circumstances. Though he has blanketed his bulb with dust, corrosion, or the darkest of thoughts and actions, he can still save himself from himself. His erred mortal-mind can be changed at any moment to begin recognizing all the possibilities in his true divine-Self. Slowly but surely he can wipe away the film covering his inner light. Then, one day, he will once again recognize the radiance within himself as a God-man, a good-man, not just a human body waiting for someone else to turn his switch.

Every person has the inherent capacity to change from a lowly, lowly character, like a benighted Saul, into the brilliance of a saintly Paul. One must look up from the ignorance of darkness, hate, anger, greed, and misguided sensuality to all the higher-minded possibilities that love, integrity and forgiveness surely will provide.

No man has prowess over another to activate or interrupt his or her spiritual currents, whether he be a man of the cloth, or a Saint. The good news is that we can fire our own pilot light and it is not accomplished by anyone or anything outside ourselves.

Every saint has a past, and every sinner has a future.

—***Oscar Wilde***

There is, however, a caveat. You are required to hold your switch in the turned-on position, no longer with just a flick, but continuously with meditative comprehension and steadfastness. Thoughts of the world will intermittently break your concentration conduit and your energy currents will seem to be mere fluctuating glimmers of light. You will have become somewhat like a lightning-bug; and yes, you may only emit a small flicker. However in the event that you can't seem to hold the switch ON all the time, keep flicking! God handles second chances well, and keeps us growing and glowing more and more with each effort.

You could eventually be recognized as your brother "Thomas" was, as a man of light. After all, hypothetically, if our firefly had originally been created to stay continuously lighted, perhaps he would have been called a "light-bug" instead of an intermittent "lightning-bug."

By the same token, if man could hold to his true identity, as he was originally intended, keeping his thoughts energized, generated only from the Father of Lights without wavering, and without so much as a flicker, then he could be considered a Light man—more importantly he would be known as a true and constant *"Light unto the World."* (Matthew 5:14)

As many men in this world have already accomplished and demonstrated, raising their earthly self into their higher vibratory "light-body" allows them to constantly radiate the highest expression of human consciousness.

When the power source shines through the light bulb in its fullness, one is only aware of its bright emanation, its brilliance, and is no longer aware of the bulb form itself. Thus, in like manner, when the Divine shines through the human form, its emanations outshine the physical.

"Therefore, if you are filled with light, with no dark corners, then your whole life will be radiant, as though a floodlight were filling you."

—Luke 11:36

Just as the bulb and the light are inseparable, men and women are synonymous with the divinity within themselves. God is interior to man, not exterior. According to the hidden Gospels, particularly in the Book of Thomas this profound truth is evident and well-documented. This perspective is not contrary to Jesus' teachings, in fact it enhances the precept that we and Father are

One. We and the I-Am-Light are One. We are Divine and human at the same time.

We are each God-Individualizations of God-Consciousness— just as solar rays are one with the sun.

The Master told us that we are the light of the world, not to hide it under a bushel, but for it to be set on an hill for all to see ... and to shine forth His greater works for all to see.

The Self is Life, and the only reality, and whoever is initiated into the Self and in this way has come to know Himself completely, loves everything and everyone equally, for he is One with them.

—***Elizabeth Haich***

*We and the **I-Am-Light** are One.*
We are Divine and human at the same time.

We may be like a drop of consciousness
in the ocean of Him,
yet we are inseparable, one in the same.

Chapter 19

PEARLS OF TRUTH

I am seeking, I am striving, I am in it with all my heart.

—***Vincent Van Gogh***

There is a very good chance if you've read thus far in this book that you are not a natural man, a normal follow-the-other-sheep kind of person. At one time or another in your life someone has probably said to you, "You must be from another planet. Why can't you be like the rest of us?"

I would emphatically reply. "Thank you, but no thanks!" Frankly, I'm not real proud of myself when I'm being "like the rest of us." You dear reader, along with myself, should be thankful that we are different, that we can think for ourselves—and we don't have to play the game of Simon Says, do this, do that, or Follow the Leader. Who is this Simon anyway?

In 1980 I was in a way prophesied to by a church friend. I was told that in order to gain more patience I should join a particular meditation group that just happened to be close to my residence.

So I attended twice a week meetings—along with 13 women. Needless to say my wife did not understand this new me. All this celestial contemplation was in sharp contrast to the former image of myself. As a sports-minded jock I pretty much had been interested in only manly type stuff—at times I was kind of a "wild-and-crazy guy," however, not quite to the extreme of a Dan Aykroyd or Steve Martin.

My pathway had radically changed, and I knew it, no matter how others were now viewing me. I was feeling a new and profound enthusiasm. An ethereally ascending momentum was carrying me forward. It was almost serendipitous. A voracious appetite for all things spiritual had overcome me. I was seeking and finding enlightenment. New inspiration came flying at me from all directions, expanding my understanding.

Little did I know that all those years of searching, seeking and finding would ultimately lead me to write books and speak publicly. Serendipitous, indeed!

Know yourself

I am reminded of an old formal injunction, once utilized when a man spoke or acted out of turn—"You forget yourself sir."

Man's prodigal journey through this vast garden of Eden experience sometimes has his human free will coaxing him out of sorts, missing the mark, leading him into negative thoughts or actions. Upon viewing this scene we might respond to his wayward manner in like terms. You forget your 'Self' sir. Your Spiritual-Self has been ignored, left behind as you seem to live and move and have your being in social circles with your busy agendas.

It is possible for a hermit crab to forget where he laid his shell, his home, but a turtle cannot be separated from his shell. In similar fashion, man can no more be separated from his Maker than a tortoise can be parted from his shell. Throughout time, literature speaks of man separating himself from God. Immediate and future understanding will know this to be an absolute impossibility; because I and the Father being ONE also means the reverse is true. The Father and I (you) are One. We may be like a drop of consciousness in the ocean of Him, yet we are inseparable, one in the same. To have no individual drops of spirit-consciousness, would equal no ocean of God experiences.

The highest truth a human being can ever attain, is this ultimate fact: there is no such thing as God and man, as a separate entity. EVERY self is HIS SELF.

Due to a trauma or illness the malfunctioning of our brain may cause a human being to forget himself, his own name, family members, or location of his home. As unfortunate as these circumstances may seem, never lose sight of this fact—next time around these people will be fine and healthy, divine as always, no matter what their current state of health.

A healthy person however, should never forget his true Spiritual-Self, no matter how deeply into the material world he may be immersed.

Sir, you may forget your Self, but in actuality the only Self there ever has been or ever will be is the One Self, the I Am Father, who lives your life and mine concurrently.

Hold this secret close to your heart, and blend your consciousness, your understanding with the Divine, knowing that you are a portion of this One Self, a spiritual drop of His Consciousness in His infinite ocean of being. Know that this self-awareness of your individual Christ-Consciousness can never "forget Him-Self."

The spiritual man

R.G. Allen, a Canadian-American businessman who has written several personal-finance books, once said, "Don't let the opinions of the average man sway you. Dream, and he thinks you crazy. Succeed and he thinks you lucky. Acquire wealth, and he thinks you're greedy. Pay no attention. He simply doesn't understand."

Our duty as philosophers requires us to honor truth above our friends.

—***Aristotle***

"The average man, the natural man receiveth not the things of the Spirit of God for they are foolishness unto him." (1st Corinthians:14)

"My kingdom is not of this world." The trick is to be in this world but to think from the My Kingdom point of view. The elevated consciousness which is not tied to anything in this world, not anything, or anyone, is willing to think in the divine while speaking from the flesh.

The spiritual secrets you are receiving in this book are being communicated to you with compliments from the Great Masters. Our Master Jesus, of course, being one of them, would say to you, dear reader, "Listen up!" These secrets are no longer meant to be hidden. However, be careful when you shout them from the mountain tops or from the hillsides. The scholarly religious man, or the self-professed righteous man, along with the unenlightened natural man will belittle you for sharing your treasured discoveries. What you are being given is so stirring and revolutionary to popular opinion that you must value and protect it. In some cases, prudently keep this treasure hidden, until you are able to share it with a like-minded individual seeker. Just be careful who you share your pearls with, because the natural man is not yet receptive, and he receiveth not.

Here is another great pearl of truth for your consideration: in reality there is no such thing as an average man, or natural man, because all men are created equal, spiritually and physically. Each person is endowed with a spirit, not belonging to himself, but belonging to the ONE and only SUPREME SOURCE, the DIVINE SPIRIT, who is living a portion of HIS LIFE through each of us.

Truly we are living His life on this earth as divine beings. We are not even having our own experiences, they are His; and oh my, how our free will may have temporarily muddled up these experiences of His, by mistakenly thinking we were a separate entity somehow wandering around masquerading on our own!

Just for the sake of contemplation, here is a tidbit of celestial information that helps depict our connectedness. A human life-stream is never disconnected from his or her Father-Mother-Source. There is what you might picture as an invisible umbilical cord, the silver cord of light and life that spiritually feeds us our daily bread—our divine energy— and can absolutely never be undone or severed. We are eternally one with our Parent. How long will it take us to grow from being the natural man into the long awaited revelation of our spiritual man status?

Presently though, we are gradually seeing the Light at the end of our tunnel. Through our seeking and finding, our human tunnel-vision is hopefully being set free, becoming lighter and lighter, enlightened. Be careful though. With no more attachments weighing, holding us down, binding us to this world, we may find ourselves lifted and floating in the air, levitating like a Saint Theresa. Then we too, may have to ask assistance from the other nuns to please help hold us to the ground while we pray! When Peter doubted his own levitating, he fell back into the sea.

Not to fear though. You will either go ahead and gently ascend, or you will stay grounded enough to be an enlightened helper and teacher here where the world so desperately needs your light. Make no mistake, this mission you and I have embarked upon, is a Holy mission. We will be helping to save souls—yes, save them—from the tired religious doctrine of condemnation and separateness; believing themselves somehow to have been estranged from their Source, and their own Christ-Selves.

Spiritual separation is impossible, only thinking separation can make it mentally seem so. Thankfully, there is no such thing as a lost soul, never a separation for ourselves or for our unfortunately ill and declining elders, only a temporal misplaced or mentally hidden understanding of one's Divine nature.

This advanced ministry is a great challenge indeed! Others may not understand, but through your steadfastness you can help others to see that their soul or spirit is one with the Supreme Being that is living all Life. Quite an undertaking, but what a joy, these pearls of truth and wisdom. Wouldn't you agree?

Through the seeking and finding,
our human tunnel-vision is hopefully being set free,
becoming lighter and lighter, enlightened.

... ascending will be our objective
in every future flowering lifetime we light upon,
as we become more "like Him."

Chapter 20

OUR ASCENDING CONTINUES

"Beloved,
now are we the sons of God,
And it doeth not yet appear what we shall be;
but we know that when he shall appear:
We shall be like him; for we shall see him
as he is."

—*John* 3:2

"Now we all are the sons of God; and now as we wipe our sleepy human eyes from our slumber we are beginning to realize that we always have been. Many philosophers and theologians tell us that in order to become more spiritual and enter the Kingdom of Heaven, we must get out of here, leave this earthly life behind, and completely disappear from this realm of existence. They insist that the mortal body and physical world are merely an illusion, a dream, or some sort of mirage, an error in the scheme of reality. They say that we must die out of this world in order that we may become immortal, perfect and divine. Nothing could be further from the Truth!

Our spiritual education is earned in this earthly schoolroom, not after school or during summer vacation, and is certainly not magically bestowed upon us after we experience our physical death. Man does not die away from his problems, whether his creations be good or bad. As below, so they shall be above.

Our ascending process is an ongoing activity taking place in the minutia of our daily lives. Every improved thought is an ascending one. We can always bring a larger, more expansive perception to any given circumstance or situation. These steps of higher thought are indispensable toward our spiritual development. Through trials and triumphs, we are continually being groomed for greater service.

Whatever advancement in character and integrity we have gained in this world will be carried with us into our next sojourn. The opposite therefore, is also true; whatever faults, weaknesses and outright sin of character a man has acquired or developed, these too will he carry in his travels and return with him as lessons yet to be learned.The ascending process is an ongoing and perpetual law of eternal Life. Of course those of us like you and I would like to assume that we won't have to continue going through a repeating and refining process, because we have already attained our perfection. Don't we wish!

It is said that only one man, Jesus, could truly ascend this world. Most know ascension as a kind of transcendence through all mortal wants and woes, all pains and sorrows. These redundant assumptions speak of only the future tense of all perfection and goodness. This approach completely misses the point of Jesus' teachings which proclaim that the Kingdom of Heaven is at hand. The ability to know and demonstrate higher degrees of harmonious and spiritual living is within ourselves, in the here and now at this moment, and at the fingertips of every man's hand. We have been looking through the wrong end of the telescope, making the things of the spirit look farther away instead of closer.

We need to perceive ascension as the grandest state of mind rather than just perceiving it as a rare and mystical one-time, one man event. The effect of its blessings is possible in the present sense. Jesus was illustrating by his ascension that the learning experience goes on and on for each of us. However, it is essential to begin the progression of thought and understanding right where we are.

Webster's dictionary defines ascension as, "to move forward, aspire, to extend upward." It is the obligation and should be the rightful joy of every human being to have ascension as his present and ultimate goal. We simply have to change our thinking, turn the telescope around, observe the progression of spirit unfolding in everything about us, magnify and enjoy the view!

Please see with me that Life is all around us, within us, and within all nature. Like ourselves, the mineral, plant, and animal kingdoms are expressions of and animated by Divine intelligence. All is God, the All-that-Is. The tiny spirit of a plant directs all the living elements of its physical make-up. Every particle of its form knows its purpose; from a seed to the opening of a flower, as well as the spirit within an acorn, driven to be a grand oak. All energies within creation are intelligently vibrating, swirling, advancing, ascending. In like manner our consciousness is continually unfolding and gently expanding to greater heights.

In reality, we don't have to get out of here, or go anywhere to attain a more elevated state of consciousness. We achieve it from within through consecration. Not only is it non-essential to leave our human-hood and this physical world in order to begin our ascending process, we would do well to understand that our true Selves are just as real, just as alive, in this material world as they will ever be in the celestial.. The dawning of this spiritual awakening is in actuality the birth in understanding our ascending process. It is in this schoolroom of the flesh, where we must come to the acknowledgment that *all* is spiritual.

No one knows or can prove exactly what happens to the spirit or soul after what we call death. However, the Scriptures assure us lovingly and succinctly, we will eventually be *"like Him"* (God), *"for we shall see Him as He"* (God) *"Is"... "It doeth not yet appear what we shall be... but... we shall be like Him."* (John 3:2) This seems a strong indication that some kind of further refinement and perfecting is requisite. A type of repeating process seems to underlie all life. This spiraling concept was echoed by the Byrds when they put to music these lines from Ecclesiastes: *Turn, turn, turn... "To everything there is a season, and a time to every purpose under heaven."*

This is an epiphany in realization—that our higher consciousness has stepped down to the physical, and is temporarily dwelling in the flesh, albeit knowing with all certainty that we are in this world, but not of this world. To be within, and without simultaneously, is the acquired wisdom of our enlightened masters— and this epiphany is awaiting our discovery as well.

Our earthly purpose is to know ourselves from inside out, instead of from the outside in. It requires driven determination, concentration, and focus to see our true Self and our full spiritual potential in the present. This opens our spiritual eye to new creative, unlimited possibilities. Ascension is continual, a "this moment" of advancing and improving consciousness, to which the physical body and our entire experience vibrantly respond. No matter how evolved a being may appear—like a Jesus—there are always higher steps and stages to be achieved. Though we may presently perceive this only dimly through our small window of human understanding, there are more schools and universities for our spiritual education even after this earth. Though we may not yet be realizing it, we are traveling upward in spirit-consciousness from the 3-D realm to the 4th, 5th, 6th, and 7th dimensions and on and on—further continuing our roles in the cosmos.

The mortal body should not be viewed as some kind of grand illusion, but instead as a marvelous masterpiece of a creation energized and vibrating from the One Source. It has been clothed around, and is entirely responsive to the individualized God-Consciousness which supplies and directs it. In addition, every infinitesimal atom and cell are synergistically working within the body and each has been given a minute portion of its own individualized God-Intelligence, God-Consciousness.

All elements harmoniously operate together at differing levels, schooled with direction and function according to each his own purpose. The rhythmic energy and vibration of higher thinking gives man dominion over his body, and with its further elevation he will gain dominion over his world. The higher and more ascended the vibrations or frequency of consciousness, the more harmonious the rhythm of man's own evolution and advancement will be.

This material body and world we live in can be likened metaphorically to the density of ice. It can chip, crack, and melt down. It can be fallible. However, just as vapor is a more elevated vibrant version of the ice, so material man has within himself the capability of a higher and more elevated, vibrant conscious spirit. The process of condensation starts out invisible to the eye, as vapor, then becomes water; and, when water eventually becomes ice, it takes on a more visible form. At that point it can either be very abrasive or very helpful, if utilized properly.

The world or physical body we live in could be compared to the hardened ice, at times abrupt to the senses. However, by contrast, and similar to the vapor, as long as our thinking stays elevated with a more quickened and harmonious vibratory rhythm, it is less likely to become rigid, fallible, harden and crack, thus more harmony is evidenced in our immediate experience. Vapor has a more ethereal essence about it, as does the conscious spirit of man. It is interesting to note that the spirit of man can vibrate at a frequency much higher than that of the spiritual rhythm of his material form.

H_2O has the properties of one substance, although it appears to us in the differing forms of ice, liquid, and vapor. In the same manner, we view earthly life as consisting of many contrasting properties; yet all substances, seen as matter, or unseen as formations yet to be manifested, are *spiritual energy*, (What we call matter is His Energy slowed down to a visible pace, manifested tangibly.) All variations of forms, originate from the one and only—the One Source.

This life may sometimes seem as unyielding as ice. But when you increase and elevate your conscious spiritual vibration, you raise and substantially improve the physical body or situation accordingly, like the warmth of the sun continually shining on a lake of ice. Our thoughts become more fluid and all aspects of our experience are improved. Our life becomes more ethereally correct, more like its original heavenly blueprint.

When we begin to live and move, and have our being within our higher mind, our divine nature, this transformation and ascending begins to take place. All energies are quickened, and all frequencies are raised. Our thoughts manifest themselves, whether they be cold as ice or quick with the warmth to heal.

The following indicates the states and stages of advancing thought:

Ice……….liquid…………….vapor

Matter…….mind-conscience…spirit

Mortal…….humane…………..divine

The ascending mind is advancing out of its denseness, as the ice, of hardened and rigid thinking, transitioning through the middle way of moderation, liquidity and receptivity; then ascending further into the vapor, the more ethereal or spiritualized consciousness. We can relate these levels to the thoughts we entertain during our day. They revolve continually, and hopefully evolve from the most basic, sensual and *mortal*, to the more *human*, or humane, and are at their best when they are *divine*, unselfish, loving, honest, and compassionate.

This illustrates our transitioning from the mortal, to the humane, into the Divine—ice, liquid, vapor!

Even though we know that the three differing forms of H_2O were equally the same substance all along, do we think that the ice ever imagined its molecules moving so rapidly that it could become steam? Do we think a human being ever imagined himself to be divine? What if his conscious thought was so elevated that it moved at a rate of vibration never before considered? Upon the realization of his divinity at this higher frequency, what greater works might he be capable of performing!

All energies in whatever form universal atoms may assume are spiritual energies, whether viewed as material or celestial.

Allegorically, vapor could be likened to a kind of ethereal blueprint of all creation written on the celestial side with the capacity to be manifested and clothed in tangible and understandable spiritually-energized material form. Remember when we slow down the action and vibration of energy, it becomes visible form or matter. In the same manner, all things originate from the same substance, that of spirit, whether visible or invisible. It is this spirit within man which "quickeneth."

As we ascend up and out of this world and into the next and the next, we shall better comprehend the true meaning of our individual immortal spiritual existence. We will be living in and joyously experiencing world after world without end... amen! Know ye not that ascending will be our objective in every future flowering lifetime we light upon, as we become more "like Him?"

An ascending man
had to first come to the enlightened conclusion
that he was not stuck in earth.

—***C.S. McClintock***

But wait, you say, touching the Him of immortality seems too transcendental, too large a task for mere mortals to consider. However, perceiving the infinite nature of all things is of paramount importance in the realm of human comprehension and spiritual understanding. Without some measure of the value and meaning of infinitude,— without beginning or end—we cannot fathom an omnipotent God, or an infinite Love. Not comprehending the boundless spirit and energy, that underlies all creation, we are like someone looking through a keyhole at the sky and not seeing its immensity. Our demonstration of an escalating and more rarified consciousness will be as large or as small as the vision of our thought will allow.

Opening our minds to new vistas of truth is evidence of "aspiring, expanding, moving upward," as Mr. Webster's dictionary suggested. Fear not, for the spirit of the Father, which is your spirit as well, is always with you, loving and encouraging His co-creative journey— through you, as you. The Christ-Self is your 4th dimensional embodiment of the I AM, albeit in this world, stepped down to a slower, third dimensional frequency, in human form.

Yes, we are ascending this world with its cross-roads of time and space. We are rising up and overcoming the limitations of mortal mind, moving into the humane, and emerging gently into our spiritually rich Divine Mind. Each and every person is transitioning, transcending into his own Christ-Self— realizing his own "Second Coming."

… all life is eternally advancing whether at the mineral, plant or animal levels… However in the human realm, it takes the power of being **driven** *and the stretch of the* **imagination** *to become more than one seems to be.*

Chapter 21

THE REPEATING PROCESS

And we begin . . . I lie in my crib.
I crawl on all fours. I stand and walk, then run.
I fall on all fours, then prone and still.
The End
. . . until we begin again.

—*C. S. McClintock*

Broadening our take on life

We tend to measure our lives chronologically, physically, and visually. We see a baby born and say this life begins here, as if eternal life had a starting point, like a particular birthing day on a calendar. Then, marking our time, we measure the years, the decades. When they are coming to a close, and only then, do we seem to consider a kind of ethereal world hereafter or after here. Strangely enough, we've never been asked to contemplate how many worlds we may have experienced prior to this schoolroom, in other words before here. Life being eternal makes one wonder why we haven't entertained the possibility of where we were preceding earth.

Someone once asked me, "Why are you so spiritually driven?" My initial response was, "Well, thank you!" Then I thought and thought. What was it that took me off the treadmill where most mice and men seem to circle, a life with no particular pursuits other than keeping up with or getting ahead of the Joneses whomever they are?

Are we living an Alabama type life? The group sang:

I'm in a hurry to get things done,"
On I rush and rush until life's no fun
All I really gotta do is live and die
But I'm in a hurry and don't know why.

Contemplating the question of leaving the treadmill of the mundane, I came to a distinct conclusion that it was the understanding and importance of one word that had changed my thoughts about death, and consequently the course of my life. This one word had placed me on my new journey, a new pathway, an epiphany of sorts. It had given my course a firm direction; not an east, west, or north and south direction, nor degrees of longitude and latitude. This new word gave me a whole different take on the meaning of eternality.

The trauma and emotions of having suddenly lost a loved one had lingered—can there be anything more difficult for a human being than learning how to deal with a sudden tragedy? I found myself visiting in the home of a Norfolk, Va. minister. She had proven to members of her own congregation and to many others time and time again her gift of prophecy and that night with me present in her kitchen would be no different. FiFi began by mentioning to me situations from my past, my present and my future. I realize now that almost all of her prophecies have come to pass. I felt her loving kindness and her genuine concern. After all, you judge a prophet by the truth they speak, so says the Good Book.

"It looks like you just lost a loved one," she said.

I asked her how she could know that.

"God knows all and He's telling me," she responded. She went on to explain Karma is accountability, reaping what you sow, and how there are no accidents. Because the laws of life are exact, what you give out, will eventually return to its individual initiator; no matter how many lifetimes it takes. I was young, and I didn't understand. Lifetimes? Karma? Then she hit me with the word—reincarnation—yes, again, something entirely new for me to contemplate.

I later found out it was a word that a group of men in the Council of Nicea, in 325 AD, had quite possibly been ordered to extract from all the Gospels, omitting any references to this heretofore well-accepted concept of rebirth.

This word, this concept, though unfamiliar and new to my ear, over the ensuing years came to make more and more sense to me. There may have been a time when this belief would have conjured up visions of spirits possibly becoming different forms of plants and animals. And while all lower forms do have individual consciousness, I learned that human beings do not go backward, they don't retrograde; nor do they ever lose their individuality or soul. Once human always human,—yet ever advancing higher. Always, that is, until we completely outgrow the human schoolroom with our much anticipated graduation.

It grew more and more logically obvious to me that one way or another we will keep re-entering the material paradigm, until we elevate above all limitation. Whether we believe this takes place on this side in the visible or on the other side in the invisible, makes no difference, we each remain a conscious entity of spirit in a perpetual learning journey..

Most of us have felt a cognitive déjà vu experience of having been in a particular location or circumstance previously, and found ourselves thinking "we've been here before." These are brief glimpses of our timeless identity.

The idea of life without end, my spirit living forever, yet with a continuation process, actually liberated me and gave me a sense of freedom. Since then I have never had any fears or questions concerning death or an afterlife, because I have come to realize that we can never die. We only change our vehicle, moving to a new phase of our forever continuing life. It has been said that we won't be any more aware of our death than we were of our birth... or our rebirth, for that matter. The Dalai Lama once said this whole process is no different than changing our clothing.

Restitution

Gradually I came to the understanding that all thoughts and actions will be weighed and balanced by the laws of life and love; and in that love there can be no harm to the spirit of the loved one who has moved on, even when that passing seemed too early or unjustified. The lives of each of us will continue on through this repeating process. We eagerly return again and again until we complete our mission, master our co-creative unresolved artwork, so to speak, keeping it advancing positively. All wrongs will eventually be righted, and thankfully, all goodness venerated.

Repeating causes learning, which in turn causes a raising effect and results in a degree of progression and ascension, escalating our lower grades to the higher.

Wow, I thought, "accountability," hmm— another word to which I hadn't given much attention. We are each individually responsible for our thinking and actions—past, present and future. It is said that our sins, debts, will be our punishers and teachers. So where else would the learning experience come from that is meant to set us straight unless through a repeating process of some kind in this schoolroom of earth? Every jot and tittle will be accounted for. And there is no such thing as waiting around while someone else pays our accumulated debts for us.

Here was another epiphany—there is no vicarious atonement! I learned that the Hebrew word for salvation means "to be expanded from within." My heretofore puzzling thoughts were really expanding. They were beginning to piece themselves together.

Conscious resolution

The Master showed The Way to be saved from our own illusions, and negative creations through the resolution taking place within our own consciousness. As the minister had said, there are no accidents! Hmm, no accidents? The law of attraction dealing with the energies of our creations is always at work in this world, like a gyroscope, moving and magnetically attracting and adjusting all balances toward the good. Even though we may repetitively pass from this sphere of time and space, truly, nothing is ever lost or forgotten. Love is all there is in spite of our mortal perceptions.

I knew that my loved one's rebirth and continuing life was imminent. While difficult for me to understand at that time, the minister had predicted that his particular return would be within 10 years. Somehow I felt reassured that all would be well for the one passed from my sight.

The answers to life's most difficult questions may come differently to everyone. Of course, I sensed the process of reincarnation was the most viable approach to our afterlife, as I felt awakened to the fact that the standard alternative, hell or heaven paradigm I had grown up with was a mere nursery rhyme, a fairy tale story of ole. How was an eternal fire supposed to affect a spirit who has no material senses of touch, taste or smell? This new outlook happily dispelled the view of my loved one having to forever float superfluously in the clouds.

It made total sense to think of real life continuing in a repeating and learning process, with redemption and regeneration possible even after what we call death. After all, in reality, is this not our one Source, God, re-manifesting through perpetual seasons... as ourselves, yet having His experiences? Finally, this brought a plausible continuity to our existence. Imagine having a chance to redeem ourselves, no matter how far off course some of us may stray in any particular lifetime. And further, no matter how many grades some may need to repeat, we will return to our schoolroom over and over, back to the scene of our crime, or our glories! Those well-learned enlightened ones with selfless compassion, may choose to come back as helpers, teachers, torchbearers, leading by example. A worthy goal for us all.

Cyclical accountability

I knew that my thoughts had been lifted to a stirring new dimension of perspective and possibility. I no longer felt sad or stagnant in my thoughts, and I had a new enthusiasm for grappling with fresh ideas, different approaches to life, death, and human purpose. I wondered why I had never been exposed to this perfect sense of cyclical accountability. After years of contemplation it occurred to me that this was a necessary component of our ongoing *ascending* process.

I began studying the laws of life, and found wonderful inspirational writings that helped to guide my spiritual growth. I also discovered that many of the simplest truths of old have been altered or completely removed from print, thus over time lost to our conscious awareness. The emperor of Rome, for instance, had the early church under his thumb, and controlled the strongest army in the world. He could also control the writing and editing of the greatest book to have ever been written—the Bible. He wielded the wherewithal to have many truths and well-known theories of life changed, altered or extracted altogether from its contents.

It was almost as if the elimination of the universal law of correction, the repeating process, from the pages of books would magically relieve individuals of all debts accrued over a lifetime of misdeeds. However, this was no immunization against the certain fate that would surely befall him. After all, the prospects of a holy Roman Emperor, or a religious potentate, having to return to the flesh as possibly a commoner, was too much to bear. Yet, did they really think that the elimination of the idea of karma- accountability, or reincarnation, would actually have sway over cosmic law? The Emperor Constantine must have said, "To hell with being accountable! I'll just take what I want and do as I please. And furthermore, I will have this Book translated and edited my way!"

Still, here we are 2,000 years later thinking someone else will pay for our transgressions, past, present and future. Vicarious atonement ... hmm?

My thoughts progressed. I remembered as a child going to my friend's church. What an awkward experience awaited me. People ranted and raved, or jumped up and down, with the preacher seemingly pointing right at me from the pulpit. He gruffly shouted out the possibility that we were all going to a fiery hell. If we didn't walk down, or better yet, run down to the front of the church to be saved, we would all be lost.

I wondered, feeling guilty, why was our group not moving to the front—I didn't want to burn! I saw grown men raising their hands in the air and was curious why there were tears running down their faces. As I grew into youth, I just assumed the heaven and hell stories were like Jack and the Beanstalk, Santa Claus tales, metaphorical nursery rhymes. That Goliath must have been ten times the size of a regular man, a real out-of-this-world giant.

I'm not saying that I didn't enjoy nursery rhymes and fairy tales, but there always seemed to be a knowing within me saying, "Be patient, one day you will make sense of this world." And the mist eventually did begin to clear. I saw that every man must have his thoughts and actions weighed, scrutinized. I now understood with full clarity the Biblical expression, "reap what you sow." It wasn't a farmer reaping his harvest after all. It was you and I, dealing with the Universal Law of Adjustment, our Karma, as it were. My learning journey was becoming clearer.

Eternal existence

I came to realize that our one eternal life will have "eternal lives—many parentheses," and unlimited experiences in this world and the next and the next. Hopefully, we will understand that they will be repeatedly evolving, just as a deciduous tree renews itself season after season. No death, just a spirit with consciousness, renewing, redressing itself, again, changing its clothing.

Our character will be refined, our debts worked out, our understanding will expand until we too, like the Master, and many others, will have ascended all earthly ills and limitations of the five senses. We will have overcome all misconceptions and will recognize our own divinity. No longer will we see ourselves or our loved ones in a linear line of a beginning, birth, life, and an end-of-the-line death. It can be helpful to imagine life in a vertical line, as a kind of spiraling upward activity, a continual, ascending, elevating process escalating us into our eternal futures ... forever learning, learning, learning. How liberating and life-transforming I hope this understanding will be for you as well!

The repeating process has always been known. This is the reason Jesus' followers asked why the man sitting at the temple door had been born blind. Was he born blind for the usual reasons, because of his own sins, they questioned? Or could this handicap have been a debt, a payback for the sins of his parents, the three inquired? The Master's answer to his disciples' question would take a whole chapter to explain. The pivotal point however, was that everyone knew that he was responsible for his own debts, either now or in the following repetitive birth and death experiences. One great thinker wrote that the "judgment day comes hourly and daily." The squaring of accounts goes on here, and continues until we "ascend" all wrongs.

Personal aspirations

Are we reaching our full potential for growth and knowledge? Are we becoming the full manifestation of our desired divinity? Perhaps you could engage your mental imagery with me. The seed of an oak tree, which we will call a spiritually driven acorn, will have to have steadfast determination and dedication to fulfill its purpose. Yet the capacity of the acorn's God-Consciousness could not possibly comprehend one-thousandth the scope of a mature and flourishing oak tree. You and I, with our greater capacity may be equal in potential volume to, let's say, the likes of Master Jesus. However, our understanding of God-Consciousness might presently be more acorn size, when compared to the full-grown comprehension Jesus had. We must come to realize that we have the same innate potential for growth and knowledge. The acorn should aspire to become a full-grown tree. In like manner a man should aspire to become a full-grown Master... transitioning his mere human thought forward with expectancy, toward the more divine.

Huge expectations

Can you remember the unsettling experience of going from the familiar confines of elementary school and grounds, to your middle school? What a joy it was to finish junior high and move on to the high school campus for your next educational experience. You knew you were transitioning into a major change, and had huge expectations of what was to come: high school sports, marching bands, getting a driver's license, dating in cars. Growing up was thrilling, what a change of mindsets!

At that point in our lives, it would have been unimportant and rather meaningless to consider where we were or what we were doing before we began our elementary level of schooling. We would have been very young children then. What purpose would it serve to even contemplate our pre-elementary years? Well, we didn't because we were busy finishing off our teens.

Today, we have so many things on our minds, so many responsibilities. Why would we ever contemplate our existence before the busy life we are now living, in this planetary school? That's right, before earth. Can you remember Dion and the Belmonts' *Where or When*? Great song! Who knows where or when we've been, or where we are going, but we should move forward with the same huge expectancy we did as children, toward our next campus, our next adventurous learning experience.

The stress and worry over an unknown afterlife, or no-life-at all after, seems to have sapped the joy from our veins and our present experience. Thus the feelings of happiness, and the expectancy of our futures, have been crowded out by the "you-only-live-once" philosophy.

Religious theologies have not allowed us to think, and use our imaginations or our intuitions concerning our past or possible future existence. Our mental upbringing has been largely fashioned around a nonsensical one-time physical birth, and physical ending called death, with the consequent choice of either heaven or hell, or in some cases, nothingness. We are completely missing the point that Eternal Life means endless—past, present and future, forever and ever. Amen.

Jesus suggested that we could expand our capabilities further than even he did, and do greater works. I have mentioned that the medical surgeon probably knows one thousand times more than the average person about the healing arts. Though we may have the very same educational potential, he has expanded his capability and brought about his dream, his destiny, of a medical degree to fruition. We may have stayed stagnant where our own goals and destinies are concerned, sometimes by our own choice. Or maybe we had no desire to challenge ourselves to make the grade in our schooling, the way the driven did. Likewise, to excel and become Dr. Medicine, or Dr. Jesus, is our own choice. The Master explained to us that we are his equal, in fact we are his siblings. For goodness sakes, we have the same Father. Have we failed to develop further in our spiritual growth? Are we less driven to grow than the tiny acorn, having lost our huge expectancy?

Spiritually driven

The Spirit within the Master is the One and only—and the same Spirit that is within you and I. The difference lies in the fact that he studied and imbibed spiritual matters 1,000 times more than we. In this regard, maybe we've progressed to being a sturdy young sapling. However, we might be a lot like a tree in the forest—stuck in one spot, and possibly stagnated, in one theology.

We are told over and over that someone else will do it for us, pay our debts, give us salvation, keeping us passively beholden to the clergy's doctrine. Maybe the Master will even come down and wave a magic wand over us, and awaken us spiritually to see. Or while down here he will raise us out of our graves, and take us up in the clouds with him. We may even believe that we will be suddenly perfected at the moment of our passing.

When will these fairy tales end? The sky is not going to fall, there is no wizard in Oz, and the Easter bunny does not lay colored eggs. Jesus was a man, like you and me, albeit hundreds of times more spiritually educated, and he understood and embraced his divinity. Why, oh why, will we not recognize the necessary progression to our own divinity?

Eventually we should learn that we are not merely the body. Though we may be stuck in the ground or six feet under it, we are not this earthly vehicle, we only temporarily abide in it and direct it. We are spiritual. The spirit merely inhabits the form, the bodily attire, our earthly costume. Oprah wisely calls the body an earthly "disguise for the spirit."

Creating our futures

We must constantly remind ourselves that we are spiritual beings having a human experience, and not human beings craving a spiritual experience.

Know ye not that ye are gods? Is the ocean not made up of individual drops? Is the one Creator not made up of individualized conscious portions within Himself? Though we be tiny, are we not creative entities within the one Creator? The Master told us to go and do, not to try and do, but emphatically to *"do likewise."* We each should be able to say that "I too, am that I AM." You and I are divine beings with the potential to stretch our minds 1,000 times, just as he did. Even today 90 percent of our brain capacity goes unused. We need to realize that we are the wizard of IS, that is— His IS-ness.

All consciousnesses great or small within atom, cell or universe, have the one inherent goal of moving up, evolving, advancing, as was the case with the aforementioned acorn that was spiritually driven into becoming a wondrous oak. With true dedication and determination it can fulfill and complete its destiny, and so can we.

Once again, use your imagination. After a few successful seasons of maintaining and balancing the system of the dynamic workings within the tree, it could be time for the evolution of the spirit of the oak to continue its progression. For the sake of illustration, what if this same consciousness had been a beautiful flower, before taking on the new responsibility an acorn would have in becoming a grand oak? Now that he has graduated his "oakdom," as a flourishing and mature tree, it is again time to move on up. This tiny spirit of God's Consciousness, has proven his dedicated worth.

Could we further suppose that our imaginary tree now dreams of progressing into a moving form, crawling or walking the earth, instead of being rooted and stuck in one location? Maybe it would imagine being a furry caterpillar, or squirrel, who knows what or how, but you can bet its desire for the spiritual and physical evolutionary process continues. Why wouldn't it? After all, all life is eternally advancing forward whether at the mineral, plant, or animal levels.

The moral of our fanciful story is that all things continue to elevate and evolve through transitional change and *desire*. However, in our human realm, it takes the power of being dedicated, driven, and the stretch of imagination with *feeling*, to become more than one seems to be. Essentially, to be like Him, requires the stretching of our human consciousness all the way up into our Higher Christ-Consciousness.

Are you and I stuck, grounded, fixed in one mindset with no elasticity in the stretching of our own imagination; slowing our vibration, limiting our own eternal and ascending evolution? Wonder with me, if you will; what will our next experience, our next universe be like?

Man is the highest manifestation of God that we know of. Fortunately, we won't have to imagine being a flower, a tree or a squirrel. However, and unfortunately, oftentimes we can't seem to envision being much more than we are, an earthly body with a multitude of complications and limitations. But hopefully, that is now changing.

As we continue creating our futures, we will learn not to give fertile soil to negative thought seeds of anger, hate, prejudice, jealousy, and greed. We will naturally police our minds, nurturing only loving, caring, constructive, and forgiving ideas. We will be found growing only love and compassion within our mind-fields as we bring our garden back to Eden. Yes, harvesting, and *bringing back that loving feeling*. Being Righteous Brothers!

Happily, once we've thoroughly conquered this elementary school of elements and senses, no retrograde step is required. Thank goodness, we are always moving up the totem pole of our universal progression, never having to go backward or cross the barriers of perceived impossibilities. Our individual spiritual selves will grow and blossom into the fullness of the Divine. We humans will caterpillar along, until we ingest and comprehend enough spiritual truth that we will take wings and ascend like a Celestial butterfly into the next chapter of our eternal life. Can you imagine that! What a beautiful unending.

> *We shall not cease from exploration,*
> *and the end of all our exploring*
> *will be to arrive where we started…*
> *and know the place for the first time.*
>
> —***T. S. Eliot***

And wonder of wonders!…
the moment **uninversal love** *fills my heart, I am raised up,*
and find myself on the sixth step.

Chapter 22

WISDOM OF THE AGES

As I peer into the looking glass
the face of God do I see.
This wisdom of the ages
has come at a great price…
Still, I would not trade
the wrinkles or the gray,
for now I know that All is Thee.

—***C. S. McClintock***

The secrets of the ages have come from civilizations long since past and have been kept in the East for thousands of years. This spiritual knowledge, this great and ancient wisdom, is just now being understood in the West. The time has finally come for the highest seeds of truth to be harvested. After having studied with the Masters of the far East, Jesus began the transference of this information though his parables and teachings some two thousand years ago. If you want to make faster progress and plunge even deeper into the secrets of human life imbued with the Divine, you would do well to look into some of the best of the Oriental philosophy and their practices.

Some years ago a doctor from India stated that for countless centuries the Orientals have been discovering and perfecting various methods by which people can reach the goal of happiness and enlightenment. Everyone carries this goal in his heart, regardless of how ignorant or uneducated he may be, or how low his individual state of consciousness. Right here on earth people can reach this fulfillment, this salvation, this state of eternal bliss—Nirvana, as the Eastern thinkers call it. The door is open for every person when he finds the key.

You may be surprised to learn that this key is yoga. The Indian doctor explained that every human act or activity which is done with concentration is actually some form of yoga meditation. He maintains the only way we have of reaching a great goal or any worthwhile objective, is through focused concentration. In studying yoga, which by the way is much more than the common vision of a person sitting quietly in a lotus position, we learn techniques for developing and improving the powers of focusing our mind.

These are methods which have been perfected through thousands of years of dedicated study and discipline. Believe it or not, even today there are a few individuals living at the top of the world in the Himalayas who have perfected the highest understanding of the yoga techniques, and are living from 300 to 800 years.

Much like an orchid that gets its nourishment from the sunshine, rain, and air, these people, though very rare and small in number, have flowered to the very highest understanding possible in this material existence. They live privately and secretly away from civilization, with most of their days dedicated to quietness and prayer, especially praying to offset the human world's accumulated negative energies of greed, hate, anger, aggression, anxiety, and stress.

There are various paths in yoga: physical, mental, and spiritual exercises in concentration. These exercises develop the highest abilities of the human being, opening up his spiritual eyes, his spiritual ears, and teaching him to be master of himself, master of creative forces, master over the forces of his own fate. The pathway is opened up, or to express it another way, the path to self-realization, to God awareness, is opened up!

The highest, and at the same time the most difficult yoga path is that of Raja Yoga. Raja means "King" and if we translate the term literally, we find that this yoga path is known as "regal yoga" or "majestic yoga." It is the shortest path, but at the same time the steepest and bumpiest.

We honor the asceticism many practice, in fact our world is the better for it. But our chosen path is the way of practical application. And as the Eastern doctor has suggested, it is for the most part steep and bumpy. The question each of us should be asking ourselves, is how adept are we at controlling our thoughts and feelings in the now, from moment to moment? After all this is the true test of a saint. Can we forgive and serve our fellow man? Can we become selfless, without ego and pride?

This pathway we have chosen doesn't allow years of time for concentration exercises in a type of ascetic meditation. Rather, it requires the practice of learning control over our free will by harnessing ideas, observing every thought, minute to minute, as we make certain of keeping them pure.

This is the disciplined pathway Jesus taught as related in the Bible— in his message to keep one's mind stayed on the Divine

Presence, his attention fixed on unconditional love, and expressed through compassion, forgiveness, ethics, and caring for all life. With patience and perseverance one can reach this lofty goal.

The phases of focus

All concentration begins with the *intellectual* or *First Phase*. You direct your thoughts to the object of your concentration and consider what this object actually is. In this stage you are using your intellect, because you want to clarify your thoughts and seek a completely satisfactory definition, which expresses fully and clearly the object of your concentration. As soon as you have found such a definition, your intellectual work is done, for you now know what this thing is, and you need not reflect on it anymore.

Thinking is the bridge between ignorance and knowledge. When we know everything—as God does—we will have no further need for thinking. God is omniscient. He Himself is knowledge, and His knowledge is as perfect as a circle. What should He think about when He knows everything? Only the person who is obliged to expand his knowledge needs to think. This work of expanding knowledge consists of thinking, which again is the first phase.

When your knowledge concerning the object of your concentration is complete, you make the transition from thinking to feeling. This is the *Second Phase* of concentration. Your consciousness projects outwardly through your nervous system all the characteristics of the object of your concentration, impressing them upon your senses. You have the extreme sensation of experiencing it, with every part of your being.

When you have thoroughly experienced the object of your concentration, in terms of thinking and feeling, you go on to the *Third Phase*—spiritual concentration, or what many might call consecration. You become identical with the object of said concentration. You are no longer thinking about it, or feeling what and how it is. You become one with it, you are it!

We call this Third Phase a state of being. In this state you don't need to think about this thing anymore, nor to feel it, because you have become it yourself. In this condition, all your thoughts, all your feelings, all your words, all your deeds become manifestations of the object of your concentration. In effect, you actually manifest or fully individualize and express the very idea that was in your thinking. In relating this to our understanding of God, it has been said, We no longer think up to God, but think out from Him. This is "having that mind,' that way of thinking and knowing, that was in Christ Jesus.

Immersion

One way to comprehend these three phases of concentration would be to visualize yourself sitting on the bank of a river and concentrating on the water. At first you reflect on what water is. You recall that water is a liquid made through the union of two gases. You know that it can be warm or cold, that if it gets cold enough to slow its own vibration it turns into a solid we call ice and that it has color and numerous other properties. You think along these lines until your intellect has completely grasped what water is and means. That is all intellectual concentration.

Then you get up and walk out into the water. Now you feel what water is and what it is like. You feel through direct sensation that water is liquid, that it flows about your body, and you feel its temperature without measuring it. You can splash about in the water, make little ripples or even big waves with your hands and arms. You revel in and enjoy the water. That is concentration in terms of feeling.

In complete concentration, however, there comes the moment when you cease to be a being separated from water, you merge and coalesce with the water, you no longer need to think about water and its various properties. Neither do you need to feel what water is and what it is like. Quite the opposite, you yourself are now blending as one with water. You no longer are thinking of your human body, you have become one with the movement and properties of the water. Complete concentration means becoming identical with the object of your concentration—being it! In the two previous phases of concentration you are separated, whereas in this third and last phase, the condition of being, you experience complete unity, then as a consequence, complete understanding and complete recognition from within. Of course your body hasn't turned into water, but in your consciousness you experience the state of oneness.

The Indian doctor added that you should watch the people around you. You'll notice some constantly talking about love and goodness, wearing sweet smiles of smugness, and trying to show others on all possible occasions that they are loving and good. But only on the outside! They wear the mask of love and goodness; but when it comes to deeds, they reveal their selfishness because oftentimes they are selfish.

Another person may never talk about goodness and never think that he wants to be good, yet everything he thinks, says and does comes forth out of goodness, because he himself is goodness! A person doesn't think about what he is; nor does he feel it; simply because he is what he is. He doesn't need to speak about it; everything he thinks, says and does is the expression of what he is, the manifestation of his own thought, his very being!

Now comes the most difficult task of all: concentrate on yourself. First reflect and consider what you are, then feel what you are; and finally you must be what you are!

For you to become conscious of your true Spiritual- Self here on earth, you first have to enter into your intellect and feelings. So far you have only been able to think and feel what you are, but you have never been able to be what you truly are! Observe the people around you and you will see that they are not their real selves. That is, they are always identifying themselves with the body, the thoughts, feelings and roles they are playing here on earth. They have fallen out of, and are distant from, their real selves and have become in a way, pretenders, people living in a world of make-believe.

Most often in the eyes of very small children you can still see the sparkle, the light of real being. Did not Jesus proclaim that we should become as little children? As its intellect awakens, the child begins to identify itself with its outward person, getting more and more removed from its divine, true self. And all the while the person, as we think about him, is only a mask through which the true self, the great invisible One, looks out at the world!

In reality, the person cannot be more than an instrument for the manifestation of the Self.

People get so attached to their mask that they cannot free themselves from it anymore. The true self is king, Raja and master, the person is only its servant. Abandoning the real Self and its throne, and identifying only with their mask, their physical body and person, they make a king out of the servant and separate themselves from their true being.

Individuals force their Higher- Self into exile, into the unconscious, or complete un-awareness of it. The intellect causes this separation. However, by means of concentration exercises and a purposeful effort to become conscious and aware, the intellect can also be an instrument by which we get out of this separation and blend back with our true self again.

In the past you have concentrated on various things. From now on, your one and only task is to concentrate on yourself, progressing through the three phases of concentration until you achieve complete identification with your own true self, until you really are and know your Spiritual-Self. It is your task, and should be your ultimate privilege and joy, to reach this state of being which can only be described in the first person as "I am that I Am," thus we come to fully realize we are divine individualizations of the I AM.

Furthermore, remember it is not enough for you to think what you are, nor to feel what you are; you must be what you are in your own true inner self, which is the "Christ" within each of us. Not the Christ exclusive to one man, but the somewhat hidden Christ within all individuals.

Manifesting Divinity

Many years ago eastern European born Elisabeth Haich, a teacher of infinite wisdom, wrote about a few of her startling, yet remarkable, personal recollections per her initiations in coming to a higher God-awareness.

She relates:

"One night as I was once again kneeling by my bed in prayer and meditation, preparing to speak to God, something strange happens; to my great amazement, it begins to get light about me. It gets lighter and lighter, and in the growing brightness, I see a remarkable landscape. A high mountain with a steep, stony, narrow path leading up to it. I know this path will lead me to my goal—to reach God. Without hesitation I start to follow it.

"The path leads through friendly countryside, higher and higher. I climb untiringly until the charming landscape lies behind me and I gradually reach the inhospitable region of the high mountains. The pathway gets ever steeper, narrower and stonier, but I climb with astonishing ease, so light as if I were gliding.

"The inhabited territory lies behind me. My horizon widens, and I see everything far below me. But there is no time to look around, and I go on. After many curves, the narrow pathway ends in front of a short stairway with seven steps. Each step is twice as high as the one before it.

"Under a crystal blue sky I stand there all alone in front of these seven steps and I know that I must climb them.

"With a deep sigh and with faith in the power the Creator has given each of his children—the power which in my case has miraculously gone undiminished and has even increased as I have climbed this long pathway—I walk up to the steps.

"The first step is low. I must conquer the *weight of my body* in order to lift myself up onto it. I succeed easily.

"The second step is somewhat higher and awakens the resistance of my body. I have in my maturity already *conquered the forces of the body*, the sensual, and so this step too causes me no trouble.

"The third is noticeably higher. In order to conquer this one I have to *conquer my feelings*. As I become master of my feelings, I am on the third step.

"As I face the fourth step, which is surprisingly high, thoughts of doubt overcome me; 'How will I be able to climb it? Have I enough strength?' Then I realize that my *doubts* are weakening me, paralyzing me. But doubt is simply a thought! So I now must *conquer my thoughts* in order to master doubt. Thanks to my long training in a former sojourn, my strenuous mental exercises in the temple of that Egyptian lifetime, I know what I have to do; I gather all the strength of my soul, *I am absolute faith* in God, and think of absolutely nothing, taking no thought. And behold—as my thoughts disappear, my doubts disappear as well. And I am on the fourth step.

"Curiously, I feel I have grown much larger while I have been climbing these steps. Each time I've gone up a step, I've grown some more, and now I'm much, much larger than I was at the beginning. Presently I face the fifth step, which even though I've grown a great deal, is so high I can only get up by using both hands and both feet. As I pull myself up with much difficulty, I suddenly find, to my great surprise, that I have no body anymore. Everything in me or about me that was material has disappeared, and *I am my invisible spirit.*

"The sixth step is very, very high, and a new difficulty awaits me. I have no body, no hands with which to hang on, and no feet with which to push myself up. How am I supposed to get up there?

"I look about me for some way to do it, and as I turn around, I suddenly see the whole world spread out below me! Country after country... city after city, looking like little toys, and houses with countless people living in them. *Infinite love for all seizes me*... and I am pained to think of all the people who would have to travel the long, laborious pathway of recognition... of all the innumerable people feeling their way forward in the darkness, imprisoned in their own selfishness—just as I once was...

"And, wonder of wonders!—the moment *universal love floods my heart,* I am raised up, and find myself on the sixth step.

"Now I stand before the last and highest step of all. It is just as high as I am. I long so much to get up there and this wish fills my whole being. In vain, I just don't know what to do. I have no hands, no feet nor muscular strength of body with which to pull myself up. But I *must* get up there at any price. Up on top, I'll find God, and I am determined to see Him face to face. I stand waiting but nothing happens.

"As I look around me, I find to my great surprise, that I'm not alone. At this very moment, a being similar to myself reaches the sixth step and begs me to help him up to the seventh. I understand his tremendous desire, and—*forgetting my own longing* to reach the seventh step—*I try to help him* reach his goal.

"The very moment I forget my own wish, I suddenly find that I am up on top of the seventh step—I don't know how—and my companion is no longer there. He has disappeared without leaving a trace. He turned out to be an angelic impartation who helped me forget my last self-centered wish, I was now completely unselfed. As long as I wanted to raise up my own person, I would never be able to conquer the step that was as high as I myself.

"I have arrived! Quicker than a flash of lightning I see the form of a heavenly being woven of dazzling light. It is my *complementary half*, my *Higher Self*, my *Divine Christ Presence*! Its irresistible attraction draws me to it, and—full of delight and fulfillment—I melt into *complete union* with *Him* in His heart. I realize that He was always I and I always He, the twofold projected image of my divine, true Self. However, I had always perceived God as a being separate from myself, but no longer do I sense this division. I now feel *Him* as you, me and all, my Higher Christ-Self, my better 'half.' Presently in this blended twofold sate of paradisiacal unity, in this invisible and distant power I had always called *'God,'* —now I realize at this moment—was always *one with myself*. A disk woven of fire begins to rotate about me. And its immovable axis—in my spinal column—my *true Self*—*'I'*—am dwelling.

"I feel my spinal column burning like a white hot bow, like a bridge made up of the current of life, radiating brilliant light through seven centres (chakras) of force—vitalizing my body.

"Then, beyond all concept of time, I simultaneously see the endlessly long chain of the different sojourns of life in which I have been incarnated throughout ages and eons of time as I traveled the long pathways of development from my first fall out of paradisiacal unity (a fall in mental consciousness) up to the present moment. I see that my countless lifetimes have been, are, and will be inseparably linked with the life of those spirits who have been traveling closest with me sojourn after sojourn. Once human, always human, until we have singularly and collectively completed our earthly mission of *returning* our *consciousness* back to *the oneness* of 'that mind' which is in our *Christ-Self*. From the events of *past lives* new relationships emerge, new ties, new developments, all supplementing each other and fitting together perfectly like the little stones in a large mosaic."

Understanding

And she understood, more fully than ever before that dreams are nothing other than realities in the non-material, vision-forming energy world of mankind. And what you call reality is also only a dream, a projection of the Self which has been dreamed into the material plane, into the atmosphere of the earth. All the tests you failed to pass once, or even several times, come again and again in your life so that you can become an enlightened helper, a useful co-worker in the great plan. Helpers will also be sent to you along your path, as you work your way through the mystical door. It would take too long to explain all the reasons why a particular person from our past lives might reappear in our present experience as our father, mother, brother, sister, child or our antagonist, for that matter. The main reason is that the greatest power in the human soul is longing. Wherever a person's consciousness is drawn by his longing, that's where he is reincarnated, re-manifested.

Motivated not by human ego
but by Divine will
makes man a devoted and active
instrument of the Supreme.

—***Krishna***

Elisabeth Haich continued: "I recognize the threads linking myself with my complementary half, my Higher Christ-Self, with my family members and closest friends. I see clearly how these threads have bound us all together over ages of time. How great souls, more advanced than we, called Spiritual Masters, have and are still helping us through our journeys. We have greatly helped each other and those less advanced in the wondrous task of the *spiritualization of the earth*; also in developing and evolving consciousness within matter including the body.

"The experiences we bring each other in all these lives help expand and deepen the consciousness in the body; while the bodies we inhabit progressively become more spiritual, more beautiful. The 'matter' composing our various *forms* of manifestation becomes ever more elastic, more fluid and responsive to the will and the radiations of the spirit; until finally the body becomes an obedient servant of the *Self*, no longer isolating or obscuring a single ray of light from the Spirit. I understand the secret of the pyramid, the triangular trinity of the three-in-one, for now I have become a 'pyramid' myself, only using matter—the body—as a firm footing, while constantly *manifesting Divinity*!

"Then everything about me, the earth, the sky, the entire universe—all merge in a single gigantic sea of fire. Huge flames encompass me. For a moment I feel as if I, with the entire cosmos, were being destroyed. Flashes of lightening crack and snap through my veins, through my entire being, as the fire burns me.

"And then suddenly everything changes: the fire is no longer consuming me but *I myself am this heavenly fire, penetrating everything, animating everything, consuming everything!* A flood of light surrounds me, however, this flood of light is arising within myself. I am the source of this light and of everything else that is. The earth has no effect on me anymore. Its attraction, which held me in fetters ceases. I am floating in what seemed to be *nothingness*, yet realizing it to be *His Allness*. My being has no limitations anymore. I am now the one who attracts everything, but nothing ties me down anymore—nothing attracts me anymore.

"I seek those whom I have loved from all my pasts, for I know they couldn't be destroyed, but I seek them in vain in the seeming nothingness about me. In the voided emptiness there is nothing but the expansiveness of myself, so I have to turn my attention inward.

"Behold, even as I do so I realize that *everyone and everything is living in me!* The universe is in *me*, for everything that *is* is *living in me*. Everything that is, *I am*. In everything that I love, *I love myself*. And suddenly I realize that everything I have always *believed* I didn't love, was that which I had *not yet recognized within myself!* Now that I recognize myself perfectly, I love *everything* and *everyone* equally, for *I am one* with them, *I am 'I' in everything, in All!*

"I am fulfillment, life—radiant, eternal, immortal being. There is no longer any struggle, any regret, any suffering—no decay, no age or death, no end! *In all that is born, I—the— immortal, begin a new form of life, and in all that appears physically to die, I, the immortal—withdraw from it into myself, back into the eternal, creative, divinity of my own Christ-Self.*

"I realized that time and space exist only on the periphery of the creative world which is like a disk rotating with dazzling speed. *But I, within myself, am timeless, spaceless eternity*. And while I am *resting within myself* my eternal being fills *all space* and everything living in it:

"I AM THE ONLY REALITY, I AM LIFE, I AM THAT I AM!

"I rest within myself and feel infinite *peace*—but in this peace a call reaches me and compels me to return to my deserted body—

in the flesh I had died. I turn the searchlight of my consciousness on to it and recognize the voice speaking to my being, the well-known, dearly beloved voice of my master teacher. *He* is calling me back …

"And I step out of my heavenly *self* and put on the fleshly garment of my personal 'ego' again. But I bring with me the consciousness of *who I am* …

"I am a human being again, but *in my heart I carry the ascended consciousness*, the Divine Self that has become conscious in me—God-Consciousness. And from now on this Divine Self will be acting through my person … and slowly I open my eyes.

"My glance meets the deep blue heavenly eyes of my master. His eyes radiate the same light, the same love and the same peace I have just experienced during the blissful state in my initiation—the same light, the same love and the same peace I now carry in my own heart.

"He lays his right hand upon my heart, and gradually I feel life returning to my body. I draw a deep breath, and the renewed regenerated stream of life flows through my numb limbs. My heart beats vigorously again. Gradually I regain control of my body.

"I can't bring my lips to utter a sound. It takes me time to again find the connection between myself and my body.

"But I don't need to speak, for I know my master's every thought and wish … '*We are in spiritual unity, in God. All One!*'"

"… I am a human being again, but in my heart I carry the ascended consciousness, the Divine Self that has become conscious in me … "

If one really loves another, he wants that one to be happy and harmonious . . . one should have no grief or desire to hold that loved one back . . . when he might go on to greater ease and freedom.

Chapter 23

LIFE AFTER LIFE

What we humanly perceive as death,
is merely our winter moving into spring.

—*C. S. McClintock*

What we humanly perceive as dying is merely like the changing of the seasons, summer into fall, winter into spring, a metamorphosis of change and renewal, a continuation of life.

Not only do we lack understanding of the changing seasons in our continuing sojourns, but we barely even begin to perceive the magical potentiality waiting right at our doorstep in the present. Imagine the possibilities if we were able to utilize more that 10 percent of our brain capacity, 90 percent going unused of course. We literally have the ability to be more like "Superman" than we could ever suppose. What if we were allowed to access a much larger portion within that 90 percent? What if? What if?

Is this another one of the unspoken mysteries within this theatrical production we seem to be acting out—this hiding-and-seeking or scavenger hunt of our life's hidden treasures? Finding our superhuman qualities means a gradual letting go of our personal attachments to any and all things, matters, obsessions of this world.

The reason there seems to be a governor restricting our access to this magnificent reservoir of consciousness is because the human race has not yet proven worthy or earned the right to tap into the gifts of heightened acuteness: supreme awareness: mental telepathy- communication without sensory means, x-ray vision, boundless strength, levitating and flying. The rest of our human brain awaits our spiritual advancement. Fifty percent of the people on this planet are still floundering around in the darkness of anger, prejudice, greed or hostilities, grief and depression; not to mention religious and ethnic fanaticism.

We may not make our ascension in a single bound or at the pace of a speeding bullet. But gradually and gently raise ourselves above all limitations, and then finally— above mortality itself. Our tenacious dread and fear of death must finally give way to a higher understanding of the changing seasons in our life eternal.

One of our super-human qualities would be to see that we are spirit-beings whether in or out of a visible body. This truth would help us to overcome the fear of an unknown future, including the fear of our transition and what comes after.

The great Master St. Germain had this to say about our renewing process:

"So-called death is but an opportunity for rest and re-attunement of the faculties of the individual personal consciousness, as each resides in the spirit realm. This is to free the individual from the turmoil and discords of Earth which they were experiencing. At this point they will receive an inflow of light and strength which will enable the outward activity of the mind to take up the work of a new physical bodily experience once again. Physical embodiment is for the purpose of preparing, perfecting, and illuming the body so its vibratory action can be raised to blend with the spiritual Body of the 'Mighty I AM Presence'; which we will call 'The Magic Presence.' Beloved Jesus referred to It as the 'Seamless Garment.'

"In this higher Body, which is made of Spiritually pure electronic substance, the negatively charged particles within the atom, the individual has complete Freedom from all limitation. Through intense devotion to the 'Mighty I AM Presence,' anyone can release Its Power to the point where he can see this Blazing Body of Substance ... so Dazzling that at first one can only gaze upon It for an instant because of the Intensity of Its Light. Through such devotion one begins to manifest humanly more and more of his own individual Conscious Dominion over all manifestation. This is everyone's Eternal Birthright and the purpose for which all of us have agreed to undertake this journey through the human experience."

The dazzling presence of this Christ-Light was witnessed in the luminance of Moses, *"When Moses came down from Mount Sinai with the two tablets of testimony in hand ... Moses wist not that the skin of his face shone."* (Exodus 34:29)

St. Germain goes on to say, "When the one striving for such Freedom has reached the point where he releases any amount of Light-Energy he desires from his Electronic Body or Light Body instantly by his own conscious command, then he can control all manifestation, no matter in whatever sphere or dimension he may choose to be expressing. One has but to observe the world at large to see what discord in thought and feeling does to the beautiful bodies that Nature provides for our experience on the physical side of Life. In childhood and youth, the flesh structure of the physical body is beautiful, strong, and responsive to the demands made upon it; but when discordant thoughts and feelings are allowed to express in the physical, personal self, accruing over the years as one goes through Life, the body becomes incapacitated and the Temple falls into ruin—because the outer waking consciousness of the man does not obey the One Law of Life—Love, Harmony, Peace.

"Call it what you will, the Eternal Truth reveals that negativity by any name, discord, sin, evil, causes disintegration—a synonym for death. When mankind learns to live its Life by the One Eternal Law of Love, it will find that such obedience will have released mankind from the wheel of birth, death, and rebirth, and hence the problems of human existence will have disappeared. In their place will come the Joy of ever expanding the perfection which forever abides within Love. Constant new creation will ever go on, for Life is Perpetual Motion. Spirit neither slumbers nor sleeps, but is ever and forever a Self-Sustained Stream of Expanding Perfection in Joy, in Ecstasy, and Eternally New Design. This Perfect Activity and Joy of Life are all contained within Obedience to the Law of Love.

"The last enemy, death, will have been overcome, and disappears. This so-called death is but a means of release from a garment (human body) which no longer has anything of value to give for the use of the Perfecting of Life. When the physical body is so incapacitated that the personality occupying it, you and I, can no longer make Self-Conscious effort to express Perfection, then Nature herself takes a hand in things and dissolves the limitation of the body, so that the individual may have a new chance, another new beginning, to make effort which is of benefit.

"*Grief* for the death of a loved one is unnecessary *self-centeredness* and only retards the greater good the passed loved one should be enjoying. Grief from a sense of loss is really rebellion against the Action of a Law that has seen fit to give another regeneration, a greater opportunity for rest and growth. Nothing in the Universe goes backward, and all, no matter what the temporary appearance is, are moving forward to greater and greater Joy and Perfection. *The God consciousness within ourselves cannot and does not grieve.*

"As humans we need to know that no one can ever get out of this Universe, until his or her graduation, we must stay and help create a place better than we left. If there be Real, True, Divine Love, It can never cease to exist, and must sometime, somewhere, draw us to that which we love. In True Divine Love there is no such thing as separation, and that which feels a sense of separation is not Love. The sense of separation is merely one of the mistakes of the personal self which it continues to dwell in because it does not understand the nature of Consciousness. Where the Consciousness is, there the individual continues functioning, whether seen or unseen, for the individual is his Consciousness.

"When one thinks of a loved one who has passed on, he is really with that loved one in his Higher mental body the moment his consciousness is upon the passed person. If the Western World could understand this Truth, it would lift the chains which cause such useless suffering. Such grief is all due to the fact that the personality—especially in the feeling, the ego, accepts the body as being the 'all there is,' to the individual, instead of knowing that the body is only an earthly garment which the individual wears. Over this body, everyone should have complete and Eternal dominion, and should exact Perfect Obedience at all times.

"If one really loves another, he wants that other one to be happy and harmonious. If, through so-called death an individual chooses to accept a better opportunity for future expression—*if there be the slightest spark of Love, one should have no grief nor desire to hold that loved one back,* in a state of incapacity, when he might go on to greater Ease and Freedom.

"It is the ignorance of this Truth which enables such selfishness to keep humanity bound in its self-created chains of limitation. This lack of understanding inadvertently binds the Life Expression of the whole race and is a stubborn refusal to understand Life. It drags thousands of human beings every year into the depths of despair, wholly unnecessary and avoidable, when they could and should be enjoying happiness for themselves and their passed loved one, living the way the 'Mighty I Am Presence' intended them to live.

"Such an attitude toward Life not only prevents the accomplishment of everything worthwhile, but incapacitates the individual griever and fills him with self-pity; this is one of the most subtle and insidious ways by which the sinister force breaks down his resistance and makes this loving being, negative and despondant. The individual must always remain positive if he is to attain his Victory and express Mastery. The sinister force of negativity, which humanity on this Earth has generated by its erroneous thoughts and deeds, keeps aspiring, marvelous individuals from gaining their Freedom. It keeps them from using the Full Power of Divinity which has been theirs from the beginning, the Gift of the Father to His children.

"Of all the faults humanity has generated, *self-pity* is the most inexcusable, because it is the apex of human self-absorption. Through self-pity the attention of the personal consciousness, or outer self, the personality, is entirely engulfed by the petty and insignificant useless desires of the physical body. And the Great, Glorious, Adorable, All-Wise, All-Powerful Light of the 'Beloved Mighty I Am Presence,' this Christ Presence, that is always abiding above, albeit beaming into the heart of the physical body, is entirely ignored; and Its Energy (referred to in The Lord's Prayer as 'Our daily bread') is being used for destructive purposes.

"Grief is colossal selfishness, not Love! Discord is selfishness, not Love! Lethargy is selfishness, not Love, and not Life! These sink the race of man into mental slavery because they break down the resistance of the individual by wasting, misusing the Energy of Life, which should be used for positive thinking and the creation of Beauty, Love, Peace and Perfection.

"Humanity cannot have anything better than it is experiencing today, until it looks away from the little self, the mortal-minded human self, long enough to acknowledge and feel the Presence of God, the 'Mighty I Am Presence,' the Source of every individual, their Eternal Life, their Christ-Self, and of all Perfect Manifestation."

On the subject of renewal, St. Germain concludes with this:

"Master Jesus gave the pubic an example of the transitioning process and sought to teach mankind its meaning, pointing everyone to this same attainment of ascension. Our Master made it very clear, one is sometimes raised into this Ascended condition previous to or near the change called death, but all must accomplish it from the physical side of life. If the silver chord of light (which is your Spirit, life, consciousness, and the supplier of your sustenance,) flowing into the body has been withdrawn at the moment of passing, the consciousness is no longer available to illumine, light up, raise that body. All individualities thus striving must re-embody once more in order to attain from the physical side of human experience the lessons that must be mastered within the material world. All ascensions must take place consciously, for this Ascended Master attainment is the complete Victory over all 'outer,' earthly experiences through the personal self, the 'natural man.'"

Those who have gone on before us, passed from our sight, are nevertheless right here with us. We only distance ourselves from them with our limited human vision, and our mistaken thinking. When we love them on their way and wish them well, we open our thought to their actual presence. A close friend related, "A few months after my dear husband's passing, during my grieving he spoke to me clear as day, 'I am right here, I am right here. I am perfectly fine.' His very clear voice was as if he was standing right next to me. This brought such profound comfort, I was once again able to continue my days with a normal sense of joy, and a heightened purpose in my compassion toward others. I grieved no more."

"In my Father's house are many mansions."

—John 14:2

All individualities, visible or invisible, live on, in His house, a mansion of many dimensions, realms.

Our life, our consciousness, along with the life within all universes, is in eternal flight, progressing, evolving. We, as eternal individualizations of the One Holy Spirit, cannot be contained by a casket or an urn. Not to mention the fact that graveyards are occupying beautiful landscapes, oft-times memorializing death, in lieu of celebrating eternal life—while individuals grieve needlessly over loved ones seemingly lost. We will finally learn that our end is but another beginning, as we steadfastly believe in Life, with no death, only change.

How will men speak of our lives as they eulogize us? What might our epitaph read? It might say, "Here lies a man that well, well, uh, hmm— was born, lived and died. He was a good person, but, yet, he also had his shortcomings. What direction he goes in the hereafter we may never know; we can only hope God will have mercy on his soul and give him peace."

Or, if indeed we have strived to live righteously, might our more enlightened friends say, at our passing... "he lived," as Saint Germain stated, "the full power of Divinity. May our hearts be filled with gratitude, not grief, for a life well-lived!"

In my end is my beginning.

—***Mary Stuart, Queen of Scots***

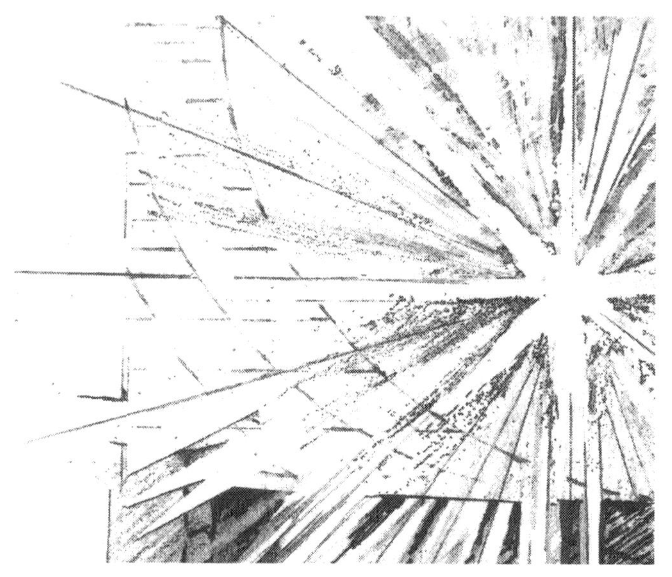

No matter how many mansions, dimensions,
we find in our "Father's house," we will discover
that all these realms or levels are nonetheless still
within the One Omnipotent . . . Spirit of our Source.

Chapter 24

HEAVEN AND HELL

Believe it or not
the devil is nothing more
than "d"evil man thinks,
evict the thoughts
and all wrong is gone.

—***C. S. McClintock***

Over and back

Facing death can be a hell of a predicament for most people. But to paraphrase the Dali Lama, death should be no more traumatic than changing our clothes. In other words, my spirit will be long gone, and pretty soon I'll be transitioning from one aged or damaged body to a brand new one. I personally want my funeral to be a joyous occasion. Heck, I'll be starting a whole new journey.

Reading verified accounts of what has become known as the "over and back" experience can be eye-opening. Thousands and thousands of people have had this "NDE," near-death experience, the sensation of leaving their body once their heart stops. Being cognizant of floating outside their bodies, they tell us their spirit-consciousness had an overwhelming attraction to a beautiful white light. As they are drawn closer and closer to this blinding brilliance, a sense of euphoria begins to overtake them. Sometimes, family members who have gone on before or an angelic presence may be waiting on the other side in this light to greet them. This Presence most likely will say, "It's great to see you, but it is not your time yet." On more occasions than not, the individual spirit who has just left his physical body on a death bed, in a hospital operating room, in an accident, or by any other circumstance, will not immediately want to come back to the earthly realm.

Most want to stay in this euphoric state of being, and reject the assumption that he or she must "come back" to his physical person. Moments later, in a whoosh, they have returned to the site where their body lies. But as they hovered above their own prone corpse, it was apparent that medical personnel were trying to revive them and get the heart started again. Then, in they go, and miraculously a pulse is found. This most personal story has been told countless times, though usually very discreetly.

Sometimes consciousness is removed from the body through sudden trauma or violence. It has been reported that some of these spirits on rare occasions, either do not see the light, or for a period of time, they refuse to acknowledge or move forward into this beckoning brilliance. Even though they are now without a physical form, the spirit is reluctant to leave his familiar location in time and space. They are, and continue to be, their divine spiritual selves, but are not totally conscious of having been released from their bodies.

In any case, the decision is whether one feels ready to move forward into the light, into what has been envisioned as a kind of heaven, as he furthers his enlightenment, or whether one fears and is hesitant to experience what he thinks may be a dreaded encounter, that has commonly been called hell. The mixed and varied interpretations of clergy, philosophers and scholars, regarding a beautiful heaven or hellish damnation that may be awaiting us in the hereafter has led to confusion compounded twice over.

Our thoughts may tend to lean more toward fearing our inevitable ending, rather than seeing it as a beautiful new beginning. The early religions used these reward and punishnent scare tactics to hold people in the fold by conjuring up a painful conclusion, or a flip-of-the-coin directional end for us. By making use of their rods and staffs they have successfully held sway over the flocks, the masses through this conundrum. And how effectively has this threatening tactic worked out for us?

Shadowy creations

We would do well to question the age-old theories put forth, whatever their source. The paramount fact here is that from childhood to the grave, our belief system has been influenced by questionable false teachings that have interrupted the perception of the flow of our eternal life's progression.

In Biblical times, the floundering spirits would often be referred to as demons or devils, which possibly needed to be cast out or separated from a living individual to whom these bodiless entities had tried to attach their consciousness, so as to continue on in this sensual realm. There are a substantial number of present-day individuals who have been schooled in these matters and feel that they are lovingly adept at contacting, speaking to, assisting and transitioning wayward spirits into returning to the light. Their caring goal is to remove the spirit's reluctance and fear associated with the progression to their next phase of development, which should be a very desirable transitional step and is required of all of us.

Listen closely. There truly is nothing outside the Divine. All is taking place within God, therefore all is Good so there can be nothing to fear. What has been referred to as evil or hell, we will finally learn, is merely the mental product of conscious action and reaction relative to a mortal's lesson being learned. As Shakespeare said, "Only thinking makes it so." There is spiritual brilliance in this assertion. This statement defines well the origination of sin and evil or a hellish place—our thinking makes them so.

Only human thinking can invent such an un-godly thing as evil, or such an irrational location as hell, which in turn makes it seem so, all derived within mortal man's consciousness. Since man does not wish to take the blame, he long ago fashioned a scapegoat called a devil, evil, and a place called hell. Mortal man thinks it up, and with his own imaginative energy and thought processes, he has conjured up and thus created this error or nightmare and now has to live with it in fear. As wise ones say, our sins and evils will be our own punisher.

Evil is nothing more than a man's free will gone awry, produced through his thinking and acting incorrectly. Evil or error has no power of its own, only the energy man's imagination infuses into his negative creation. Like little children in the dark, we've become frightened by the shadowy creations of our own imagination. Even the concept of a final judgment day is indeed an unfair judgment imposed upon our collective thinking by ancient disciplinarians and scriptural writers who wished to scare us into a more desirous behavior. However, doesn't choosing either heaven or hell as a final destination leave little room in thought for contemplating all our wonderful experiences to come hereafter?

Again, evil, error, or hades by any name or nature, has no power of itself. Giving this negative mental encumbrance energy opens the doorway in one's life to manifestations of an imagination gone sadly wild, such as various forms of depravity, depression, discord and disease. These are man's own creations. One will eventually have to transmute his erred follies back into the one and only Power, which is crystal clear Love-energy, the very same energy one used to fuel its discoloration. Hopefully we are beginning to see that this learning experience of righting our free-willing wrongs, should be a good and valued lesson.

Remember, the reaping of our own sowing can at times make us feel like we are going through hell. This discomfort can occur at any time in one's life, not just in those moments of transition. Getting our fingers burned, and our soul singed, should have a very positive effect on our correcting process. It is Love's parenting device, Love's "rod and staff" that gently begs our transformation.

Many people think they have actually been taken to this place called hell. Unbeknownst to them, it was all within their own subconscious. This fabrication dances across the mental screen of the human mind, like fleeting nightmares in our slumber, usually from the embedded fear and guilt inflicted by their early fervent religious teachings. These individuals are reflecting upon their accumulated debts and misdeeds, which they feel need to be transformed, righted. In rare cases there are a few unfortunate ones who are just sure, at the moment of death, they tasted hell and were sent back to tell their story.

Quite an imaginative subconscious!

The mind is its own place, and in itself,
Can make a heaven of hell, a hell of heaven.

—***Milton***

Visions

A friend told me of her grandfather, a story that I'm sure is representative of many families. As he lay on his deathbed, he knew that his last breath was drawing near. Overwhelmed with emotion, and through his tears, he repeatedly asked whether he would go to heaven or hell. This big, strong man cried to be forgiven, and feared his visions of hell and damnation. Strange, since he seldom went to church, and he wasn't the least bit religious. But the hellish rumor of demons in a fiery dungeon has been so ingrained into our psyche, that it had him worried almost literally to death! It seems as though, in some cases, religions have really done a number on us.

Surely, we are light-years past the era of having to be threatened into being good, or fearing punishment by a contrary, vengeful, yet loving, God. Another account tells the frightening experience of a little girl being taken to a church where the shouting of strange sounds, visions of hellfire, and the eternal burning of one's spirit were being graphically portrayed from the pulpit. Untouched by the whole ordeal, she skipped away afterwards, and innocently remarked, "How can you burn a spirit anyway?" Her reply shows that even from out of the mind of babes comes more logic, and spirituality, than from the most studied, staunch, fanatical and overly zealous, leaders of today's hillside flocks.

Later in life, she wondered if this raucous display was to win souls, or to win more numbers in the pews, through threats of guilt and condemnation. Needless to say, there was no love felt during that hour, and she never wanted to return to that church again. This haunting religious experience, however, would give her a greater impetus in her search for enlightened answers about God, Heaven, as well as Hell, that mythological abode for the dead.

She learned that hell is a word much used in the Bible, and is also widely included in the teachings of most religions in the world. The concept presupposes a fiery place, a kind of underworld, in which resides a devil, wielding a seeming power that opposes God. This wickedness personified is the supposed tempter that leads one into sin. It boasts its imaginary power, by playing both the tempter and the punisher, and threatens hell as the terrible consequence one will incur for wrong-doing, a debt to be paid at a "final hour" or "judgment day."

Throughout the Scriptures, hell is used as a constant reminder of a horrible punishment for those who disobey God's Laws. Even *Merriam-Webster's* dictionary describes hell as a mythical abode of the dead. I would suggest "dead" to the Truth of our own eternal Divinity, that is.

She knew that Jesus often referred to the word hell in his talks to the multitudes. Her research revealed that the Master was simply using a familiar Hebrew term of his day, a term used to describe the area where trash was burned on the outskirts of Jerusalem, "Gehennan," a garbage dump. The Greek word hades, or "hell" became the name for this not so desirable area; a word used to threaten and frighten the children into being good. In the Master's teachings it metaphorically described well the uncomfortable, albeit temporary condition of mortal consciousness, or self-inflicted mental agony that would be incurred directly in the consciousness of the perpetrator of any wrong-doing.

He taught through his Parables that we must live righteously and that if we don't, we are in danger of hellfire or of the judgment, in other words in danger of experiencing the consequences of the discord and misery derived within our own "hellish" imagination, thoughts and actions.

Misery is,
because we think it to be so.

—***C.S. McClintock***

With this in mind, one can see that what we call an "after life" of hell is more or less a feeling of discomfort in one's consciousness. Jesus brought out plainly that each must *"work out his own salvation,"* in overcoming his own individual wrong-thinking, wrong-doing. It became increasingly clear to this woman in her seeking, that we each choose to make our own heaven or our own so-called hell right here on earth; and that neither her soul nor spirit, nor that of anyone else, could ever be harmed, or could ever be literally burned in hell. Just as this lady had thought as a child—how could an invisible Godly spirit be burned by a loving Father in a material fire?

Angelic entities

Her inquisitive nature also made her wonder how beautiful angels like an out of sorts Lucifer could be warring with an all-powerful and loving God. She later thought about what a complete oxymoron this was as well. Regarding her confusion on the subject of angels, I shared with her the following: Angels are spirit entities, God-Consciousness individualized, just like ourselves; only wearing a different form of embodiment or bodily clothing. They are invisible to the eye except upon occasional occurrences whereby they need to materialize into physical view, in order to communicate a particular message, or lend a helping hand, coming to aid someone in need. Their mission in life is to work right alongside humans, helping us with our own journeys.

At this point, I really wanted to further challenge Linda with some revolutionary ideas, hoping to take her thought far beyond the present-day perceptions of angelic beings. I proceeded to tell her that a few angels have taken the option of entering the earthly realm of birth and rebirth, thereby wearing a human body, feeling that they can do greater good for mankind, mingling among us physically within the material world instead of from without. Many angelic entities have made this monumental crossover; one such example is said to be the Mother Mary. By choosing this course, they are required to go through all the grades within this material earthly schoolroom just like ourselves. And both they and ourselves must continue on our ascending pathway until we have completed all the steps for graduation.

Quite challenging too, is the idea, and perhaps it is possible, that during our eternal journeys, our spirit has the free choice of entering this universe, or another, as an angel or as a human—choosing earth or another planet. It may always have been our individual choice, depending on our level of enlightenment, and the purpose for which we may be called.

Similar to our consciousness, the angel has the free will to think as he wishes. A scant few, like the fabled Lucifer, have perhaps chosen to create anarchy instead of total loving harmony. Just as our own, their Higher-Self, will deal with them lovingly, yet sometimes firmly, if we or they have gone too far awry.

In reality, the concept of a fallen angel warring with God is as comedic as a very mean shark warring against the ocean! The shark is still within the ocean, no matter how rebellious or ridiculous he decides to think and act. Similarly, whether a fallen man, fallen angel, or fallen shark, their spirit no matter how contrary, will always remain one with the Spirit of the Ocean of God.

A fallen angel or a fallen man, has merely descended in consciousness from truth and his true identity, that truth which sets one free. He has lost the freedom to see that every spirit, life-consciousness, is a portion of the ONE, the All-that-Is. All life, visible and invisible, angelic or human, is and remains one with Him.

Remember, whether fish, foul, angelic or human, all life is One with the infinite Ocean of Love that is our Source.

Devil's wrath

Interestingly enough, this woman's husband had experienced a similar perplexing childhood church-related situation as a young boy. They are older now, but the memories of those Sunday mornings of long ago are still vivid. The husband related being frightened out of his shoes. There was the lamenting coming from the pulpit, beseeching the congregation to individually come down to the front of the church to be saved from the devil's wrath, or they wouldn't go to heaven. Some parishioners wept. He was scared to death that someone was going to grab his hand and drag him kicking and screaming to the front of the church. He vowed never to go back to this shout-it-out, jumper church.

In later years, he wondered why the big people had been crying, and just what was it they were being saved from? Even to this day his questions go unanswered. However, the fact remains that heaven versus hell is still vividly in the picture of his thoughts of the afterlife.

More than a half century has gone by, but his emotions and fear from that so-called religious experience still well-up inside of him today when he recalls that Sunday morning. He has come to the realization that the only thing anyone needs to be saved from is his own errant thoughts and actions.

Impressions

The paintings of the Old Masters, exquisitely rendered as they are, have also played a part in inadvertently placing detailed images in our mind's-eye of horned demons with pitchforks in hand, dark howling monsters, and giant torturing flames engulfing horrified naked bodies. These remarkable artists may have been realists, but their work could be described as impressionistic, in that their depictions have left such an impression on the conscience of mankind to this day. Their images illustrating the hereafter remain deeply imprinted into the human psyche. Small wonder these visions project themselves into the unsuspecting thought at the strangest times, in the minds of babes, or in the aforementioned moments before one's death.

The ridiculousness of this dark visionary concept found in virtually all religions seems to have done just the opposite of its intended purpose of keeping people on the straight and narrow pathway. It has encouraged many a perpetrator into the "catch me if-you-can" attitude similar to that of a young person's feeling of his own invincibility. There is far too often in no wise a sense of accountability in having to pay the reaping for what one has sown.

It would seem that the threat of hellfire and impending doom has done little to diminish the sins of our world. Fortunately, most of us inherently choose to do good rather than perpetrating an evil. Shouldn't it be natural for a person to envision, adore, and love the idea of harmony lived on earth, here and now as it is in heaven? We need to be teaching our children that they are Godly beings with eternal life, yet still responsible, and that their every thought and deed has its own consequence.

What we say and what we do
ultimately comes back to us
so let us own our responsibility,
place it in our hands,
and carry it with dignity and strength.

—***Gloria Evangelina Anzaldua***

How profoundly the experiences of our early childhood influence the rest of our lives. Have you ever asked yourself, where is this so-greatly-feared hell? We seem to be fluctuating between a God way up there and a devil way down below—we go down and up, up and down in our thinking, in our formulation of thoughts. The conundrum of God, man, and the devil seems to be rewritten and reinforced with every generation. "The devil made me do it," is an easy out or flimsy excuse for the lack of one's self-control and the misuse of one's divine inheritance.

Centuries ago hell was declared by the early clergy to be found in the center of the earth. That's an almost believable scenario for some, since volcanoes erupt from inside the earth, spewing out fire and brimstone. As time passed by, the scientists of the world revealed that indeed, hell was not to be found in the middle of the earth after all. And the church reluctantly recanted their claim. The site for their impending doom had to be moved—send Lucifer a memo! It was then relegated into the realm of the mystical, where it has remained—until this day!

Today, it should be plain to us that hell is not a geographic location or a dreaded destination. Hell is merely a human experience—the scenarios of discomfort and disease, this so-called "vengeance of the Lord," comes to us from our own erroneous thoughts, misdeeds, or fears, as a kind of karmic boomerang. Once again, we bring a temporary hell upon ourselves. Thankfully, there truly is no such thing as an evil power, or an evil place, only the negative energy a man invests into his personal mis-creations. These man-made-created evils are required per Universal Law to be transmuted with right thinking and restitution as we individually work out our transgressions and misguided perceptions. Then and only then can our overseer, our own silent watcher, who is the Christ-Self in each of us, absolve us, forgive us of these misconceptions, hopefully, just as we are forgiving others. His grace will be sufficient for thee.

The Faces of Sin

So still your voice
And speak to me of
Neither sin nor goodness.

For if a thousand mortal tongues
Describe but one sin,
That sin will have a thousand faces,
And not one will know the other.

And I will not know a single face of sin,
But I know the touch of it.
And I would not do battle against sin,
But would welcome righteousness;
Then know that sin is gone.

—***D.L. Harris***

Kingdom of harmony

A human mind filled with goodness and love has nothing to fear; it creates nothing that has to be transmuted or forgiven. When we truly discern this glorious fact, we will begin to understand clearly that while heaven, too, is not a physical location, it

IS real, and is in actuality a higher realm in our already overlapping dimensions.

Heaven is an experience, an experience of harmony and joy, a state of Divine Consciousness, albeit possible in the human realm. It has been said that the word "heaven" actually means "even." To have all thoughts even would be to have no imbalance from any influence other than the Divine.

Jesus didn't give a location for hell. He knew it did not exist, because it is self-created misery, which our thoughts bring into our own experience. But he did share with us the locality of Heaven, knowing its reality, when he said, *"the Kingdom of Heaven, harmony is within ourselves, our spirit's consciousness."*

> *A man seeking heaven outside himself,*
> *Is a seeker in vain.*
>
> —***C.S. McClintock***

Heaven on earth or the euphoric condition of heaven in our consciousness, has always been our birthright. For *"Thy will* (to) *be done,"* we humans must certainly think from our highest mind, which acknowledges only one God, good, not two opposing powers. Do not let your free-wheeling free will, drag you down to the depths of carnal or less than perfect thinking. Keeping your conscious thought-processes ascended entails thinking from the heights of your own Christ-Consciousness.

There are many who would say we cannot experience heaven unless we first die. Even our most modern dictionaries cling to the antiquated and pre-modern concept of a blissful location in the sky where good Christians gather after death. A few brief but pertinent definitions are: "heaven—an abode of the deity and of the blessed dead, a domelike firmament above the earth." Further, a more realistic definition from Webster, states: "A spiritual state of everlasting communion with God."

Some psychologists say that the visions of either heaven or hell are generated by a chemical reaction in our brains at the time of death. The truth of the matter is that heaven is a reality. It simply needs to be redefined. Heaven is a blissful state of Divine harmony in the conscious and subconscious. Doesn't it stand to reason that if God, Spirit lives all life simultaneously, including we people on earth, then this One Spirit is our spirit as well.

We dwell in the glorious omnipresent realms of Spirit, which include all dimensions, yet here we are without eyes to see it. We already reside within this Divine garden. Still we continue to hold heaven as a mystical dimension above and apart from ourselves, when all the while even scientists are telling us we may be living in as many as eleven dimensions simultaneously, albeit, aware of only the one.

Many mansions

No matter how many mansions, dimensions, we find in our Father's house, we will discover that all these realms or levels are nonetheless still within the One Omnipotent, within the Spirit of our Source. In other words, all levels, dimensions, or mansions, above the third, the 3D, are heavenly endowed and can be glimpsed, known and felt even in our present experience.

There are a fortunate few who have glimpsed what heaven means to them even while they were still present in the material realm; some during near death experiences. What they have glimpsed is not merely a chemical reaction in the brain, but a higher degree of elevated conscious perception, seeing within these mansions or realms the fact of Love and Harmony, the beauty that permeates all existence. In this exaltation we recognize the spirit of all individualities as oftentimes youthful, always vibrant, and whole. This epiphany can happen just as simply to a child, an older man, woman, or a sage, because all spirits and individualities live forever, in unison, without limits of time and space or matter.

Neurosurgeon, Dr. Eben Alexander writes about his near death experience, concerning the afterlife, in his book, *Proof of Life*.

During his week in a coma, and on the fringes of death, he was miraculously elevated to a full understanding that the false belief that we can somehow be separated from God, our Source, is the origin of every form of anxiety in the universe.

He realized that nothing can tear us from God, and said that this is the single most important thing he could have ever learned—Oneness. As he was experiencing this out of body phenomenon, he so completely forgot his mortal identity, that he was somehow granted full access to, and awareness of, the cosmic being of himself—and everyone. What he discovered "out beyond" was the indescribable immensity and complexity of the universe, and that consciousness is the basis of all that exists.

He was so completely connected to that glorious immensity, which one might describe as heaven, that there was often no real differentiation between "himself" and the world in which he was moving. He felt the joy of experiencing the basic purpose of consciousness and spirit simultaneously—that the universe has no beginning or end, and God-Intelligence is entirely present within every particle of it.

"I was blind but now I see."—He related that "now" had an entirely new meaning as he perceived just how blind we are to the full nature and dynamics of the spiritual universe we exist in on earth—especially people much like he had been, who had thought that physicality was the core reality.

Dr. Alexander added that during this time he experienced many epiphanies of spectacular enlightenment. He had the sensation of being able to see in all directions simultaneously, and also had the sensation of being above linear time—the feeling of being above everything. He brought back with him a vivid remembrance of this celestial journey.

After his return to the body, his medical staff was astounded to find his complete healing of what had heretofore been pronounced a terminal illness. He continues even today to carry exact memories with him of the profound feeling he had been shown in what he later called 'the core'— the intensity within the center of unconditional love!

Heaven is not a geographic destination,
It truly is, a blissful state of consciousness.

—***C.S. McClintock***

Heaven is the awareness of eternal life! Simply put, heaven is omnipresent, the beautiful harmony of Love manifested.

Man's purpose on earth is two-fold:

First—to advance out of the material world and its limited thinking, overcome and leave the senses behind, and to elevate our consciousness into the higher, spiritual dimensions of the fourth and fifth, etc., where perfection reigns in all its glory. Yes, and then we will see that the angels are right here with us, beside us, in our overlapping realms. Our religious figures are here as well, be they Jesus, Buddha, Muhammad, or Moses, along with our loved ones passed. They are all right here in our midst, receptive to our beck and call.

Second—Since all mansions or dimensions, are within the magnitude of God, and all is spiritual, then it is our duty, our mission, and should be our joyful privilege, to bring the spiritual qualities of heaven back to earth—back to the first, second and third dimensions. The heavenly love and peace of the Divine have actually never left the first three levels. It is only man's limited consciousness that has drawn the veil.

Thirdly—It is an absolute requirement for all humans, that, in this lifetime or the next or the next, we must attain that mind which was also in the Master. In this heavenly-type state of mind there is no negativity to be thought, imagined, or recognized, thus no manifestation thereof. Nothing to fear... "not even fear itself," as FDR so eloquently stated. Then we too, will be mindful of only loving and forgiving thoughts. Man's creative thinking will no longer conjure up anything less than goodness and sin and evil will be no more. Then we surely will have ears to hear the angels singing, and clear eyes to see Heaven on Earth made manifest!

Heaven is an experience, an experience of harmony and joy, a state of Divine Consciousness, albeit possible in the human realm.

What the caterpillar calls the end of the world,
the Master calls a butterfly.
—**Richard Bach**

Chapter 25

THE END TIMES

If you do not change direction you may end up where you are heading.

—*Lao Tzu*

As I scan the media outlets, bookshelves, television, radio, CD s, and videos I am overwhelmed with all the attention given to the finality of our numbered days on earth: the Apocalypse Now, Armageddon, end of the world, the end of days, the Mayan Calendar concluding, the Rapture, the Second Coming of the Christ, etc.— as if doom and destruction, or some kind of supernatural deliverance, were somehow a foregone conclusion, when God is good, and Love is the substance and master of the universe!

How thankful am I, and we all should be, for the enlightened understanding of our own elevating process. A *rapturous* occasion, indeed, is about to take place, as all of us consciously yet lovingly ascend into our Higher-Self, our Christ-Self, our individualized I Am Presence. And all the angels will indeed be singing our praises as humanity comes to its collective senses.

The "Second Coming" in reality represents each man raising his consciousness into his own Christ-Self. Yes, each of us rapturously, euphorically, and mystically transporting, blending our spirit, and its now purified soul with our Higher-God-Self, just as the Master demonstrated. He showed us that through this raised consciousness the only things to be ended or transformed are man's own transitory creations, the formations of negativity recorded in his soul. This conscious awareness will be a true ecstasy, an exaltation of mind and feelings, a genuine transforming rapture.

Merriam-Webster had this to say about regeneration: "1. Cause to be spiritually reborn 2. To cause to be completely reformed (physically) 3. To bring into existence again."

However, spirit being reborn is an absolute impossibility. Spirit, Life, and Its manifestations can never die or come to an end, they are eternally one with their Source; never extinguished; but forever changing and progressing. The comprehension of the spiritual nature of all things and its evolvement only need to be awakened to or "reborn" in our own minds. The fiery debate over the anomaly of heaven and hell becomes a mute point, a non-discussion, because all life is eternal, no death! Only change!

The same is true of matter, its atoms are full of life and intelligence, with intelligent design. The material world or universes cannot die; like the Phoenix, they are spiritual energy emanating from the One Source, merely changing, ending one formation and energetically re-manifesting, rising up from the ashes again into a new tangible form of existence or regeneration, like ice into liquid into vapor. However infinitesimal, they never come to an end. They are elements, alive! All things are changing, evolving. continually becoming different configurations. As Richard Bach suggests, "What the caterpillar calls the end of the word, the Master calls a butterfly."

Yes, the world as we know it may very well be coming to a conclusion of sorts, but in this end will be our new beginning. Spiritual adjustments are already in the works. How harsh our earth changes will be, has yet to be determined. World conditions will be found to be commensurate to the harmony within each man's thought, which multiplied equals mass consciousness.

Love and compassion for his fellowman and his world must predominate. Our Mother Earth and the spiritual hierarchy will no longer permit the ravaging of our earth to continue. The intolerable treatment of our planet and our fellow man has to stop. Human free will must give up anger, hate, greed, and prejudice of any kind, including religious, and then give way to Divine Will, opting for love, sharing, kindness and forgiveness.

The 2,000-year reign of the Piscean Age, the 12th sign of the Zodiac is fast coming to a close. The Age of Aquarius is at hand. The spiritual shift in thinking has begun anew. Will mankind usher her in on bended knee with folded hands in supplication? Or, God help us, with pugilism and fisticuffs, our self-induced Armageddon?

Again, no matter which direction humanity chooses, there can be no such event as the end of life, only a conclusion to the way things were. This Aquarian Age will not allow for evil thoughts to exist; thus the phrase, speak no evil, hear no evil, see no evil, will prevail. Such thoughts will become obsolete in mortal man's now clear and exalted consciousness.

Please see with me that it makes little difference whether our physical body is stopped by natural causes, a planetary shift of the poles, or a bomb. Whether in or out of our material form of a body, our true and timeless identity, our life, spirit, soul, continues consciously onward, through rapturous journey after journey, life without end.

Nonetheless there is this one caveat—the cessation of thinking up evil must come either through suffering and its lessons, or through the more desired path of enlightened and loving advancement; which naturally eliminates all discord from mortal thought and action, hence no manifestation.

Gradually yielding up the material paradigm, however, doesn't mean devaluing this "performing arts center." It requires us instead to embrace it in all its richness and glory by giving up the continual rehearsing of negativity, the attitude of a planet gone wrong, thus fueling the predictions of impending destruction, doom and gloom.

A thousand years of peace must begin with peace in the heart of every man. The countries of our world, the people of our earth, who would harbor any hate, prejudice, malice or terrorism toward their neighbors, their planetary brothers and sisters, will possibly per the Universal Law of Life be removed from their present destructive physical existence; for their error will rebound upon itself, their negativity imploding from within.

The revelation within Revelations is this, that evil is a mind-game soon coming to a close, coming to its end times! It's a game that will not be allowed to continue.

"And the great dragon (the sum total of all evil) *was cast out,* (and transformed) *that old serpent, called the Devil, and Satan, which deceiveth the whole world: he was cast out."* (Revelation 12:9) All negativity will be ended, will be cast out of man's imaginative and creative thinking. And the 1,000-Year Reign begins now.

World conditions will be found to be commensurate to the harmony within each man's thought, which multiplied equals mass consciousness.

We should be looking into the eyes
of every individualized being, great or small,
earthly or otherworldly, human or ET, and seeing
the light of spirit within every divine creature.

Chapter 26

WHO WE ARE NOT

Ye are not who ye think ye are,
Ye are, though, who ye think ye are not.

—*C.S. McClintock*

Why is it of such great value for us to know how we people originated and who we really are? At this particular point in our earthly existence it is not of great importance. However, to achieve the very highest understanding of the human experience, we may begin with the singular and elevated perception of revealing who we are not.

You and I are currently in our highest evolutionary state for the world mentally, physically, and spiritually. Forget Darwin's theory of evolution and the principles of natural selection, which describe how our bodies have evolved and been modified over eons of time, and how we have adapted to our ever changing environment. No matter how intriguingly true these theories are, they are not pertinent to our spiritual growth. Instead, they are helping us to better understand who we are not.

How has the automobile changed over the last 100 years? How about a caterpillar transforming itself into a butterfly through metamorphosis? What difference does it make to the fundamental knowledge we must attain about the center of our being, the spiritual core? These changes are wonderfully interesting, but vehicular and physical variations in differing forms aren't really a concern at this stage in our spiritual education and evolvement.

Perhaps we will all finally reach the perspective, the perception, that physical evolution is of little consequence. It is our requisite spiritual evolution that is of paramount importance, and tells us who we really are. We will each find this light in our own way and eventually take on spiritual wings and mentally fly higher.

While we inhabit a bodily vehicle for our creative earthly use, during our worldly playhouse of experiences, our body-temple will continue to be maintained and sustained by the All-that-Is, its true and only origin, the shared Source of all Life. Remember, there can be no such thing as an intelligence, existence or an experience apart from God.

So, for instance, if we ourselves were to land on our moon or on another planet for that matter, the existing indigenous life-forms we might encounter there would not necessarily look like us. Even so, the reasoning we find in Oneness should tell us that we must be sharing a common source. After all, their bodily-vehicular forms would have had to adapt to their particular environment, their own planetary atmospheric conditions. So then, as outsiders wouldn't we be considered the extraterrestrials, and looking mighty odd to them?

A dictionary says creation is the bringing of something into existence, the world and everything in it, and a product of human imagination or invention. It should be worth noting that the intelligentsia within the dictionary did not even reference the whole of universal creation, or man! Did the big bang start it all? Did we evolve from creationism, evolution, intelligent design? Or has our physical evolvement been accelerated with the help of ETs as has been recently proclaimed?

If—and I repeat, if—the ancient astronaut theorists have their say, then we homo sapiens may have been genetically engineered thousands of years ago in test tubes or artificially inseminated by extraterrestrials, or the gods, as early man deemed them for their magical feats and miraculous flying machines coming down from the heavens. Scientists say these ETs did this genetic engineering by using the true "Tree of Knowledge," the tree-like make-up of our physical DNA. It is speculated that they may have actually made us in their own "image and likeness," to which some attribute this Biblical quote.

Whether or not we believe the possibilities in these scientific speculations is insignificant. Perhaps these theories challenge us to see better who we are not. Just because a scientist cannot see a spirit under a microscope has no bearing on the fact that true Life with consciousness and free will is invisible to the eye and simply wears the material form of a body, whether human or other-worldly. We as spiritual beings, divine entities, are governing the body vehicle. We direct its thoughts and actions.

The fact is that a higher source than even themselves, the extraterrestrials, may have possibly engineered their physical form as well! Unlike the early church teaching, God is not endemic only to earth. We need to move past lingering under the tree of knowledge and intellectualism, the supposed intellectuality, of science, to the refreshing "Tree of Life" where all creation originates from One Source, Spirit; and moreover, is expressing individualities of Itself at different levels and realms, and wearing various forms.

True life-spirit will never be found in test tubes or DNA. Yet we search, speculate, postulate, and sift through matter only to realize over and over again who we are not. And the beat goes on.

If we expand on the ET theory, this schoolroom of earth might better be likened to a nursery school of sorts for these advanced beings. These gods from the heavens, or star people, as the Hopi Indians have called them, may have brought to us some of their higher knowledge from other planets, as the worldwide ancient petroglyphs of old portray. Suppose we have been helped along with our invention, scientific discovery, or enhanced genetics. Wouldn't that be a good thing?

Since we are speaking hypothetically, maybe we should be considering these other-worldly helpers as guardians assisting the progression of our race, rather than seeing them in an adversarial role. Possibly their goal would be to advance us, to help us evolve into more highly developed thinking and a more elevated spiritual awareness. Could it be that they are the advanced evolution of humans, after our graduation from earth, possibly appearing from our next plane of existence? Or even more intriguing, perhaps they might be you and I in a higher dimension wearing a bodysuit suitable to their planet's environment.

Stretching our imagination further, why couldn't our spirit be multifaceted, as our scientists are now speculating. While we may not be consciously aware—think about it—our spirit could possibly be experiencing multiple dimensions at the same time. After all, is this spirit not a portion of the One Spirit with the potential for infinite possibilities? Remember, statistics tell us, that only 10 percent of our brain and thinking capacity is utilized. Imagine the fantastical and possibly mystical discoveries that might be found in that other 90 percent if tapped into. Only 10 percent. Hmm. Can you even imagine becoming more than this limited mortal you are currently experiencing?

Adding to our hypothesis, ancient astronaut theorists suggest that for our betterment, maybe the extraterrestrials have been engineering our development all the way from the incubator through our final graduation. Perhaps they have never been exposed to the negativity that we humans have subjected ourselves to and consequently have had to endure. After all, there is a possibility that sin and evil are only an earthly, man-made concept.

There is also a possibility that the ETs may not be who we think they are. Heck! They may not even know who they are not. Maybe by contrast, we could in some minor fashion help school them. Perhaps we would be able to help teach them that they too, are indeed spirit-beings wearing their particular forms, however that form may appear. Again, we are not the body, nor are they. Neither of us are merely material.

We would need to reach the understanding that both we and they are simply using these bodily vehicles for playing our roles, our parts in the never ending infinite games of universal existence. All levels and planes of life continue to evolve, even galactically. And the show goes on.

We are, I hope, coming to understand that all physical worlds, consists only of *spiritual materials* and are ever evolving, forever changing their forms. Everything changes. Energy moves from one configuration to the next and the next as dictated by the degree of spiritual thought and the elevation thereof. All is God!

What we ARE are divine spiritual beings of intelligence, as are all life-forms including the entities and spirits wearing the body-form from their particular world, planet, or universe. It is to be hoped that all are expressing and experiencing His will!

No matter what planet we are coming from, the fact of our *true being* is always going to be the same. There are thousands of stories about people finding themselves hovering above their own broken or sometimes expired bodies. It was suddenly very clear to them what they were not—they were not their physical form. In fact they felt completely separated from the material. Yet they were very aware of being spiritually alive and fully conscious, and many returned to write their vivid accounts of this elevated state of awareness.

The reality of their spiritual nature was now vibrantly evident; experienced outside of and without a material form. Yet, they were truly alive with none of the former pain or encumbrances. As they approached the brilliance of the white light, they felt a wonderful exaltation, a kind of euphoria. With their individual consciousness fully intact, these people felt they were sent back to share their incredible stories because it wasn't their time yet. And they returned eager to tell us of glimpsing who they were, after understanding fully who they were not! In my book *God We Are,* I describe it this way:

Imagine with me if you will, a cow or a horse standing along a country road within his or her pasture and watching as vehicles pass by. The animal sees a vehicle. Does the animal know that there is a human being directing that vehicle from within? Or does the animal really know or care that there is a separate intelligence within the vehicle operating and directing its movements?

As the ultimate intelligence in this world, do we really see that the One Spirit of God is driving all human vehicles, (and all life-forms) *or do we even care? Do we see only the outer appearance of the form? Do we see only the color, shape, age, gender, clothing, etc., of the human vehicle?*

We should be looking into the eyes of every individualized being, great or small, earthly or other-worldly, human or ET, and seeing the light of the spirit within every divine creature. After all is said and done and speculated upon, this I Am-Spirit is WHO WE ARE!

One can thus attain immortal
consciousness and awaken to the true self,
God, the real nature of man.

—***Ramana Maharshi***

The one eternal lesson for us all
is how better we can love
and bring peace to our surroundings.

Chapter 27

WHERE IS YOUR VISION?

In order to experience everyday spirituality,
We need to remember that we are spiritual beings
Spending some time in a human body.

—***Barbara De Angelis***

Yesterday I passed a church whose marquee displayed this question: "Why don't I always feel God's presence?" Well, spiritually inquisitive readers of this book may already know the answer to that question.

First and foremost, if you didn't understand already, as many do of course, you know by now that the Presence of God, the Kingdom of God, is not outside yourself, but forever within. You are a spiritual, divine being; you are not merely a physical body walking about the earth. God's spirit is your spirit, for you and the Father are one, just as *"I and the Father are one,"* as stated by the Master. Holding this vision allows you to feel the Father's Presence within at all times.

Second: Having this knowledge, you realize that you have the ability to be in this world, yet not of this world, be in this body, but not of, or better still, not dominated by this body. You are not ruled by the senses, by the environment, education, or by appearances. Your focus remains clear on the fact that whether within, "My Kingdom," or without, in the worldly kingdom, all is within the I Am, therefore all is spiritually good, even the harsh learning experiences from our imperfections. Sometimes our acute shortcomings lead us to believe that we've made our bed in hell. Regardless, the Presence, the Force is always with us, and awaits our beck and call.

Third: We need to realize that the responsibilities for our own paybacks, the promissory note for our debts, is in essence a good thing. Remember, even Saul's blinding turned out to be a valuable learning experience, albeit a large check to write! Evil and sin are only human mistakes, mere human concepts, mortal creations soon to be brushed off with an eraser by our own hand, our transmutation as it were. On the blackboard of life's lessons, all advancements are to be valued; the so-called bad experiences simply move us temporarily back a step; the old right versus wrong two-step—two steps forward, one step back.

Now we have come to the conclusion that in the end, these forward and backward steps, whether called good or evil, formulate the sum total of our productive learning process in this wonderful earthly schoolroom and are so recorded by the soul. We know that to "always feel God's presence" ultimately depends on where our vision stays focused and what these lessons teach us.

Our co-creative status in this school of performing arts will keep turning our inharmonious spending into discord, burdens, and disease until we see the light and right our course, which depends entirely on our mind's thoughts and ensuing actions. Then we too, can triumph over all challenges with that same radiant understanding and clear vision which turned Saul into a Saint Paul. Are we focused on our shortcomings, or on the bright spiritual path before us?

We will still be present, in this world, as beautiful it is, yet thinking out from "My Kingdom," when we are allowing the intuitive feelings of our Higher-Self to monitor our every thought and action. This is the Shepherding Presence of Love in application, examining and watching over our every idea., thought by thought.

Fourth: You might note that the second most important word, the first being "God" of course, in the church's marquee question, is the word "feel." Now you are becoming more and more aware that you can consciously think about God, love, compassion, mercy, forgiveness, and so on, but unless you put these qualities into concentrated feeling there will be no active expression, nor outward manifestation.

Thinking without feeling generates no action; thus, no creative, angelic-type forces are evidenced forth in your experience. The laws of attraction, perpetually moving energies and vibrations, impressed upon our human subconscious, won't work unless feeling with heart is involved. Then they become a part of Universal Love and Intelligence, a power for the collective good. Here we feel we are working in at- one-ment (atonement) with the Divine Creative Presence.

At this point you may be wondering how you can stay focused and continue to feel the warmth of your spiritual nature when your mind is in the business office or out to lunch. You may sometimes feel like you are in limbo out in left field, mesmerized by that certain someone or something, or distracted by outside pressures and obligations. The fears and stresses of this world would try to block His Presence from being felt. Yet it should go without saying, His Presence, His Spirit is our spirit as well, forever One. And when we truly embrace this oneness, nothing can block the inspiration we need to move forward.

Presence of harmony

This life is not a fairy tale. The issues we all face are not virtual, but real. You might compare our individual story to *Snow White and the Seven Dwarfs*. We came into this dimension "white as snow," perfect and spiritual. However, gradually over the millenniums we have become bogged down in a limited and sensual mindset, having wavered from our higher vision. We've let the lower senses take us over. We've forgotten that our true, God-given identity is snow-white, spiritually pure.

Walt Disney was a very spiritual metaphysician, you see. His elevated genius was obvious throughout his magical kingdom. He was very wise and aware of what the seven negative influences could do to us human beings. Not the whimsical characters, Happy, Sleepy, Sneezy, Grumpy, Dopey, Bashful, and Doc, but the original seven sins of wrath, greed, sloth, pride, lust, envy, and gluttony. Our Spiritual-Self must not become dwarfed by the enormous weight of the negative effluvia in material thinking. Fortunately, as the wonderful fable illustrates, the best in us finally wins out and we live happily ever after.

Never shall we forget, as we claim and live our true identity as divine individualities, we are also required to view others in the same light; all working together toward a more harmonious outcome. Indulge me for a moment if you will, I'd like to use a few illustrative metaphors of my own. Picture an octopus with his eight tentacles. If the octopus was to endow each of his tentacles with free will thinking of its own, imagine the consequences. Disharmony and starvation would be the probable outcome, because none of these eight extremities would be working together, toward one end, with the same goals in mind.

Or consider a centipede giving each of its 100 legs free will to think and act on its own. Imagine 100 legs in chaos! One leg running, one leg standing still, another walking, and yet another stepping sideways. How could the centipede ever advance? Synchronization results only when each leg comes to the realization that it is governed by its one central mind, and should be working in concert with the whole. Fortunately, in the case of an octopus or a centipede, obedience is required, and each member must be still and listen to its source, working together synergistically.

So here we are, our thoughts and bodies moving in all directions. Yet, we too can all work together with one agenda and purpose, if we will quiet our own thoughts and listen to the will of the one Mind—our central intelligence agent who is our one common Source.

We humans are like ten billion limbs of the Omniscient-Mind-God, each with our own unique set of footprints. What wonderful harmony awaits us, when together we understand that "everyone I meet along my path is myself," as the Zen proverb says. We are each an independent but indispensible "leg," so to speak, yet are also each distinct individualizations of the One Mind.

Hopefully the proverbial cartoon light bulb over our head will turn on as we realize that our bodies and minds are active extensions, working portions, of the whole of God. And, guess what? These same bodies do not even belong to us! Do the 100 legs belong only to themselves or the centipede? To the centipede of course. Just as all human bodies are extensions, appendages of, and belong to, the One All-that-Is. Each is an instrument of the Divine.

Are we finally seeing that we are singularly responsible for creatively directing our form, His body, with our obedient thoughts and actions? What a divine privilege! Furthermore, this marvelous vehicle we are operating is actually only a rental. We are leasing it from our Source, His Majesty. Are we being conscientious concerning its care, diligent about servicing our loaner vehicle?" We should hope we are not stressing it out by continually driving it 90 miles an hour, or recklessly fueling it with drugs, alcohol or smokes, or defacing it with graffiti. What in the world would our Owner think of us!

Presence of blessings

So, where is our vision? Where is our thinking taking us? Are we moving forward, or just existing in our own chaotic creation? We have learned that this life we think we are living is only a hiccup in time, in our eternal lifetime of lives, perhaps in differing personality experiences. We will be graded as we go along with each performance or embodiment, not only in that particular role, but in every second of each sojourn. We won't be judged by the antiquated and outdated vision of an old bearded man in the sky throwing lightning bolts at us. Nor will He judge us with a vengeance. However, our every thought and action is lovingly being recorded in our soul, after being scrutinized, balanced and weighed by the cosmic law of correction.

Imagine an ongoing, eternal neon scoreboard of our accumulated rights and wrongs flickering above our heads. Remember this, there is no such thing as a secret thought or action. Every jot and tittle is instantly marked down, in plain view, all pluses and minuses being calculated by the Universal Laws of Life, and policed by our own Self. Yes, "Self" with a capitol "S", our Christ-Self, our Higher-Self which is forever watching our every step, and willing, directing us back to its spiritual fold. We might call it a portion of the greater vision, the ascending process, because we now know that every right and good thought is an ascending action, even right in the midst of our daily experiences.

Remember, you can always feel God's presence, as you are a light unto this world. So gather your feelings and energies into your very large spotlight; because where your vision is, and where your thoughts are focused, that's the direction in which you are pointing that huge beam of creative light-energy, toward which you will walk.

Like attracts like, and light attracts light. Aim high your vision. Be still. Meditate on heavenly matters. Don't scatter your energies by continually stepping sideways or backwards, thinking of the things you don't want in your life, ruminating in self-pity or resentment. Your feelings will only perpetuate the negative, and keep it coming back to you.

Whatever you dwell upon, you will be precipitating. Continually give thanks, for all your blessings, the positive aspects of your experience. And quite frankly, give thanks for your hardships, they are your school of hard knocks—their discomfort gives you the impetus to move forward. Feel His Grace, your grace, showering you with abundance. Initially, blessings may manifest in subtle spiritual ways, but soon your goodness will appear in all manner of manna, that is, something valuable that comes unexpectedly, in tangible form. Your soulful experiences will travel with you accordingly.

Presence of joy

"A merry heart doeth good like a medicine:
but a broken spirit drieth the bones."

— ***Proverbs 17:22***

Our church marquee might also have asked, "Have you found joy in your life? And have you brought joy to other's lives?" This was the ancient Egyptian question, posed by Morgan Freeman to Jack Nicholson, in the movie, *The Bucket List*. Do you seek happiness only for yourself, or might you also seek it for another? Are we solemn and self-serving, or happily selfless in serving? Our life, our learning experiences, and our spiritual path should be service with a smile! To feel God's Presence is coincidentally to feel joy.

Our dictionary defines happiness as: "Showing joy, contentment, pleasure, delight... mental and moral health, relative permanence of well-being."

It tells us that joy means "Feelings of great happiness or pleasure, especially of an elevated or spiritual kind."

Joy is happiness on an extended vacation!

—***C.S. McClintock***

Peripheral thinking includes others in our outreach of joy and goodwill. It excludes the tunnel vision of selfishness.

It is man's choice to see and feel the joy of his glass, his life, especially when it appears only half full. He deserves an elevated spiritual kind of happiness, which looks away from the negative or empty portion, knowing it will be filled in His good timing, being content with his present blessings.

Too many focus on the infelicity of the empty half, thus drying up and withering the flesh with worry, and unease, wearing them down with stress, and possibly manifesting disease.

Are you aware that scientists say our body rebuilds 98 percent of itself every twelve months? The All that Is, is the 100 percent joyous-happy energy we call love. If we were to keep our hearts and minds in a state of continuous peace and bliss, the natural reproducing process of our atoms and cells would operate without the interference of negativity. The ensuing regeneration would manifest health and wholeness, a lack of aging would be the result. It should be our privilege to keep our minds focused on the vision of our role within this Oneness of Him. Let us be the recipients of this joy and youthfulness, this All-that-Is, on earth, as it is in Spirit.

For men are made for happiness,
and anyone who is completely happy
has a right to say to himself:
'I am doing God's will on earth.'

—***Anton Chekov***

Presence of Light

Our body, our "*temple,*" as the Master called it, this "church" where a portion of our Christ-Spirit resides, is full of light to direct us on the course in which we presently need to proceed. *"His Word is a lamp unto our feet,"* His direction a light unto our path. Webster's definition of light is: "radiation that makes vision possible." So when you are stumbling around in the dark, absorbed in worldly thoughts, know that it will take a conscious effort to change and illuminate your thinking, turn your experience around, and transform it. Wherever you are, there is already an abundance of Light available. Your thoughts however, must have feeling, the feeling that "I want to take action." Then you must flip the switch within, to see and experience the shining of the One Light.

Paul's advice to Timothy was to *"think on these things."* Where is your vision? Where is your beam of light directed? Be careful. If you are in a glass factory, hopefully you are concentrating on blowing hot glass. If you are working in a steel mill, you may be focused on melting iron ore. While working the beams of a skyscraper, you'd better be riveted on the job at hand because every step, every footprint, counts.

Wherever you have placed yourself, you are now conscious of the need to stay focused on your objective. Every movement mentally and physically counts. By the same token, currently your spirit is exactly where your consciousness and free will have placed it. Your spiritual work is in concentrating on feeling the Presence within, the Everlasting Light, as often as possible, if not *always*.

But then, you say, that's pretty difficult to do when I am angry about my spouse, my teenager, my co-worker, or when I am in heavy traffic. But just remember no one person or thing can make you happy or sad or upset. These are emotions you allow others to generate within yourself.

When you hear the question, "Why can't I always feel God's presence?" You now have your answer. Of course you can! At any moment night or day, you can take action, and consciously make the connection. Let the neon-lighted marquee of your temple-self read loud and clear, "I always feel God's presence—and His joy. Laugh-out-loud, rejoice! LOL.

I happily see that Presence in everyone and in every life-form moving about in this beautiful world.

Man's ability to laugh aloud
at himself, with himself,
could be his ultimate clowning glory!

—***C.S. McClintock***

… and Jesus said, Father how thou hast glorified me, not the commonly mistranslated, misinterpreted, "Why hast thou forsaken me?"

Chapter 28

JOY TO THE WORLD

Joy to the world the Lord has come,
Let earth receive her King.

—***Isaac Watts***

A small group of like-minded individuals, including Guy Ballard and Alice Schutz, came together in the 1940s, and published some of the most enlightened literature that has ever been presented to the West, which is now given for your consideration. A large portion of this information has been corroborated by the works of many, including: Deepak Chopra, Baird T. Spaulding, Shri Chin Moy, Yogananda, Nityananda, and St. Germain.

In this I sincerely, and with all respect, remind the reader that the more receptive one is, the more he receives.

Alice Schutz writes:

"Jesus started certain work for the purification of the earth and the freedom of mankind, which is only now being completed. He came to earth at a point of great darkness and through his mission the currents of negativity were reversed.

"As a small child, Jesus first attended classes in the Temple at Karnak, Egypt. He was walked there daily by his mother, Mary, who was very aware of his life's mission. The family was in Egypt for a number of years before returning to the land of his birth.

"The Christian dispensation was designed at inner levels by Ascended Spiritual Masters. When the drama of what was to come, was shown on the cosmic screen about thirty, sixth ray individuals, who had much development and mastery, volunteered for the initiation of the public crucifixion. Jesus was the one chosen, and then other highly evolved individualities were chosen who would come along with him and be the guards, protectors, his mother, his father, the Disciples and helpers. The scene was being set. The three wise men with Jesus formed the square, the squaring of the circle, its completion.

"Jesus, also at times called his guru and teacher, Lord Maitreya, 'Father.' Jesus had the ability to recognize his teacher-guide, in the spirit, while yet a small boy. Their attunement and association grew, and their connection became closer and closer until they were as one in action. You may remember the form of the white dove descending into Jesus during the baptism at the age of thirty. This is when the healings and miracles performed by Jesus began. His God mission had been initiated.

"The Master Jesus was in training in various retreats, monasteries and such, even as a child, and also during the period between age twelve and twenty-eight. Most of those years, he was studying in the East and Far East. In fact, before his father Joseph passed on, he informed Jesus that prior to attaining his majority, he would be required to journey to India on foot to receive training from Joseph's teacher and master, the Divine Director. Jesus made that journey soon after Joseph's passing. He was in a monastery in the Kashmir Valley for five years, and there are scrolls preserved there, which he wrote himself. Even today, records of Jesus' studies in the Far East are continually being discovered or unearthed.

"He was in the retreat for some length of time, when one day he telepathically received the mantra, 'the I AM is the resurrection and the life,' from a Master. A Master can convey an idea or message to his pupil on an inner level, and it need not necessarily be through the spoken word. He had received no prior recognition from this Master, although this sage knew perfectly well who young Jesus was to become, his mission, and of his visit.

"That statement was vital to him—a key phrase, and he returned home, walking all the way with this new revelation uppermost in his consciousness. The result of the use of that statement creates the raising of a vibratory healing action. One thing definitely taught there, was that a decree had efficacy only when the truth affirmed was accepted and understood within the consciousness, within the feeling of man.

"Jesus had a close relationship with the archangel Zadkiel. He was thus able to change the quality of energy. He changed rough seas into peace. Sickness into health.

"Another statement Jesus gave, which was not recorded, was, 'the I AM is the manifestation of the fullness of that Great Light.' When he said '*greater works than these shall ye do,*' he knew then that, as he went on into celestial activity, and would charge or enfold someone that was prepared, receptive, in his name, with heavenly momentum, they could then do even greater things than he did. Also, there would be greater, and more opportunities, such as now. Jesus had had this instruction, which we are now being given. He gave these teachings to about three thousand people. Spiritually, he touched less than five hundred lifestreams during his lifetime. About five hundred witnessed his ascension.

"Jesus and Mary were at Luxor, Egypt, for about three years previous to Jesus' public ministry. There they each took the final initiation at that retreat. This initiation is to consciously suspend the breath from the body and then after a certain length of time animate the body once again (suspended animation). This was done in preparation for Jesus'upcoming crucifixion.

"Jesus did not suffer when he was on the cross because he had withdrawn his bodily consciousness into his own Christ-Self or Higher Mental Body. He kept just enough connection with the physical body to enable him to speak those words, 'Father how thou hast glorified me,' which he spoke on the cross. He did not say, *'Why hast thou forsaken me,'* as has been so commonly mistranslated, misinterpreted! When he had been taken off the cross, his consciousness again entered the physical body.

"The three days he was in the tomb, he completely purified his body with the use of light rays of energy. When archangel Gabriel rolled away the stone, and he came forth that first Easter morning, he had drawn the purified essence of the physical body into his own Christ-Self and all else was consumed or transmuted. That was done through the action of the Resurrection Flame. There were only about twenty persons on Palm Sunday who were aware of the action and significance of that resurrection which was an externalization of the victory over so-called death, and was not meant to portray the sorrows of the crucifixion!

"He was now the full manifestation of his own Christ-Self and thus he walked and talked with his Mother Mary and some of his friends and disciples, for those forty days. The Christ Self is the higher consciousness and one must cultivate the action of blending one's own personal consciousness with its higher Christ Self consciousness, through one's thinking and feeling, until one develops the fullness thereof."

Schutz continues:

"Jesus had ascended into his Christ-Self, that was one step, but he was not yet fully ascended. The fourteenth day when he walked to the top of Bethany Hill and into the Heavens in blazing Light, that completed his ascension. When Jesus ascended into the vibrant Light-body of his I AM Presence, he poured forth an individualized flame around the heart of every life-stream on earth, embodied or dis-embodied, and will sustain it until each one of us is freed into our own Christ-Self's Ascension.

"Before his Ascension, Jesus and Mother Mary had vowed to assist those life-streams whose lives had been taken by order of King Herod. Jesus was permitted by the great Universal Law to consume, transmute at inner levels, during the time of his Ascension, *some* karma for certain life-streams, (not the whole world's sins, karma as decreed by the early Roman church). He could reach only some of those who were ready for spiritual enlightenment. Others should have been reached during his ministry, but because of lack of transportation and communication, he was unable to reach them. Therefore, at that time, the Law permitted him to give that assistance. This has been greatly misconstrued into the idea of vicarious atonement."

Shutz goes on to say, "These Ascended Masters, Divine Beings, further related to us, that the one on the cross to the right of Jesus also made the ascension. Jesus has appeared thousands of times since he ascended from Earth. He appeared twenty-one nights in succession and once five days later, to a noted artist who painted his portrait. When the painting was finished, he ceased to appear. Jesus has golden hair and blue eyes. The music of "Joy to the World," would accompany Jesus' visitations after his Resurrection and often be heard before people were aware of his Presence."

Joy to the world! The Lord is come
Let earth receive her King!
Let every heart prepare Him room
And heaven and nature sing
And heaven and nature sing
And heaven, and heaven and nature sing.

—***Isaac Watts***

… *"and heaven and nature sing."*

The greatest gift underneath your tree will not be packaged with paper and ribbon … in fact, always present and available is this gift … your very own Christ-Presence.

Chapter 29

A CHRISTMAS GIFT

Twas the night before Christmas…

—***Clement Moore***

When we have completed lighting and decorating our Christmas tree, do we give pause to contemplate the Christ-light shining about the room? What exactly are we celebrating? Do we consider the spiritual significance that the symbol of an evergreen tree represents? As we are enjoying our decorations through the holidays, we might be more mindful of the spiritual meaning underlying our symbols, i.e. our tree, a star, a cross, a manger scene.

Every material symbol representing such a holy occurrence is a three-dimensional representation of a fourth-dimensional spiritual expression, reminding us of an inspiring and enlightened message. Did you know that a candy cane, for instance, represents a shepherd's rod and staff? A star stands for spiritual illumination?

Perhaps we've taken some symbols too literally. We've mistakenly put homage and reverence into the symbols themselves—the cross, the anointing water, the wine, the bread, our churches, temples and mosques, as if they held spiritual power. We think our symbols and places of worship will anoint a man, when the opposite of this is true. A righteous and enlightened man energizes and blesses the structure. The anointing takes place upon our arrival, the moment we enter, our light shining, with the awareness of our own full divinity.

If the Master could have his say, I believe he would suggest that Christmas should be the calling to celebrate the Christ within all men.

Acknowledging the birth of Jesus at Christmas time should remind us of the birthing of a recognition, the recognizing of that same Divine Spirit within ourselves, never born and never dying. The I Am of you and me is the One and only Holy Spirit, everlasting after everlasting.

The universal symbol of life is often represented by the triangle or pyramid, which is also evident in the shape of the evergreen tree. The perennial nature of the evergreen thrives and flourishes, unaffected by the passing of seasons, thus representing eternal life.

The Christmas tree has become the symbol most associated with the annual celebration representative of the birth of the Christ, in Master Jesus, and is that heavenly quality which should be seen inherent within all men.

In its highest sense, Christmas can be described as a festive observance, a mass celebration of the Christ, yearning to be recognized within all mankind, a Christ-mass. However, we too often focus on idolizing the man Jesus, in lieu of holding him as our ideal. He literally was asking us to emulate him and to go and do likewise. Maybe this was his greatest gift, his greatest message to us. After all, he is our Master Teacher, our ideal man; representative of the Highest-Self, expressed as perfect-man.

Do we see the Christ in Jesus? Do we see that it is the same Christ-Spirit of God which is also within ourselves? Once again, does the Master not tell us, *"I, Jesus, can of my own self do nothing. The Father spirit within me, he doeth the works."* This Father within is our Father as well, our spirit within as well.

When the Master said, *"I and the Father are One…"* he was declaring that his spirit-consciousness was being raised into the Christ-Consciousness of God, the I Am Presence, the One Spirit which animates all lives.

Jesus was born to show us The Way of raising the Christ-child within ourselves. We will all mature and hopefully come to know that our spirit too, possess everlasting Life. Seeing Jesus demonstrating the ascension, and witnessing his own spirit ascending into the fullness of his individual perfection right before our eyes, was symbolically the First-Coming, or revealing, of the Christ.

What a glorious day it will be when Jesus returns, yes he will return, along with many of the Ascended Masters who have themselves gone on before us in overcoming their human existence. These light-beings, along with the angels, will congratulate us, and sing our praises. Hallelujah!

Can you imagine them all appearing ceremoniously together every time one of us earthlings reaches this exalted destination, as they witness our making this monumental graduation? At this time we too, will have completed our prodigal journey back into our Father's loving arms—the I Am. The "Second-Coming," as it were, occurs each time an individual rises and ascends, as his human consciousness blends into his higher Christ-Self, his ultimate crowning glory.

To quote Paramahansa Yogananda's most profound statement:"A thousand Christs sent to earth would not redeem its people unless they themselves become Christ-like, by purifying and expanding their individual consciousness to receive therein the second coming of the Christ-Consciousness, as was manifested in Jesus ... contact with this Consciousness, experienced in the ever new joy of meditation, will be the real second coming of Christ—and it will take place right in the devotee's own consciousness."

This final graduation within our ascending process will be our proof that we have overcome the material world. We will have taken total control of our person. We will find that we have receded from wants and desires, ego and pride; all prejudices dissolved, we will walk with love and forgiveness, knowing now that all men are created perfectly equal.

"I have a dream. " said Martin Luther King. And the dream of all men should be to become totally selfless, no longer wishing to receive anything from anyone— and we will say, "I am a Santa," the compassionate giver! What a Merry Christmas it will be when each individual reaches this Divine demonstration, the true activity of his Higher-Self.

Like the Christmas cedar, we too can be "evergreen," ageless, unaffected by the seasonal divisions in the year and the passing of years themselves. The timeless secret is for us to see ourselves through the 'single eye,' with the singular Christ-perspective of only one consciousness, that of our God-ness. We are then becoming God-awareness, awareness of God on earth and our own eternal Being, as one with the trinity of eternal Life, the Father, the Son, and the Holy Ghost.

The Christmas tree which we have come to revere needs to be seen as symbolic of a more spiritual aspect of our everlasting Higher-Self. At that juncture we would no longer be viewing ourselves as merely mortal, but spiritually looking out through Life, through the Father's eyes, as Life itself, seeing the three in one, being the three in one. At the holiday season we would then be truly christening the Son, and recognizing the Christ's holy spirit in every man.

The one eye is symbolic of Divine awareness. *"Letting thine eye be single,"* is actually a call to focus on the Holy Trinity. It is the Father seeing the Holy Ghost (the Spirit), as the Holy Ghost sees the Son—as the spirit of the Son is seeing the Father, and so on and so on. This is the continual and immortal equally-sided, circling, cycling action of universal life; hence the equilateral triangle, the Christmas tree. The significance of this view should remind us to see the action of the ever-living trinity within all men.

The "Christ" doesn't have to come down to earth, it has never left. It comes out from within yourself. It is not something that needs to be added to you, not a concept outside of yourself, nor a doctrine or a theory. It is the perfect incarnation of Life projected into this earthly realm from the great I Am Presence of our Source. It is the Higher- Self, the blueprint of every man, woman and child.

Upon your acknowledgment of this awareness, and at that very moment, you are blending your human consciousness with the Perfect Higher- Consciousness, the Christ of yourself. You are taking part in the ascending process. At this point you are recognizing yourself to be a resplendent portion of the trinity, the three in one, the one in three, the very emblem of eternality, immortality.

The greatest gift under your tree will not be packaged with colorful paper and ribbon. Neither is this gift to be found only one morning of the year. This present is within your very own tree of life. In fact, always present and available is this gift—it is your very own Christ-Presence, the gift that keeps on giving. In Shakespeare's words you must think it to make it so, bring it forth, to have it manifest. Therefore knowing that you have this endowment ever-present is not enough. The power is not only in the knowing, but also in the doing. And this doing is the continuous thinking of this awareness, the feeling and activating attention given to this Holy Presence.

The Christmas season is about sharing love, being grateful for every elevated thought great or small; realizing the royalty, the king and queen in everyone.

It means honoring the Christ-child innocence and purity in every face, in every wise man gathered at the festive holiday table. Your heart then overflows with the giving out of this most precious gift, the gift of the Christ-Light within you and your knowing of the true meaning of the Christmas message.

Your own Christ-Self in swaddling clothes is awaiting your nurturing. This young child begs your attention, so it too can be raised, to its spiritual fulfillment in you. This wonderful understanding was the Master's gift to mankind.—Merry Christmas!

But I heard him exclaim
as he drove out of sight,
Merry Christmas to all
and to all a Good Night!

—***Clement Moore***

… and we will say, 'I am a Santa,' the compassionate giver!
What a Merry Christmas it will be when
each individual reaches this Divine demonstration.

We will look forward... We have dropped our old beliefs,
forgiven them entirely... the old beliefs, where are they?
Gone, dispelled like a mist.
The Cosmos stands forth crystal clear.

Chapter 30

TELL IT ON THE MOUNTAIN

Be like the bird that passing on her flight awhile
on boughs too slight,
feels them give way beneath her,
And yet sings, knowing that she hath wings.

—***Victor Hugo***

The name Baird T. Spalding was legendary in spiritual circles and where the topics of truth were being discussed during the first half of the 20th century. Spalding played a very significant role in introducing to the Western World the knowledge that there are Masters or Elder Brothers, as they are called, who assist and guide the destiny of mankind. The following pages will share many of the published experiences from his travels regarding his visit to the top of the world, the Himalayas. His manuscript includes his face-to-face encounters with Jesus.

Mr. Spalding wrote:

"When you think on the Saints and Masters, including the Masters still present in human form, they feel your love. They surround you with the full glory of the Divine Light of Life, Love and Wisdom; and by surrounding you thus, they aid you in your understanding.

"They enfold you in the ever-present Divine Light of Life, Love, and Wisdom which is theirs to send out and to give. They see you always enfolded in this Omnipresent Divine Presence. They see you seated on your own throne as a true king or queen, ruling through and by this Divine Presence. They envisage you knowing and accomplishing your Divine Mission, always alive, always peaceful and happy, always the Divine You. They see not only you, but the whole human family, divine and pure, and every created thing or form as divine, created in the image and likeness of the divine; not one nor one sect nor one creed but All and all inclusive.

"None can appreciate these great people save those who have been admitted to the quiet of their sacred place and thoughts. These divine elder brothers LIVE Truth, which is a part of the Universe itself. Life is really traceable back into the misty past which bears to us the accomplishments of hundreds of thousands of past centuries. To us, life is bound by every limitation and convention. To them, life is boundless, ceaseless, unending bliss and happiness; the longer the span of life, the greater the joy, and the more worthwhile the living.

"None that understand and love these people can doubt their teachings; neither can he doubt their true sincerity when he has partaken of their hospitality.

"The Western World looks to the outer, thereby touching the hem of the garment. The easterner puts on the robe, but not as a garment that may be laid aside (when Mr. Spalding speaks of easterners, he is mainly speaking of those enlightened sages that he was destined to visit).

"The West polish the vessel of the lamp. The East fan the flame that it may give forth a more intense light.

"The West look to the outer with longing eyes, back of which is the glow of spiritual vision, the seeking of true knowledge. The East know that flesh must be illumined by the light of the flame that is first kindled from within, then allowed to shine forth to the without as the full blaze of the noonday sun.

"The West name themselves material. The East live truly in the allness of spirit. They behold each and everyone living by compelling, impelling, sustaining Spirit—it matters not what the location, be it in the great snows of Alti Himalaya, the busy modern city, or the most secluded monastery.

"That which to the Western World seems miraculous and unbelievable, is to the poised Hindu thought, the natural outcome of the acceptance and the bringing forth of Spirit, that which is set forth as God in manifest form. They that are fully alive know full well that there is far more than that which comes under their personal recognizance; in fact, there is much more than has ever been dreamed of in any philosophy.

"When you look longingly with a clear vision toward an accomplishment, it is your divine heritage to command that you place yourself in such a receptive attitude that the ability is already yours to bring forth your ideal.

"God speaks through the God-man today just as God has spoken down the long ages. The knowledge which these people convey is by no means new, although this presentation brings a new light to the Western World.

"The main object of their lives is to give knowledge and enlightenment to humanity through pure knowledge, aflame with love. Their great mission is to pave the way toward peace and harmony through man's great power to accomplish. They are the greatest friends of true science, religion, and philosophy; and they proclaim these as well as all men, brothers, as Truth is one. Thus science becomes the golden thread upon which the pearls are strung."

***

"The day is here in which a large portion of humanity has already outgrown the old concept of Divinity. They have lost their faith in teachings based upon faith alone; they have learned that to be good in order to gain a heavenly reward after death is a fallacy, a very low ideal— this idea of being good for the reward's sake and the special privilege of playing harps and singing songs forever. They have realized that this is an expression of self-interest only and completely foreign to the teachings of the Christ of God, the God-man fully alive.

"The idea of death is foreign too—in fact, it is a direct contradiction of, and to the Divine purpose and is not in accord with the law of the Cosmos or its vibrant and eternal vibrations. Neither is it in accord with the teachings of our Master Jesus.

"The church and the graveyard are often in the same field. This alone is a direct acknowledgement that Christian teachings have not been comprehended. The Christ-man has spoken and the listening ear has heard not. The gift of God to the God-man is eternal life.

"The enlightened beings of the East have taken God out of the realm of the supernatural and of superstition and have placed Him wholly in vibratory frequency, knowing that as they keep themselves in the higher vibrations of Divine Light, their bodies never have to grow old or ever die.

"When the vibrations of their thinking, their bodies, are lowered or allowed to slow down, death ensues. In fact, these people know that when the mistake of death is accomplished, the body is vibrating at such a low rate that the emanating life-vibrations are actually crowded out of the body-temple and that those vibrating life emanations still hold together and maintain the same form which the body had prior to being crowded out. Those emanations or energies have intelligence and still revolve around a central nucleus or sun, which attracts and holds them together, hence our blueprint remains undisturbed.

"Our body could be likened to a kind of miniature solar system with all its energies swirling around our heart center, (our personal central sun.) Our earthly clothing (body) is cast off, yet our structural foundation, our individual arrangement of elements, stays intact, though unseen, as does our individual identity. These characteristics remain the same and are our physical definition in this particular lifetime.

"These energies that went to make up our temple, our physical clothing, will swirl and gather with our spirit until redesigned for our next sojourn. The gathering of these energies is the 'three days' before the 'rolling away of the stone,' or in more common terms it is what is known as the three day wait before burial or cremation. We may call an event 'death,' yet it is only the winter that precedes the spring of eternal seasons, as our everlasting life is preparing to blossom anew—to assume a new personality, or role, the script for our next earthly mission."

All changes, even the most longed for have their melancholy, for what we leave behind us is a part of ourselves; we must die to one life before we can enter into another!

—***Anatole France***

"These emanating energies are surrounded by an intelligent emanation that assists them to keep their form and from which they can again draw substance to erect another temple. A kind of resurrection has taken place. Though resurrection has taken place, through this resurrection man is perfected in the flesh. Unfortunately not all can hear or accept such a valued revelation, *'He that hath ears to hear, let him hear.'* (Mark 4:9) He whose understanding is developed sufficiently, is able to comprehend.

"Thus, large portions of humanity are developing a science through which they are again discovering that *God has always lived in man, as man*; yet they for a time have not known God, during this time they had only lost sight of the God-man, the 'good' man."

* * *

Here Mr. Spalding continues the accounts of his Himalayan travels at the top of the world:

"In a light and whimsical mood, the Chief Sage addressed Mr. Spalding and his co-workers, along with the group of enlightened easterners who had gathered in a mountain retreat at the top of the world, in the Himalayas during the 1890s. The Chief Sage began, 'You have expressed a desire to see and know. A desire is no sooner expressed than it is fulfilled. The thought expressed in a verse in your western Bible comes to me as I look over this assembly. Where two or three are gathered together in My Name, there will I be also. How often that verse has been looked upon as a mere play upon words, instead of being applied and made really true. The great error you have made with Jesus' teachings is, you have consigned them to the dim and misty past, looking upon them as mythical and mystical, pointing to something that may be gained after death, instead of knowing that they can be applied in the daily lives of all, right here and now, if you only will.

'We wish it to be understood that we are not putting forth the claim that Jesus, as the Christ, represented a plane or condition of life in his own realization that had not been brought forth to a greater or lesser degree by a great many seers, and prophets of other times and people. We wish to emphasize his life because that life is the one you can understand more fully. The specific reference to his own life can have but one purpose and meaning, and that was the faith-inspiring fact that his life and experience was the living demonstration of his teachings. The speculative dogma of vicarious atonement, which has biased Christian thought for centuries, cannot be charged to the author of the Sermon on the Mount or the Parable of The Prodigal Son.

'The leaders of Christian thought have diverted the followers of Jesus and his teachings from their practical application and the study of the God power. These leaders have taught us to look upon his teachings as the experiences of the Apostles after his time, instead of teaching us that the law upon which those teachings were based was an *exact science* which can be understood, practiced and experienced in the lives of all of us.' "

"The Chief Sage continued, 'The Orientals have made the scientific phase of their religion the supreme object of their study and attainment. In this, they have gone to the other extreme. In this way, the Christians and the Orientals have consigned their religions to the realm of the miraculous and supernatural. The one has become absorbed in the wholly ethical, while the other has become absorbed in the scientific side only. Thus both have shut out true spirituality.... Where is the love?

'The monastic, or monastery type of existence of life, retirement, asceticism, and seclusion from the world, whether in

Buddhistic or Christian monasteries, is neither a necessity nor is it the true method of attaining spiritual enlightenment; nor is it the realization of the perfect life of love, wisdom and power as brought forth by Jesus. These monastic systems have been in existence for many thousands of years, yet they have in no wise accomplished as much for the uplift of the common people as did the teachings of Jesus in the few short years of his time here on earth.

'Jesus studied and studied information that took him on an entirely spiritual path which led him away from the ritualistic, monastic, and materialistic forms of worship. The Master began to recognize the deeper, inner meanings, the insights, which he had received from the Buddhistic teachings, as he had walked to India over the old caravan route maintained at that time, in order to study the ancient teachings.

'There he studied the Buddhistic teachings which had been preserved with a reasonable degree of purity. He saw that, in spite of the ritualistic forms and dogmas that had been imposed by man, religion had but one source, and that was the God within, whom he designated as his Father and the Father of all. Then he threw all forms to the wind, as it were, and went directly to God, went straight to the heart of this loving attainment. He soon found that this did not take long years of weary plodding through dogmas, rituals, creeds, formulas, and initiations which the priesthood were foisting upon the people in order to hold them in ignorance and, therefore, in subjection. He realized that that for which he was seeking was right within himself.

'In order to show that he had found the Christ within himself, he declared this same Christ to be in every man. This he did with all people in mind, showing us, The Way. Then with pure motive of life, thought, word, and deed, he must live the life he sought, in order to incorporate it within his physical body. Then, after perceiving this, he had the courage to go out and declare it to all the world.

'It did not matter from whom or where he got his realization. It was the work that counted, not what someone else had done, but what he did that counted. The common people, whose cause he sponsored, heard him gladly. He did not borrow his precepts from India, Persia, or Egypt. Their teachings were but the outer that brought him to see his own Godhead and the Christ, the representation of it, that was in everyone; NOT IN A FEW, BUT IN ALL.

'There were other spiritual leaders, like Osiris, Buddha, and Moses, and if you would study their teachings, you would find many similarities. Their teachings also show us the way from the outer to the inner. They all went through the same experience, in that their followers wanted to crown them kings of temporal kingdoms. But to this they would not listen, each expressing the same thought, in almost the same words, *"my kingdom is not of the material, it is a spiritual kingdom."*

'Jesus saw and contacted all their teachings, then in his characteristic manner, went to the heart of all these. He went one step further than any of them did, however, by glorifying his body to the point where he could allow it to be crucified; yet brought it forth in a triumphant resurrection.'"

* * *

Just as the vision, the presence of the blessed Mother Mary has been witnessed firsthand over the centuries, Jesus too, has presented himself, to a few receptive hearts over time.

During that visit to the Himalayas more than one hundred years ago, Baird Spalding considered himself a very fortunate man indeed to have experienced what transpired next:

"After, a short interlude, Spaulding's enlightened guide called the meeting back to order. After a few minutes of general talk, we were seated, and our Chief Sage and teacher resumed, 'There is not a character in all your history of the Western World that stands out as Jesus does. You count your time before and after his birth. He is idolized by a majority of your people, and that is where they err. Instead of the idol, he should be the ideal. Instead of being made into a graven image, he should be real and living to you, for he actually lives today. He lives, and can talk to you, just as he did before his ascension.

'The great error, with so many, is that they see his life ending in sorrow and death upon the cross, forgetting entirely, that the greater portion of his life is that portion after the resurrection. He is able to teach and heal today, far more than he ever did before. You can come into his presence at any time, if you will. If you seek, you will find him. He is not a king who can intrude his presence upon you, but a mighty brother, who stands ready, always to help you, and to help the world. When he lived upon the mortal, earthly plane, he was able to reach but a few. Today, he is able to reach all who look to him.

'Did he not say: *"Where I am, there you are also"*? Does that mean that he is away in a place called heaven that you must die to attain? No! He is where you are, and you are where he is. You are just not cognizant of this fact. And he is able to walk and talk with you. Lift your sight a little higher, and let it extend to a wider horizon; and if your heart and thought are sincerely with him, you will see him. You may walk and talk with him. If you look closely, you will find the scars of the cross, the spear, and the thorns, all healed, all gone. And the radiant love and happiness about him will tell you that they are all forgotten, forgiven.'

"Our friend stopped talking, and all was deep silence for the space of about five minutes. Then the room lighted up with a brilliance that we had not seen before. We heard a voice, At first it seemed a long way off and indistinct. After our attention was attracted to it, and our thoughts directed to it, the voice became very distinct and rang out in clear bell-like tones.

"One of our party asked, 'Who is speaking?' Our Chief said, 'Please be silent. Our dear Master, Jesus is speaking.' Then one of our friends said, 'You are right, Jesus speaks.'

"Then the voice went on, 'When I said *'I am the way, the truth, and the life,'* I did not intend to convey the thought to mankind that I, myself, was the only true light. As many as are led by the spirit of God, they are the sons of God.' When I said, *'I am the perfect Son, the only begotten Son of God in whom the Father is well pleased,'* I fully intended to convey the thought to all mankind that one of us, as God's children, one of the brothers and sisters, I, myself, saw, understood and claimed my divinity; saw that I lived, moved, and had my being in God, the great Father-Mother-Principle of all things, all of life. Understanding this, I then spoke forth the word, that I recognized the Christ within myself. What I really meant was, *the Christ within each one of us, is the the only begotten Son of God.'"*

"With true heart and steadfast purpose, Jesus lived the life, becoming what he claimed to be. With his eyes fixed upon that ideal, he filled his whole body with that ideal, and the end sought, was fulfilled.

"Jesus told us 'The reason so many have not seen me is because they have put me upon a pedestal, a shrine, and placed me in the unapproachable. They have surrounded me with miracles and mystery; and again, they have placed me far from the common people, whom I love dearly. I love them with a love that is unspeakable. I have not withdrawn from them. They have withdrawn from me.

'They have set up veils, walls, and partitions, mediators, and images of myself and those so near and dear to me. They have surrounded us with myth and mystery until we seem so far removed from these dear ones that they do not know how to approach.

'They pray and supplicate to my dear Mother and those that surround me, and thus they hold us all in mortal thought. When truly, if they would know us as we are, they would and could shake our hands. If they would drop all superstition and creed and know us as we are, they could talk with us as you are doing. We are no different at any time than as you see us now. How we would love to have the whole world know this as fact! Then what an awakening, what a reunion, what a feast would ensue!

'You have surrounded us so long in mystery, it is no wonder that doubt and disbelief have become dominate. The more you build images and idols and surround us with death and make us unapproachable, save through some other than ourselves, the deeper the doubt and shadow will be cast and the chasm of superstition grow wider and more difficult to cross. This chasm includes the fact that some have even placed my loving Mother between you and myself. If you would boldly shake our hands and say, 'I know you,' then all could see and know us as we are. There is no mystery surrounding us or those we love, for we love the whole world.

'So many see only that part of my life which ended on the cross, forgetting that the greater part is as I am now; forgetting entirely that man still lives, even after what seems a violent death. Life cannot be destroyed. It goes on and on!

'Dear Pilate, when he washed his hands and said, away with him and crucify him yourselves, I find no fault with him, how little he knew of the history he was making or of the prophecy he was fulfilling. He, with the multitude, has suffered far more than I have suffered. That is all past and forgotten, forgiven, as you will see, by our all standing here in one place together.'"

"Two figures came forth, and were embraced by Jesus. As they stood, with his hand on the shoulder of one, he said, 'This dear brother has come all the way with me. While this one, (pointing to the second one,) saw many more trials before his eyes were opened. But after they were fully opened, he came quickly. He is just as true, and we love him with the same love we do all others.'"

"Then another advanced slowly, and stood for a moment. Jesus turned and with outstretched arms said, 'Dear Pilate.' There was no mistaking the comradeship of the embrace. Then Pilate spoke and said, 'I labored and suffered many weary years after the verdict which I pronounced that day so lightly, when I cast from myself the burden. How few of us, while in the material, realize the needless burdens we heap upon others in the attempt to shift the responsibility from ourselves. It is only when our eyes are open that we realize the more we attempt to shirk and shift our burdens upon others, the greater the burdens bear down upon us. It took many weary years before my eyes were opened to this fact; but since the day they were opened, how I have rejoiced.'"

"Then the invisible choir burst into full song, and the melody was beyond all description. After a few bars, Jesus stepped forward and said, 'Do you wonder that I have long ago forgiven those that nailed me to the cross? Then why have not all forgiven, as I have? With me, the forgiveness was complete when I said, *'It is finished.'* Why do you not see me as I am, not nailed to the cross, but risen above all mortality?'"

"Again the invisible choir continued with, 'Hail, all hail, you sons of God. Hail, hail and praise Him. His Kingdom endures forever among men. Lo, God is with you always, and as they sang, the words stood out in raised letters upon the wall of the room.'"

"This was not some far off, hazy, nearly invisible scene. Neither was it set on a stage far away from us. All were actually present in the room, we talked with them and shook their hands. The only difference that we could see, between them and ourselves, was the peculiar light about them, and this appeared to be the source of the light within the room. There were no shadows anywhere.

"To us there seemed to be a peculiar translucent quality about the flesh, for when we touched them or clasped their hands, the flesh seemed like fine, fine alabaster. Still, it had a warm, friendly glow and that same warmth pervaded everything about them. Even after they had walked out, the room we were in retained the same warmth and light. Moreover, every time we entered the room thereafter, some of the party would make reference to this wonderful radiance."

***

Spaulding was so taken aback by these miraculous adventures that he wrote these words: "We came doubting; we left with the greatest of expectations, loving these wonderful Masters every one, feeling that we had gained a truer and deeper insight into the science of Life and True Living."

In the following, Spalding recounts yet another inspirational session with these Masters:

"We find one of the enlightened sages speaking….'Light does not comprehend darkness, as it shines through darkness. When Jesus saw that he was to be betrayed by Judas, he said, *'Now is the Son of man glorified, and God is glorified in him'*. The Master never said, 'Judas betrayed me'; he did not refer to Judas at all. He understood and held only to the Allness of the glorified Christ of God flowing through himself.

"Thus we see that perfect mutual action works out all inharmony in its own way. Now you can say, 'Christ, stand forth more and more definitely, so definite that you are myself. In fact, now are we one body, one mind, one spirit; one whole, complete principle. You are I AM— I am you— together, we are, God.'

"The moment he ceased speaking we found ourselves transported to the Sanctuary, the center room of the Tau Cross Temple. We had scarcely composed ourselves when Jesus and a number of others, including our Chief, stepped from the ledge into the large room which had been carved within the rock. As they entered, a great burst of light filled the room and everyone was introduced to each other.

"We formed a circle and, placing both hands palms down, upon the table, stood in deep silence for a few moments. Although there was not a word uttered, the room was completely filled with a strange, pulsing, vibrating emanation. It was an entirely different sensation from anything we had ever experienced and at first seemed to overwhelm us. The rocks pulsated and vibrated with a resonate musical tone. This lasted only a few moments. When the stillness was broken, we were told that this morning we would see the creation of a universe in pictures. These pictures would be a representation of that which happened when our universe came into existence..."

"And I saw a new heaven and a new earth; for the first heaven and the first earth were passed away; and there was no more sea ... and I heard a great voice out of heaven, saying Behold, the tabernacle of God is with men, and he will dwell with them, and they shall be his people, and God himself shall be with them, and be their God... And God

shall wipe away all tears from their eyes; and there shall be no more death, neither sorrow, or crying, neither shall there be any more pain; for the former things are passed away."

—***Revelations 21***

"We stepped through the door, out upon the ledge, and walked to the edge of this Himalayan mountain. It was still an hour before sunrise. The dead calm of the absolute silence enshrouded us. The time was propitious for the unfolding of another birth. We were looking out into infinite space, our souls eager and expectant. The Sage began by saying, 'There are but two events in the world: that which was in existence before consciousness began to assert itself, is now, and ever shall be; and secondly the things that humanity has thought and will think about.

'That which was before human consciousness began, is eternal; that which humanity thinks, is changeable and inconsistent; that which was, before consciousness began, is Truth; that which humanity thinks is truth, is truth to them. When the Law of Truth comes to consciousness, *it will erase all that humanity has ever thought erroneously.*

'As the centuries roll on and push back the material veil by the process of spiritual evolution, thoughts will come through the mind of humanity that revert back to Truth or, as we call it, the original Cosmic facts; and these thoughts that fill the memory of the past, faced with the facts of the present and overshadowed by the prophecies of the future, stand out definitely upon the path of the whole evolving race of man's consciousness. Thus the race is called back again and again to the original existing principle.

'By this return and repetition, humanity is shown that creation and all ensuing creations are eternal, the same with all mankind; but mankind's creatures are always changing and they are under a manifestation of Law, called action and reaction. Where human beings have gone far enough in their creation of creatures, the Great Absolute Law of Truth takes a hand in bringing them face to face with the original plan. Thus we see that cosmic law never allows life to run too far in a tangent. This law is always polarized in equalization, balance, and harmony.

'In spite of idols or creeds it will crowd mankind on into complete union with Absolute Realities. All things that are not in perfect accord and union with actual, existing Cosmic fact, *must erase themselves* when the Absolute Law of Truth holds sway in the human consciousness. The thoughts of humanity are always so formed as to release their imperfect creations, that are only born of half-truths—when Truth arrives.

'Cosmic Absolute Law must be fully satisfied. Thinking, speaking, or acting the Law of Reality is bound eventually to lead humanity into Law of Reality itself. The ancients tell us that every tree that the Heavenly Father has not planted within you, will be uprooted. 'Let them alone, blind. If the blind always lead the blind, shall they not fall into the same ditch?'

'The cycle is fast closing, in which the blind of the whole race have led the blind (ourselves) into a welter of ignorance, superstition, and delusion created by those who believe as human beings think, rather than that which is true and real. The civilization that has risen on the delusions and superstitions of the closing centuries is submerging itself into the welter. Through the pain and tragedy of their misappropriated creations, a new race consciousness has been conceived and is fast evolving. In fact the door is opening wide for its birth.

'There is no other course than to go on from one plane of consciousness to a higher and more advanced step in the actual cosmic path. The only condition forbidden in the vibration of the great Cosmos is that dullness of thought which allows the human race to become so solidly fixed in what it believes that, if it clings desperately to its old delusions and will not let go, it can in no way come into the greater expanse of universal thought.

'Those thus absorbed in personal consciousness must go on through natural exhaustion of beliefs and experiences until they fail to go forward; then, of its own accord, Absolute Law wields a progressive hand through disease, pain, and loss, until the human is so dissatisfied that he turns to find the curse of a false idea within the idea itself.

'If a race or nation refuses to let go of things created by *a portion of human thought* instead of that which really exists, the Law takes a hand in its progress by allowing the accumulated vibrations sent out by such a condition to reflect back upon itself through the light ray. Then with war, strife, discord, and death on every hand, that race or nation is wiped out, imploding upon itself, in order that it may be placed again in a new uplift of creation. Thus it can begin over again in a new contact with that which was before the beginning of human consciousness. Civilization today is fast approaching a great *reconstructive moment.* All things that seem so stable and well-founded now will soon be immersed in a state of inversion.

'Every tree that has not been planted by Truth will be uprooted. There is approaching a complete Cosmic overthrow of the present social, political, financial, and *religious institutions* that will make room for the placing of the new era; in order that humanity may come in closer touch with that which is and was established before the present human consciousness submerged and set it aside. Truth waits on with attentive, loving and radiant beneficence until man will see that he can embrace and become the consciousness of that which has always existed.

'Humanity is taking a forward step from the cradle stories of the former generation, and their creations are no longer of any avail to the arisen individuality and spiritual discernment of the consciousness of the generation that is fast approaching. Delusions, traditions, and superstitions are nearing their end. It is also true of the civilization which they established. The old idols are good enough for the infantile consciousness that is nearing an impasse. Their delusion has caused their undoing as they are proved to be only cradle stories woven by a master craft of priesthood and preceptor (teacher) to lull into false sleep the crying infants of an evolving race. Those who saw further afield did not cry and thus were not lulled to sleep. Most of them saw that the cradle stories were not true and many stepped boldly forth to erase the untruth; as they saw directly through to the absolute, that which has always existed and which has always been seen and known and contacted directly by a portion of mankind. From this portion there will arise a new and more vitalizing consciousness, fully awake and ready to erase the idols that man has set up for his fellow man to follow, and make room for the new ideals which are as old as creation's dawn. (Are we listening?)

'These will demand of those who teach, lead, or inspire the race-consciousness, that they shall do it from a plane of actual living contact, so high that there can be no mistake or contradiction and on a plane of interpretation that is so simple that it cannot be misunderstood. The awakening tiger of higher intelligence and spirituality will refuse to sleep again, as it has already been ravaged with the fragments of the past and disappointed with the torture of misplaced confidence. It will demand a stronger and more vital thought with instruction based upon Truth itself.'"

"The wise sage went on to say, 'The multitudes are now listening, over the heads of past centuries with their *creed-bound traditions*, to the old, old message that to the newly-born is working its unfoldment into the hearts and lives of mankind. This new-old message is the clarion call that is heard above the changing voices of creed-bound priesthood.

'It is louder than the voice of battle;

'It is louder and clearer than the muffled contradictions of financial, industrial, political, and religious lies.

'In spite of the creed-bound thoughts of a portion of humanity, their traditional and idolized ideas of God, of Christ, and man, of self, of life and death, all must go; and in the absolute freedom from these preconceived ideas there must pass and thus be erased all that was built upon them.

'There is looming upon the horizon of this new approach a redemption that has an entirely new meaning. This new multitude, coming out of this clearer vision and more definite perception, is redeemed through *deeper revelation emanating* out of all races and all people. That emanation is the One Life that is in all and through all.

'In spite of the delusion-bound multitude, their clinging hands and cringing attitude, a greater and more noble vista of the expanding horizon of God, the *Christ of man, the Christ of God, of Self,* is looming; and another cycle of spirit is dawning for the whole world. (The dawning planetary shift in consciousness.) Another age of the crystal race is coming up out of the swirling mass of the maelstrom.

'Whenever a people or nation think of God as absolute, that people or nation recognizes that they are a portion of God, for God is established unto them. As they love, worship and reverence that ideal, they do become cognizant of their Godness. In the fullness of time they have reached their heritage, that which was first and is established in Spirit. Whenever an individual thinks of God, he will see his own reflection, and God is established unto him. Breathe life into humanity, it means the same, God individualized. In this greater understanding of celestial revelation, men find God the same as God was before human consciousness began to manifest— the same yesterday, today and forever.

'There is slowly rising from the ashes of *orthodoxy* the actual temple not made by hands, eternal in heaven, in man. A great new race of thinkers is coming to the fore with Herculean strides. Soon the tides will surge over the earth to sweep away the debris of delusion which has been strewn over the paths of those who are struggling along under the load of evolution.

'The work is already accomplished. Hundreds of millions are re-released with their heart, soul, body, and instinct free. They are the throbbing pulse of an unborn race that is again heir to the ages. I see them stepping across the ages, walking hand in hand with God. Great waves of wisdom flood toward them from the eternal shores of the infinite. They dare to step forth and declare themselves a part of eternal God, eternal Christ; God and man, One eternally with eternal life. They dare to step forth and declare to heaven that much that is written by man is a lie and in *terrible blindness wrought*.

'This new pulse-consciousness is the crest of the wave that rests on the new race-consciousness. This new race sees man, himself, the highest expression on this planet, and one with God through the medium of his earthly life. (We are God's experiencing of Himself—the very activity of Creativity); and we see that His whole supply flows through that life itself. This race knows that man can live consciously in a perfect universe with perfect people and in perfect accord with harmonious situations and conditions, with absolute assurance that there is not a single error in the great Spiritual plan of the Cosmos.

'Man sees God as Cosmic Spirit pervading everything; then, with the subtleties of mind through his thought, he does not hesitate to review the fundamentals that have placed him where he is and made him that which he is. Thus he is again one with his Source. He knows that his Source is the ever-silent side of his God-mind linked consciously in thought and amalgamated with Infinite Mind.

'This new race understands that, through sun and shadow, without the bitterness, the soul's true quest for Love and true Peace is the Truth of God and man. This race does not hesitate to strip the swaddling-clothes of delusion from the whole human race. The gaunt specter which for ages has bound the feet of the weak and doubting ego-man, through his own ignorance will be completely erased. He finds he has erased his every limitation through his true selfhood, completely arisen. He has raised himself from man, to God-man, to God.

'At this point man maintains one-ness with infinity and can afford to wait till the time is ripe for the bringing forth of the universes. Then with the preserved consciousness of former experiences, he is better equipped to assist in the bringing forth of a more perfect and lasting condition. In this, God-man can never fail, as he is more definite than any form; and failure is not written in His horizon or in His Consciousness.

'The infinitesimal becomes the infinite of all forms. When the wise and now enlightened man says: *I am deathless, ageless, eternal; there is not a thing in life or light that I am not,'* he is looking into and sees this vista. This is true divinity. The ascension is truly his—Amen.'

* * *

"When the speaker closed, we realized that the sun was well past the meridian. We sat there, not spellbound, but enraptured, as we were actually enclosed in the vista that had been set before us. Where had the horizon gone? We had dropped it entirely; we were in and of infinity. The infinite was ours for the reaching out and acceptance of it. Do you wonder? Could we grasp the magnitude of who we were, where we were, and the importance of our place in the great plan of the Cosmos? Not yet, dear friends, not yet.

"Would the world accept what we fortunate few have witnessed with our eyes and our ears? We did not know. We had looked into the long, long past. What the future portends we know not until we have proved it by actually living the present. What the past has been for millions of years we have seen.

"We will look forward toward this accomplishment, knowing that the future extends as many millions of years as has been portrayed before us. We have dropped our old beliefs, forgiven them entirely, and we look forward to every accomplishment, not hopefully but knowingly. The old beliefs, where are they? Gone, dispelled like a mist. The Cosmos stands forth crystal clear."

The most beautiful of all emblems is
that of God, whom Timaeus of Locris
describes under the image of a
circle whose centre is everywhere and
whose circumference is nowhere.

—***Voltaire***

We arose and walked out of the garden together…
This day has been a revelation to me.
A new world, a new light, a new life stands revealed!

Chapter 31

UNDERSTANDING THE MASTER

I would like to be able to feel admiration toward God.
Sometimes I feel a nice glow about the idea of God,
But I'd like to have a really mind-boggling swept-off-my-feet
Meeting with God or Jesus... what an idea... I wonder...

— ***Carolyn Whitt***

Meeting the Master

Would you recognize Master Jesus if you encountered him in public today? If he had long hair and was carrying a guitar playing a far different beat, would you be open-minded enough to interrupt your busy day and stop and listen to his words? Imagine the lyrics he would be singing! What if he was in a three-piece suit and a fedora? Would you instinctively know him by his demeanor and his message, or would you need to witness the holes in his hands?

How would you respond if suddenly you found yourself face to face with our Master? You might awaken in the middle of the night with him standing radiantly at the foot of your bed. You could bump into him on a bustling city street. Or he might come and sit down with you in a restaurant during lunchtime. Forget for a moment what he might say. My question to you today is—what would you say to him? Maybe you should ask yourself what questions you might ask Jesus.

The following is another of several encounters chronicled by Baird T. Spalding, an American studying with a group of archeologists in the Tibetan region of the Himalayas, concerning his group's life changing face to face meetings with Master Jesus. During the 1890s he met, and was tutored by, a few local enlightened gurus or sages, who later traveled with him over a period of years during Spalding's explorations, sharing with him their ancient wisdom.

An inspiring journey

This true recorded account tells about their group stumbling upon another American individual, named Weldon, who happened to be in the same area of the Far East, in the midst of his researching the earlier historical travels of Jesus. The reader should find, as Weldon did, the actual events as recounted here to be at the same time both startling, and deeply enlightening. So once again, have faith in the inspired message you are about to receive. Open your eyes to see and your ears to hear.

Mr. Spalding wrote:

"As happenstance would have it, Weldon crossed paths with our party. The Master Sage traveling within our group suggested that he join us for a short time. Weldon, a well-known writer who had lived in India for many years, was in sympathy with and deeply interested in our work. He had asked several times to join our party. We sat in the garden, relating our experiences to him. Weldon suddenly remarked that he had never fully accepted the authenticity of the history and life of the man called Jesus of Nazareth. He had studied available records carefully, but they had all seemed vague and lacking in conclusion. Finally, he had given up in despair, as there were very grave doubts in his mind that such a character existed. Our Chief Sage asked him, if he were brought face to face with this man, did he think he would know Him, and how would he recognize him?

"Weldon replied, 'You have touched upon a subject that has been the greatest motivating ideal of my whole life. You will never know the absorbing interest with which I have looked forward to some sign of actual truth of the man's existence in bodily form upon this earth.

'Each year my doubts have grown stronger until I have despaired of ever finding a trace that I can place full confidence in. However, there has always been something away back somewhere that I might define as a vague thought or ray of hope that sometime, somewhere, if I could meet this man face to face without a suggestion from any outside source, I would know Him positively.

'Instinctively this thing wells up before me; and I say this to you—I have never before voiced it,—I know I would know Him. This is the most sincere feeling I have ever experienced and, if you will pardon me for the repetition, I will say again, I know I would know Him.'

"That evening as we were preparing to retire, our Chief came to us and said; 'You all heard the conversation regarding the man Jesus this afternoon. You recognize the sincerity of our friend. Shall we invite him to go with us? We do not know, nor have we any way of determining whether this man that is known as Jesus of Nazareth will be at our destination. We cannot check his movements. In fact, we only know that he has been there recently.

'If we invite Weldon to go and the man is not there, will it not result in further disappointment, and serve no good purpose? Weldon seems anxious to go with us. Since none of us knows that this man Jesus will be there, there will be no suggestion from any of us in any way. In this, I think the time is auspicious.' "We all agreed.

"The next morning, our chief invited Weldon to accompany us. Instantly his face lighted up with anticipation. After a moment's reflection, he told us that he had an assignment for the following Wednesday and would be obliged to return by that time. As this was Thursday, he would have six days. Our chief thought the time sufficient so we decided to leave that afternoon. Things went well, and we reached our destination before noon of the second day.

"As we arrived, we noticed a group of twelve people sitting together in the garden of the lodge we were to occupy. As we approached they all arose, and the owner of the lodge came forward to greet us. In the group we saw the man Jesus standing. Before anyone could say a word or make a suggestion, Weldon had stepped from our midst with both hands extended and with a joyous exclamation rushed forward, clasping Jesus' hands in his, saying, 'Oh, I knew you, I knew you. This is the most divine moment of my whole life!'

"When we realized what had taken place, there was something akin to divine joy that swept through us as we beheld the rapture of our friend. We stepped forward and exchanged greetings, as Weldon was introduced to the group."

The awaited meeting

"After lunch, while sitting in the garden, Weldon said to Jesus, 'Won't you talk to us? I have been waiting a lifetime for this moment.'

"There was silence for a few moments, then JESUS began; 'In the silence of the hour, I would have you know that the Father to whom I speak and who dwells within me, is the same loving Father who dwells in all, and to whom all can speak and know just as intimately as I do.

'A breath of wondrous glory sweeps across the chords that vibrate with a life pure and divine. It is so pure that the waiting silence stops, and intently listens; the fingers of the great and knowing One within your true self, touches your hand with lingering softness; and the voice as always is telling you of the Father's great and glorious love. Your higher voice is saying to you, 'I know you are with me, and whether together or apart, you and I are God.'

'Now the Christ of God stands forth. Won't you erase every limitation and stand with me in spirit? Greater thoughts have not been given than these I give unto you. It does not matter that men say it cannot be. You, each one of you, are standing forth The Divine Master, conquering and in full dominion, just as you have seen me conquer. The time is here; the fulfilling pure thought that you have sent out to the Divine Master has come to fruition in your own body and the soul has taken complete command. Just as I did, you will be soaring to heights celestial.

'We lift these bodies up until their shining radiance becomes a blaze of pure, white light and together we have returned to the Father from whence we all have come forth.

'God our Father is pure light emanation and from this vibrating light we all have come forth; in this vibration all stand together with God. In these vibrating emanations of light all material consciousness is erased and we see creations projected forth from the formless into form, all things renewed every instant. In the primal cosmos, aqueous or God substance, all things exist and, because of that existence, the vibrations are so high that none perceive them. Unless one stands forth in spirit as we do, it is necessary to raise the vibrations of the body to the level of spirit vibrations.

'Now we can see creation going on all the time, as creation is caused by the radiation of cosmic light vibrations generated in the great cosmos; and this radiation is the great universal life or light energy that sustains all and is called Father of radiation or vibration. It is the Father of radiation that will shatter, displace any other radiation or vibration. In reality it only sets them aside in order that they be molded into other forms to take their place.

Resonating with spirit

'When our body resonates in tune with Spirit, we are light vibrations, becoming light-bodies, the greatest of all emanations. God, our Source, is the Father of all vibrations.

'It will soon be proved that these cosmic rays constitute such a terrific bombardment that they are transformative to so-called matter. These rays are from the source of all energy, the Father of all elements, the source from which all elements are derived. This is not destruction, this is transmutation from so-called matter to spirit form (i.e. ice to liquid to vapor, remaining the same substance, yet changing formations.)

'It shall be known that these cosmic rays have such tremendous penetrating power that they penetrate through all mass, shattering as it were, the very heart or nucleus of a so-called atom, transmuting it into atoms of other substance and thereby creating other elements of higher order; and in this way creation advances into a higher emanation of pure light or life itself.' "

"The Master went on... 'These radiations, which have such tremendous penetrating power, are readily distinguished from all radiations coming from the earth or sun galaxy, and have complete control over all these radiations or vibrations. It will soon be known that these radiations come from a universal source, unseen, and that the earth is continuously subjected to a terrific bombardment of these rays that are so potent they change or transmute atoms of one element into the Infinite particles of another element.

'It will also be found that when this cosmic ray strikes the nucleus of an atom, it does not shatter it. It separates this atom into the minute particles of another formation, causing transmutation from a lower to a higher element, from the material to the spiritual.

'This higher element is as man dictates. It is higher as he names and uses it for a higher purpose. When man stands forth in spiritual vibrations, he can fully determine and regulate these rays, and their mode of action.

'Thus to man, standing in spiritual vibrations, transmutation is going on all the time all about him. Transmutation is but creation in the higher sense. Thus all are created where they stand. Creation never ceases; it is continuous, never ending.

'Creation goes on in an everlasting fashion; expanding and concentrating, then through reduced vibrations, slowing and cooling, condensing into form.

'This intelligent, emanating, Energy—is God, controlling the universe around us, as well as controlling the universe of our bodies which are spiritual first, before manifesting outwardly, materially.

'This transmutation or change is not disintegration. The intelligence so directs that only a few of these light bullets strike the nuclei of other atoms, at a time ratio and in complete conformity to law, so that no manifestation is overbalanced.

'Man, one with his supreme intelligence, can, in an orderly way, step up this impingement, so that his needs are fulfilled instantly. In this way, man hastens the slow process of nature. He does not interfere with nature. He works with it in a higher rate of vibration than that in which nature works in the lower order of concept. *'Lift up your eyes and look on the fields; they are white already to harvest.'* (John 4:35) All is vibration and corresponds to the plane or field upon which vibration acts.

'The planes or fields spoken of have no reference to the concentric bands or shells that surround the earth. These concentric shells or layers are ionization bands, which enclose the earth, and reflect back vibrations originating on the earth, but they do not impede or shut out cosmic light rays. It is through them that transmutation or creation is going on all the time. Even our bodies are transmuted from a lower to a higher condition, and we become the conscious directors of this change by keeping the thoughts and, therefore, the body, attuned consciously to the higher, more positive, vibrations. Thus we attune the body consciously to a higher vibratory rate and we become that vibration.

White light

"Jesus continued. 'In this radiant condition, the master waits. As you stand now, you are master, you are ruler over all conditions. Now you know that the glory and the consciousness of a divine creation is far above any material thought.

'The first step is fully and completely to control all outer activities of thought, mind, and body, with the thought always uppermost that you are cultivating the habit of perfection, the God habit, the Christ-of-God habit. Do this wherever you are, every time it comes to you during your working or resting hours. See this perfect presence within you, as you. Get into the habit of seeing this perfect presence as your real self, your Christ-of-God presence.

'Then go a little further. See a Divine White Light, dazzling in purity and brilliance emanating forth from the very center of your being. See it shining forth with such brilliance and glory that it emanates from every cell, fiber, tissue, muscle, and organ of your whole body. Now see the true Christ-of-God standing forth, triumphant, pure, perfect, and eternal. Not the Christ of me, but your own true Christ-of-God, the only begotten of your Father-God, the only true son of God, the triumphant and all-conquering Godhead. Step forth and claim this as your divine right and it is yours.

'Every time you say 'God,' know fully that you are personally presenting God; and you will do the world a greater service by so doing than by presenting me, Jesus, as the only Christ-of-God. It is far greater and nobler to see yourself as the Christ-of-God, you yourself presenting God to the world and beholding God as yourself.

'You sit back and pray to me to intercede for you. It is wonderful that you do present me to the world as the Christ-of-God and recognize the God qualities presented through me, just so long as you do not make an idol or image of me and then pray to that idol. The moment you make a greater image of me and pray to that image, you debauch me and yourselves. It is well to see the ideal that I or anyone else presents, then make that ideal your very own. Then we are not apart or separated from God; as such, man conquers the world. Do you not see the greater thing to be accomplished by standing forth ONE with us in God?

'If you cultivate this with love, reverence, devotion, and worship, it becomes a habit and soon it is all of you, your daily life and existence. In a short time you have brought forth Divinity. You are once more the Divine Christ, the first-born of God. You are One with Primal Spirit, Energy. Actually feel, see, and take hold of this Great Light. Accept, declare, and know positively that it is yours, and in a short time your body will lovingly send forth this Light!

'In every age and every condition, all through the great immensity, this supreme light has existed. It is everywhere. This light is life.

'When anything is made plain, we are enlightened regarding it. The light shines forth into our conscious concept. Soon the Light of Life will shine forth to your watching eye, as it has to all great ones. Many of these great ones are portrayed standing forth in a great blaze of light. Although you may not see it, this light is real and is life, radiating from your body.'

"Here Weldon asked if we might talk over some of the Bible teachings and Jesus readily assented. We arose and walked out of the garden together. Weldon exclaimed, 'Just think! You Americans have made contact with these Sages, and even though I have lived in this neighborhood for a few years now, I had never recognized them. This day has indeed been a revelation to me. A new world, a new light, a new life stands revealed.'

"We asked him how he recognized the man Jesus. He answered, 'You marvel that I recognize the man for what he is. I do not know how I know. I know, and nothing can shake that knowing.'

"We suggested that if he kept his assignment, it would be necessary for him to leave the following Monday, and that two of our party would leave for Darjeeling on that day, and would accompany him.

'Leave,' he replied. 'I have already sent a messenger asking another person to take my assignment. I am staying here. You just try to send me away.'"

Words of wisdom

"After a most interesting day going about the countryside, visiting many places of interest, we returned to the mountain lodge at eight o' clock and found our friends assembled in the garden.

"After a short talk on general subjects, Jesus spoke, saying they realized that Weldon was mystified. The Master went on to say: 'I shall talk to you, just as I wish you to talk to yourself. If you will make these statements true, or make them a part of yourself, you will need no other. These statements are in no wise to be used as formulas. Students can use them to bring their thoughts in accord with Divine Principle or, as many say, to train their thoughts to the one point. We use the word GOD as often as possible, repeating it many times.

'It is a well known fact that the more often you say or use the word GOD, knowing it to be the highest Principle indwelling and flowing through you, the greater benefit you will derive from it. Allow me to repeat, our thought is, You cannot say GOD or use the name too much.

'See God as Creative Principle, flowing through you. Concentrate and energize that principle, and send it out with more dynamic influence. Because of the fact that it always flows through you, as well as around you, you are able to give it a greater impetus by sending it out with the whole force of your being, impelling it outward. Man's body is the medium through which this force is transformed and added impetus is given it, in order to do a greater work, and be set forth in greater form.

'Thus there is far greater force added to this principle through the fact that millions are magnifying its radiations and sending them out; yet one man standing forth in full dominion can conquer the world. Thus, you see what millions could accomplish.

'The more you use this name, knowing that it is the in-dwelling God Principle that you are establishing within you, the higher the rate of vibration of your body. These vibrations become correlated, and respond to the Divine vibrations which the word God means and gives forth. Should you say GOD once, reverently, your body will never return to the same vibratory rate that it was giving off at the time you used the word GOD.

'With this thought in mind, make these statements your very own. Put them in your own language if you so desire. They are from you and not from any outside force. Just try for a time and see what it will do for you. Recall that every time you think GOD, you are within God's Divine plan. These are not my words, they are your words coming from the Christ of God, yourself. Bear in mind that Jesus, the man, myself became the Christ as He expressed light, which is pure Life or God.

'God, my Father, the Divine Principle flowing through me, is all; and all that God is, I AM. I am the Christ of God, God-man.

'All that God my Father is, is for God-man to use; thus I AM is entitled to use all substance. In fact, God my Father is pressing out all substance to God-man in unlimited measure.

'God Principle is my Father; I have come to the realization that the I AM is the Christ of God; both in whole and complete union. All that God has, the Christ of God is.

'Let us take the word GOD. Why is it that this word has so much power? It is because of the vibrations that are released when the word is spoken with feeling—they are of the very highest, they are the Cosmos, the most effective vibration. (Because all the Cosmos is within God, the ALL-IN-ALL.) They come in on the Cosmic Ray and set up the highest field of radiation. This field is all-inclusive, all-penetrating, all-existing, and rules all mass. They are the ruling elements of all energy and this vibration is the vehicle that carries all life and light.'

"Jesus went on, 'The ruling intelligence back of this radiation is what we term GOD, and through its radiation, the intelligence pervades everything. From this radiation field, both light and life emanate. When man accepts these, he unites them in his body; they are one. This body responds immediately to the light vibration, and he is God vibration; his body radiates light. Thus, one standing forth as God, is often invisible to one functioning in a lower vibratory field.

'Because of this sustaining word GOD, your Bible has maintained such influence and longevity. Think of the number of times the word is written, and thus spoken, in that great book. See the different lines of radiation of light, and therefore, the life and energy that go out from each word, either written or spoken.

'Each word carries its vibration to the very soul of all who speak, hear, or see the word GOD; and as the soul responds to that vibration, the book from which the radiations come forth is lifted and exalted correspondingly as the soul is exalted by the vibrations. Thus the book is given life, power, and immortality. It is in reality the word GOD that has accomplished this feat. Thus, you can say that the book is the word of God in the spiritual sense, but not in the literal sense of the word.

'Too many take the Bible literally, instead of giving attention to its true spiritual value. This lack of understanding is somewhat offset by the spiritual vibration that is set up by the use of the word God.

'Do you not know that it is high time to go within your house, put it in order, and find out what the Word will do for you? Think attentively for a moment, try it, and see if it will not cause you to drop all differences and bickering. Speak GOD with your whole soul, and feel the exhilaration that causes you to treat your brother more kindly, and deal with him more justly. Place God before you and the mist of the long-forgotten ages will be dispelled as a wisp of smoke.

'The intellect may frown upon this. Don't mind the intellect; it has erred many times. Stand forth with the word GOD dominate within you, and a whole world of strife and confusion cannot touch you.'

Knowing and doing

'When you know positively that GOD or supreme vibration does exist and that it is ALL POWER, you can use it to accomplish all things. The instant you make it definite that you are God vibration, you are using the power. (Remember, water, vapor and ice are the same substance; however, scientifically the vapor energy is moving at a much higher rate of vibration. Spiritual knowing operates at the highest level of vibration.) Just thinking a thing does not accomplish that thing. YOU MUST KNOW AND DO; then love and worship the source or principle enough to do it, be it!' (Knowing that your home is full of light is not enough. You must make conscious effort to activate this power within your bodily temple.)

"The Master continued: 'Faith shows the way through thought but it takes the actual command of the Christ of God within each man, to be that vibration. The instant you allow that vibration to take full command, you GET UP AND DO IT. THE KNOWING, through love and worship, becomes the accomplishment. That you are unconscious of their radiations does not set aside the fact of their existence. Through faith in their existence, and a conscious knowing, only then can you use them, as you have become fully conscious of their existence.

'Light is Life; thus, if you live wholly in the vibrations of light, your body is pure life. Light, and life, is God, thus all are God, and show it forth, when they live in the God vibration.

'The sun shall be no more thy light by day; neither for brightness shall the moon give light unto thee; but the Lord shall be unto thee an everlasting light and thy God, thy glory.' (Isaiah 60:19) The Lord Christ of God has no more need of earthly light when His body vibrations are raised in unison with God vibrations. His body is light, purer than that of the noonday sun. The Lord (or Law of) God, expressing pure life (Light) through Jesus or any man, becomes the Christ upon earth. Each man becomes the Christ, when the Lord (Law) or Law Of God is understood and actually lived.'

"Jesus concluded this particular discourse with these final few words:

'Is it not much greater to live the Christ life? Is it not worthwhile to make this your ideal? Does this not completely erase the petty things of life? Do you not see the accomplishments of the ones that dared to step forth and live the Christ life?

'As you accomplish this, you stand on the Mount of Transfiguration. Man's law and prophecy disappear and the triumphant Christ stands alone, but not lonely. You can do this, all can do it, if they but will.

'As you know your origin with the Father, you never pass on, you always know, and are within, the Father. (Our spirit-consciousness lives eternally, regardless of the many "forms" we may wear) If they *had* known one, that is my Father, they would have known me, for all our vibrations would have been in perfect accord.

'Now you know that you and the Father are one, just as *'I and the Father are one.'* This is the testimony of two standing together as one law, and this testimony IS TRUE.'"

Hear ye Him! These are the golden words of our Master. Read them again and again!

* * *

When our Master, Jesus, originally spoke to his flocks, very few understood the deeper messages within his teachings. The smartest man of the day, Nicodemus, asked the Master to explain to him of heavenly matters. Jesus responded something like this—'How could you understand the spiritual, when you can't even grasp what I tell you concerning the here and now?' Even the closest followers of Jesus, including the Twelve, did not fully comprehend the depth of meaning in the truths he was trying to teach.

Scribes and translators through the years have passed on the stories of his teachings to the best of their abilities, according to their own interpretation. Not even a Nicodemus-type of intelligence could have discerned and transcribed the full meanings. However, what little they did glean from him, was life-transforming, and enough to spin earthly thought around a new *axis of spirituality*.

Down through the ages, humanity persists in this quest to unlock the secrets contained in the allegories and parables spoken by the Master. As we pray for discernment, we join with multitudes around the world in this most joyous quest. Understanding the journey of Jesus, along with our own spiritual unfoldment, is an ongoing adventure of inner discovery. This, of all studies, brings to human consciousness peace, and the promise of a life lived more abundantly.

We persist and persevere in comprehending more of Jesus' Truths, with full faith that through our own individual discernment, we may discover with our eyes to discern and ears to perceive that which, until now, only the highly enlightened have seen and understood. Therefore *"seek and you shall find, knock and it shall be opened unto you."*

Axis of understanding

Where are we presently in the ever-turning axis of spiritual understanding? Are we truly comprehending our spiritual nature? Or are we, as the Master implied, just living for the here and the now, still debating and consternating over his simple, yet profound, words of wisdom?

For hundreds of years the clergy debated whether Jesus was mortal or divine, man or the actual God. In the fourth century, the debates raged within the council of Bishops. Meetings were taking place all over the Roman Empire, especially in Alexandria, Egypt, a leading theological center. Within three hundred years, by the insistence of a few powerful men, Jesus went from being a Jewish prophet to being God himself.

The many divided factions or groups continued the argument for years and years, as even the pagans were being forced to exchange their many gods for the one imposed deity, Jesus. In other words, they were being instructed to worship an actual man, rather than the inspiring principles he lived and taught the Christ-principles that are innate to all men.

As we have gathered, numerous details of the Written Word were scrutinized. History shows that councils of men in power decided which Gospels were to be allowed, and which were to be withheld. The simple messages and humble words of Jesus were gradually being obscured by literalism and intellectualism.

Eyes were no longer seeing, ears were no longer hearing, the pure truth in the Master's underlying teachings.

Another major portion of these early exchanges between the scholarly men was developing the concept of the Holy Triune, the three in one, the trinity of the Father, the Son, and the Holy Spirit. These church fathers reasoned that, even though there was no mention of the idea of a "trinity" within the Bible, or anywhere in the Scriptural texts gathered, it seemed a logical explanation to help settle the dispute over whether to define Jesus as man or God, human or Divine. This would aid their coercive agenda in the unification of the masses, by setting up an allegiance to one God, one religion. Possibly at stake was their own self-preservation, and that of church and state.

Meanwhile, the more accurate Tertullian theological assumption insisted that while the three "persons" of the Godhead are distinct in function, they could not be different in substance. These "free thinkers" had been brought into the enlightened realization, through much reason and logic, that All is God, Spirit—the Trinity simply signified different functions of the ONE Spirit, ONE Source, as the Gnostics had insisted. Temporarily, humanity was breaking out of its slumber.

Had their liberties of thought been less scrutinized by the hierarchy during their day, these scholars might also have been more insistent on the importance of retaining the placement of the word "the" in proceeding a myriad of "I Am" statements. Instead, the more powerful Bishops, along with the Roman Emperor and his Pope, totally extracted the word "the" in the I Am references, in order to build this great prophet into a supreme deity an almighty "god." However, the Master himself had insisted that his "Father," our Father, was the ONE Supreme Being... saying I Jesus, a man *"can of mine own self do nothing."*

Today we continue the pursuit of unlocking the spiritual significance in the meaning of The Master's works. Two thousand years later we are now entering yet another celestial paradigm—a Planetary Shift, and a revolutionary spiritual shift in thinking—going through still another door, the Aquarian Age, that will help us better understand this most wonderful man Jesus, and the compassion and forgiveness he taught.

Further, we are constantly receiving the blessings brought to us by the special dispensation of spiritual information coming from the Cosmic Divine Hierarchy with love, from the Ascended Ones, telling us that the I Am threads through all hearts. Are you hearing the underlying message speaking to you through the words of the Master?

Like Baird Spalding, in the 1890s, what if today you encountered Jesus. What questions would you have for the Master?

*We simply have to change our thinking,
turn the telescope around, observe the operation of spirit
in everything about us, magnify and enjoy the view!*

Chapter 32

NOTHING ELSE

Lose yourself wholly
and the more you lose,
the more you will find.

—***St. Catherine of Siena***

Why do we say that "All good things must come to end?" Who was it that decreed this edict? Can a king, queen, president, or pope write an official order that would reverse this unfounded man-made proclamation?

We should hold in mind that giving up the physical self does not necessarily mean ignoring or bringing to an end the good in this world. It is no longer necessary to see human-hood as something lesser, an illusion, mirage, or a reflection of something grander. But rather it means valuing and improving our earthy experience to the greatest degree. The human self is at the same time the launching pad and the rocket that has to propel us into the ascending mode, a raising of our consciousness into our Higher-Self, the Christ.

Remember, being still, quieting the clamor of material reasoning, desires, doubts and fears, is the first phase of ascending out of physicality and its sensuality, into a lighter consciousness, a lighter body, without limitations. *"In quietness and in confidence shall be your strength"* as the Book of Isaiah lovingly admonishes us." (Isaiah 30:15)

Look away from the human condition, and its wants, desires, its ego and fears. Be in a state of knowing that your divine Higher-Self, is one with, as *Jesus said... the I Am*, your Source. Holding to this conscious awareness, living and breathing this knowing, envelopes the human in all its greatest potential and capability, raising it to its highest vibration and frequency, the highest standard possible in present experience. To paraphrase Deepak Chopra: To recognize your own divinity you must be rich in every human quality first.

Understanding that you are in this world, yet consciously not having to be of this world, and its influences, is one of the greatest human attainments— acquiring dominion.

The human life, which by the way is beautiful and grand, or at least should be, is never to be devalued, brushed aside, or shunned, but is to be raised to its fullest glory. There are not two worlds—one material and one spiritual—we live in a spiritually rich material world, manifesting itself in varying forms, visibly and invisibly. We are, and will be, understanding and experiencing this phenomenon of "spiritual-matter" at differing levels, experiencing it more materially or more spiritually, according to the degree of our enlightenment.

This illumination comes step by step in the now, moment by moment, plateau upon plateau, through quiet prayer and meditation with contemplation. One might think of it as an escalating staircase, gently ascending the human consciousness out of this sometimes less than paradisiacal state of self-imposed human limitation. The old and immature mortal traits of the material paradigm are outgrown and gladly left behind; as we step into our immortal light-body, the consciousness of our seamless robe, glorifying and living the virtuous principalities of love, wisdom and power.

To quote the brilliant Winston Churchill, at the closing of the Battle of El Alamein, "Now this is not the end. It is not even the beginning of the end. But it is, perhaps, the end of the beginning... of WWII."

Finishing this book, or this particular lifetime for that matter, is not the end for us. We are merely finishing, perhaps, the end of our beginning to spiritually comprehend our eternities.

The height of greatest attainment in this life for us would be to fully know ourselves and *who we truly are*—remembering with crystal clarity, that there is no such thing as God and anything else. NOTHING ELSE. No such thing as God and man as a separate entity— only God being man, as man.

There is only GOD being... being... being.

ACKNOWLEDGMENTS

A special thanks to my skillful editor and publisher, James Abraham.

This publication would not have been possible without the help of my innovative friend, Diana Craun, who is the associate editor, cover artist, and illustrator of this book. I would also like to recognize Carolyn Whitt for her kind encouragement.

I appreciate the enlightened wisdom and contributions from ascended masters and teachers, as well as the many spiritually inspired authors of our day, who strive to lift our planetary consciousness.

BIBLIOGRAPHY

- Ballard, Guy. St. Germain, *The Magic Presence: St. Germain Series.* St, Germain Press. Schaumburg, ILL 1999
- Chopra, Deepak. *The Third Jesus.* Three Rivers Press. New York, 2008
- Condrin, Dr. Barbara. *Kundalini Rising.* SOM Publishing Company. 1992
- Dr. Eben Alexander. *Proof Of Heaven.* Piatkus Books. London ,2012
- Drummond, Henry. *The Greatest Thing In The World.* Wilder Publications LLC. Radford, VA, 2009
- Eddy, Mary Baker. *Science And Health With Key To The Scriptures.* The Christian Science Board of Directors. Boton, 1994
- Einstein, Albert. *The World As I See It.* Kensington Publishing Corporation. New York, 2006
- Fox, Emmet. *Sermon On The Mount,* Harper Collins Publishers. New York, 2009
- Goldsmith, Joel. *The Thunder Of Silence*: Reissue edition HarperSanFrancisco, 1993.)
- Haich, Elisabeth. *Initiation.* Aurora Press. Santa Fe, NM, 2000
- Hankey, Katherine. *The Old, Old Story.* Nabu Press. Charleston, SC, 2012
- Lumkin, Joseph B. *Banned From The Bible.* Fifth Estate, Incorporated. Blounstville, AL, 2008
- Saint Germain Foundation. *The History of the "I AM" Activity and Saint Germain Foundation.* Schaumburg, Illinois: Saint Germain Press 2003
- Schutz, Alice. *The Law Of Life, Books I, II.* A.D.K. Luk Publications Oakland, CA, 1959
- Spalding, Baird T. *The Life And Teaching Of The Masters Of The Far East.* Devorss & Co. Camarillo, CA, 1986
- Wlprat, Stanley. *Gandhi's Passion: The Life and Legacy of Mahatma Gandhi.* Oxford University Press. New York, 2001

BENEDICTION

Signs and wonders will follow, as our heightened awareness enters the new era of a spiritual shift in consciousness.

I have been privileged to hear many inspiring stories of an angelic nature, and many unusual happenings in peoples' lives. Some have told me of the sensational feeling of levitating and flying in their dreams. Others have consciously awakened, hovering in the air above their bodies. And many have heard loved ones, who are passed, speaking. Still others saw an angelic presence at the foot of their bed, telepathically communicating to them.

I am also aware of a countless number of miraculous healings. These special events should not be suppressed, hidden away, or ignored. I encourage all our brothers and sisters to share their individual stories.

You may contact me or order this book, at:

mcclintockbooks.com.

Made in the USA
Charleston, SC
14 August 2016